Domenico Scandella
Known as Menocchio

His Trials Before the Inquisition
(1583–1599)

MEDIEVAL & RENAISSANCE

TEXTS & STUDIES

VOLUME 139

Domenico Scandella
Known as Menocchio

His Trials Before the Inquisition
(1583–1599)

by

Andrea Del Col

Translated by

John & Anne C. Tedeschi

ⲘⲈⲆⲓⲉⲩⲁⳑ & ⲢⲈⲚⲀⲓⲤⲤⲀⲚⳐⲈ ⲦⲈⲬⲦⲤ & ⲤⲦⳙⲆⳠⲉⲤ
Binghamton, New York
1996

Pegasus Limited for the Advancement of Neo-Latin Studies
has generously provided a grant to assist in meeting
the publication costs of this volume.

Library of Congress Cataloging-in-Publication Data

Scandella, Domenico, 1532–1601.
[Domenico Scandella detto Menocchio. English]
Domenico Scandella known as Menocchio: his trials before the inquisition (1583–1599) / edited with an introduction by Andrea Del Col ; translated by John & Anne C. Tedeschi.
  p. cm. — (Medieval & Renaissance texts & studies ; v. 139)
Includes bibliographical references and index.
ISBN 0–86698–148–9 (acid-free paper)
  1. Scandella, Domenico, 1532–1601—Trials, litigation, etc. 2. Trials (Heresy)—Italy—Udine (Province)—History—16th century. 3. Inquisition—Italy—Udine (Province)—History—16th century. I. Del Col, Andrea. II. Tedeschi, John A., 1931– . III. Tedeschi, Anne. IV. Title. V. Series.
KKH174.S29S2913 1995
272'.2'0945391—dc20   94–46794
                                                     CIP

This book is made to last.
It is set in Caslon, smythe-sewn
and printed on acid-free paper
to library specifications

Printed in the United States of America

Table of Contents

Acknowledgments

I owe hearty thanks to Sergio Bigatton, who most generously furnished me with data and documents from the Archivio di Stato, Pordenone and from the Archivio del Capitolo, Concordia, fruits of one of his earlier researches; to Aldo Colonnello, whose friendship sustained every stage of this labor; to Francesco Zambon, who facilitated my access to texts concerning the Cathari; and to Giorgio Zordan, who furnished me with information and advice on questions connected with the defense proceedings in the second trial. Finally, I should like to express my special gratitude to Silvana Seidel Menchi and to Giovanni Miccoli for their suggestions and their constant availability for intellectual exchanges and discussion.

Abbreviations

AAUd Archivio Arcivescovile, Udine
ASPn Archivio di Stato, Pordenone
ASVe Archivio di Stato, Venezia
AVPd Archivio Vescovile, Padova
AVPn Archivio Vescovile, Pordenone
BSPn Biblioteca del Seminario, Pordenone
Ginzburg: Carlo Ginzburg, *The Cheese and the Worms: The Cosmos of a Sixteenth-Century Miller.* Translated by John and Anne Tedeschi (Baltimore & London: Johns Hopkins University Press, 1980; 1st Italian ed. 1976).

Translators' Preface

Domenico Scandella, the quixotic, free-thinking and outspoken Friulan miller was executed by order of the Inquisition in 1599 as a relapsed heretic. This modest figure, virtually unknown in his day outside the borders of Montereale Valcellina, a tiny hamlet nestled at the foot of the mountains, and a few other neighboring villages, suddenly was brought out of centuries-long obscurity and was made one of the heroes of modern historiography by Carlo Ginzburg's now classic *The Cheese and the Worms.*[1]

Ginzburg told a fascinating tale that whetted our appetites to know more about "Menocchio," and an early reviewer of his work expressed the hope that the two voluminous Inquisitorial trials against him, Ginzburg's principal source in the reconstruction of the miller's life and intellectual world, would some day be published in their entirety. This arduous task has finally been accomplished by Andrea Del Col, a historian attached to the University of Trieste, in an edition that is a model of its kind. It is a pleasure now to present to a new audience in its English vestment a book that has enjoyed notable success since it first appeared in Italy in 1990.[2]

Del Col's contribution goes well beyond his formidable philological and paleographical labors in bringing to press, in a critical edition, the complete transcripts of two trials conducted over long intervals of time by a branch of the Roman Inquisition. Few such records have seen the light of day in their original languages; they are even scarcer in English translation. The volume provides us with previously un-

---

[1] *Il formaggio e i vermi: Il cosmo di un mugnaio del '500* (Turin: Einaudi, 1976), translated into English: *The Cheese and the Worms: The Cosmos of a Sixteenth-Century Miller.* Translated by John and Anne Tedeschi (Baltimore & London: Johns Hopkins Univ. Press, 1980).

[2] *Domenico Scandella detto Menocchio: I processi dell'Inquisizione (1583–1599).* A cura di Andrea Del Col (Pordenone: Edizioni Biblioteca dell'Immagine, 1990).

known and unused documents which further illuminate Menocchio's tragic life; and Del Col's long, scholarly introduction discusses in detail the special relations which prevailed in Friulan peasant society and the cycles and rituals of its agricultural year. It also provides one of the fullest explications of the organization of an Inquisitorial tribunal and its intricate judicial procedures. But a novel feature of the present work and perhaps its most significant contribution is its suggestion, meticulously argued, that Menocchio's intellectual world must be explained in terms of the latter's reception of notions of Cathar origin. This hypothesis marks a notable departure from previous interpretations and it will be interesting to see if it is upheld by future research.

The present English edition contains the two trials in their full form, but is slightly abridged in a few other particulars. An occasional sentence has been deleted from the introduction, the philological note has been reduced and the textual apparatus to the trial has been almost wholly eliminated since problems connected with the original language were not relevant in English. The documentary appendix has been confined to letters of the Supreme Congregation of the Inquisition directly pertinent to Menocchio.

It is a pleasure to thank our good friend Andrea Del Col for his assistance and counsel throughout these labors and the officers of the following entities and governmental bodies which graciously combined their forces to further help spread the fame of their departed Friulan *concittadino*. The translation subsidy was generously contributed by the Provincia di Pordenone; the Comune di Montereale Valcellina—the Biblioteca Civica; the Circolo Culturale "Menocchio."

J. T.

A. C. T.

Introduction

On a day at the end of September, 1583, at the height of the harvest, events began to unfold which would make Domenico Scandella— whose nickname was Menocchio—known to history. The life of this eccentric, headstrong miller had actually begun fifty-one years earlier and, like that of so many others, had run its course leaving but a few traces in documents buried in notarial archives. On that autumn day the Inquisition initiated a trial against him which would change his destiny, in life, and in historical memory after his death. The priest of Montereale Valcellina, a tiny village nestled at the foot of a Friulan mountainside, in an amphitheater overlooking the plain, goes to the vicar general of the bishop of Concordia and denounces the obstinate and headstrong Menocchio. We do not know how the unstable equilibrium which had endured until then was broken, what tipped the scales in the mind of the priest Odorico Vorai. The impulse might have come from another indignant cleric, or as the result of Menocchio's own talk and that of those around him during the harvest when the peasants lend each other a hand to bring in the last crops of the year. Monsignor Giovanni Battista Maro listens preoccupied to the priest, who tells him not only of the miller's unheard-of ideas and incredible heresies, but also confesses fears for his own safety. In the village Menocchio has support, friends, and a secure position which it is risky to assail. The vicar general decides then to institute a formal trial and on the 28th of September sets the arraignment to paper: Scandella has made heretical and blasphemous statements about the Savior Jesus Christ, and not only did he impiously believe them, but even dared to preach them as the true faith. The documents show that the trial was initiated by the Holy Office, without any mention that a denunciation had come from the priest Odorico, an expedient that is not an unusual feature and conforms to the regular practice of the Friulan Inquisition of shielding accusers.[1]

Actually, the name of the miller had already surfaced in an anonymous denunciation against villagers of Fanna, sometime between June–July 1580 and August–September 1583. The gist of that document is simple enough: four persons are accused of denying purgatory, the utility of rites for the dead, of charity to monks and priests, of preaching; and two others of not believing in the most holy sacrament and of holding that "when the body dies, the soul dies." It closes with the names of nine witnesses. A second sheet has a denunciation against priest Andrea Ionima, chaplain at Montereale, without mentioning a precise charge, and against Domenico Scandella. He is accused of denying the obligation to observe Lent, of possessing a Bible in the vernacular and of quoting from it constantly. We are not told who received the document, the bishop, the vicar general or the inquisitor. At any rate, nothing came of it.[2]

In the trial records the heresies imputed to Scandella by the parish priest and enumerated for the vicar general are not described explicitly, but they can be deduced easily from the specific questions systematically addressed by monsignor Maro to the first four witnesses on 29 and 30 October 1583, who were asked about phrases uttered by the miller in the village. The judge needed to determine if they had been spoken seriously, if they were propositions in which he really believed, or if he was reporting hearsay, had lost his wits or was simply joking. Menocchio was saying disconnected, disconcerting things: the air was God; it was impossible that the Blessed Virgin could have given birth to the Savior and remained a virgin; it did not show much wisdom on the part of Jesus Christ to have let himself be killed if he was really all powerful, as was being preached; to blaspheme God and the saints was not a sin; to be saved it was enough not to harm one's neighbor, and there was no need for so many sermons and good works.[3] These

---

[1] See 3; AAUd, *S. Officio,* b. 8, fasc. 136, session of 1 June 1584. For the procedures of the Friulan Inquisition, see, for example, b. 1, fasc. 2, 3, 15. The period of the harvest lasted from mid-September to the end of October, as we can infer from the request to postpone the appearance of Francesco Pichissino until 1 November lodged by his brother Ottavio on 12 September 1584, "propter vindemias nunc imminentis": cf. b. 7, fasc. 108, fol. 37v.

[2] For the denunciation see 1–2.

[3] See 3–10.

words were only a sample, much reduced, of what Domenico Scandella was saying and thinking, a man who wanted to understand things with his own head, whose wealth consisted of his pride, four books, and a mind full of ideas. In fact, during the trial, the accused shocked and disconcerted the judges with even worse heresies. He was condemned to a perpetual incarceration the following spring, but was freed at the beginning of 1586 and confined to Montereale as his prison, enjoined to wear the yellow cross of the heretic as a sign of public infamy. He was tried a second time in 1599 because he was unable to suppress his "truth" and suffered the fate reserved for the relapsed, death.

Fifteen or so years ago Carlo Ginzburg discovered the records of these trials in the archive of the Inquisition in Udine, and studied the life, ideas and culture of this unknown miller. His book aroused tremendous interest in Italy and abroad, rekindling among historians a discussion about the relationship between learned culture and popular culture.[4] The many passages quoted by Ginzburg in his captivating work give an idea of the two trials, but nothing can substitute for the stimulating immediacy and fascination of the original texts in their entirety. They permit us to enter the very chambers of the Holy Office and listen to the words of the protagonists—accused, judges, witnesses—each with their baggage of ideology and human emotions. These documents delineate the unfolding of a typical inquisitorial trial, but they are exceptional for the heresies they record and for the tragic end with which they conclude.

The miller and the village.

Who was this Menocchio and what was he saying? The few biographical facts we have are quickly stated. Born at Montereale in 1532, he

---

[4] C. Ginzburg, *The Cheese and the Worms: The Cosmos of a Sixteenth Century Miller,* translated by John and Anne Tedeschi (Baltimore: The Johns Hopkins Univ. Press, 1980). Originally published as *Il formaggio e i vermi* (Turin: Einaudi, 1976). For an idea of the scholarly discussion at that time, see G. Spini, "Noterelle libertine," *Rivista storica italiana* 88 (1976): 792–802; P. Zambelli, "Uno, due, tre, mille Menocchio?," *Archivio storico italiano* 137 (1979): 51–90; the round table on "Religione e religiosità popolare," *Ricerche di storia sociale e religiosa,* n.s., 11 (1977): 5–380; the monographic issue "Religioni delle classi popolari," ed. C. Ginzburg, *Quaderni storici* 41 (1979): 393–697; P. Burke, *Popular Culture in Early Modern Europe* (London, 1978); P. Camporesi, "Cultura popolare e cultura d'élite fra medioevo ed età moderna," in *Storia d'Italia. Annali 4,* (Turin: Einaudi, 1981), 81–157.

had almost always lived in his village except for a brief sojourn in neighboring Arba and Carnia, and an occasional journey as far as Venice and Udine. His father was called Zuane and his mother Menega. He was married and had eleven children, of whom seven were alive in 1584: Zanut (Giovannino) was twenty-six years old, Stefano about fourteen, and then there were Daniele, Menica, Iseppia, Maria, and Giovanna. About his wife, whose name is unknown, he wrote with rough affection and sorrow in 1599: "she looked after me," and in the same way lamented the death of his eldest "who was able to keep every trouble and suffering from me." He worked as a miller with two rented mills, but from time to time exercised various other trades: carpenter, mason, teacher of abacus, and he often played the dulcimer or the cithara in the village feasts. He knew how to read and write. He also filled various public offices: he was mayor in 1581 and administrator of church property sometime before 1584 and in 1590.[5] In short, economically and culturally, he had risen above the great mass of the disinherited, and occupied a place in the esteem of his fellows. But he was known above all for his critical and original ideas. Menocchio made no mystery of them; on the contrary, he spoke about them with spirit and conviction in random encounters, in the *piazza*, in the street, in the tavern, on doorsteps, on his way to the cemetery or to Mass, coming or going from the neighboring towns, returning from the mountains. "He is always disputing with someone over the faith for the sake of argument, and also with the priest," one witness stated, and another: "He is always looking for the chance to talk about these things" and "it is his custom with whomever he is speaking to turn the conversation to matters concerning God, and always introduce some sort of heresy, and then he argues and shouts in defense of his opin-

---

[5] See C. Ginzburg, 1–2, 95–97; the names of the children are obtained from Menocchio's two trials, from the trial against the priest Vorai cited at n. 166 and from ASPn, *Notarile*, b. 488, n.c. 3786, fols. 10v, 21v (1599). The wife was three years younger. The references are at 135. For the identification of the musical instrument, see G. Pressacco, "Canti, discanti . . . e incanti. Intorno alle disavventure inquisitoriali di un organista friulano del '500," in *Spilimbèrc*, N. Cantarutti and G. Bergamini, eds. (Udine: Società filologica friulana, 1984), 254–55. On mills in Friuli, see L. De Biasio, "Dal mulino al filatoio: un singolare spaccato di storia economico-sociale udinese tra Seicento e Settecento," *Metodi e ricerche*, n.s., 6 (1987), no. 2: 5–18; D. Penzi, *Mulini ad acqua e arte molitoria in provincia di Pordenone* (Pordenone: Edizioni della Provincia di Pordenone, [n.d. but 1988]), with a list of the surviving mills and of those whose remains can be identified.

ion."[6] The interest and cultural limitations of his listeners who, to the miller's regret, were often few, served as a brake on these discussions, but fear of the Inquisition also held him back: he asserted, in fact, that "if he did not fear for his life, he would say so many things that would astonish."[7] At any rate, his words were on everyone's lips and were talked about in the taverns.

What Menocchio was going about saying can be reconstructed only in an indirect and fragmentary way through the testimony given by these witnesses at the trial. The first four interrogated by the vicar general, who were systematically asked the same questions, confirmed the priest's accusations, adding little that was new: a few variations on the pantheistic theme ("everything that we see is God and we are gods"; "the air is God and the earth is our mother"; "the sky, earth, sea, air, abyss and hell, all is God"). There were also statements that the Holy Spirit did not reign over the Church; that priests wanted to keep the faithful submissive under their control, while they themselves sported about; that after death man was like the beasts. He also rejected the observance of Lent and the prescriptions for fasting and abstinence.[8] Only the fourth witness, departing from the established subject matter, recounted at the end a fantastic theory about the origin of the cosmos: "I heard him say that in the beginning this world was nothing and that the water of the sea was whipped into a foam and coagulated like a cheese, from which then were born a great number of worms, and these worms became angels, of which the most powerful and wise was God." There was an evil one among them, Satan, who wanted to oppose God, but God overcame him and sent his son forth as an ambassador to mankind, "who let himself be hung up like a beast."[9]

The other ten or so witnesses interrogated by the inquisitor in a random way during the months following, besides repeating what already was known, not without some significant variations, added several new details: Menocchio did not believe in the divinity of Christ ("It is not true that Christ was crucified, as many say, but he was a certain man, who was then hanged"; "he did not believe that Christ was born from the Holy Spirit, but that he was the son of St. Joseph

---

[6] See 4–5, 11, 13–17, 19; the references at 4, 13–14.
[7] See 7, but also 5, 16, 18, 20.
[8] See 4–9; the references at 4, 6, 8.
[9] See 9.

or was a bastard"), nor in the pope, the laws of the Church or the immortality of the soul ("when a man dies, he is like a beast [...] when man dies the soul dies"). Similarly, he did not believe in confession and in the existence of God (God is "a bit of air and whatever man imagines him to be"; God "is a fraud on the part of Scripture to deceive us, and if there is a God, he would let himself be seen"). Nor did he believe in the Eucharist ("I can only see a piece of dough there, how can that be God?"), or in indulgences and purgatory. However, Menocchio respected the ethical norms which regulated social relations and reduced all morality to them: "Do you want me to teach you not to do evil? Do not take the property of others, and this is the good one can do."[10]

To be sure, what the miller was actually going about saying could not be reduced to just this. The discrepancy between the bare-bones, curt, disconnected statements relayed by the priest and by the texts, and the rich and complex ideas expressed by the accused during the trial, cannot, in my opinion, be attributed merely to the difference between Menocchio's public utterances and his private thoughts. It can be explained in part by the hypothesis that he had deliberately conceived of two different levels: on the one hand he used a crude sort of exposition comprehensible to ignorant listeners, and, on the other, a complex of ideas reserved for the learned, educated judges.[11] But one would thus have to suppose that for many years the miller had kept most of his deepest thoughts within himself without communicating them to a living soul. The very notion of a simplified version for the many and a more complex one for the few, itself implies the existence of a nucleus of adepts capable of receiving the most secret and most basic of his notions. Menocchio could occasionally go into things more deeply with some of the inhabitants of Montereale, as is demonstrated by the description of the origins of the cosmos which, despite the fact that it is reported at third hand, details exhaustively one of the cardinal points of his thought.[12]

The gulf between what was recounted by the peasants and what Menocchio himself told the judges can, moreover, be readily explained by the reduction and simplification of ideas when they are relayed by

---

[10] See 10–19; the references respectively at 10, 13, 16, 13, 17–18, 14.

[11] See Ginzburg, 65–68.

[12] See 9. After Scandella heard this version from the vicar general, he elaborated it with new details: see 25–26.

others[13] and, above all, by the differing legal functions performed by
the testimony of witnesses and that of the accused. The first serve the
judge to collect evidence or proof against the offender, not to reconstruct his patterns of thought and speech in their full complexity.
Witnesses almost always content themselves with responding to precise, circumscribed questions; rarely do they have a strong motive to
tell what they know completely and in detail. In the present trial, four
of them, in fact, are obviously reticent: Bernardo del Ceta, Bartolomeo,
son of Andrea, Paolo Sgiarbasso, and the priest himself, when he is
questioned by the inquisitor.[14] In determining the gravity of the
crime, a detailed confession by the accused was more important and
critical than the miscellaneous testimony of witnesses. Judges worked
to obtain it in every way possible since it was the result for which the
entire procedure was constructed.[15] Sometimes there would be only
the slightest discrepancy between the depositions of witnesses and the
interrogations of the accused, because it was in the latter's interest to
say as little as possible. But this time it is different. Menocchio wants
to explain himself thoroughly because, paradoxically, the trial is the
chance of his life to be fully understood by learned churchmen. For
years he had waited for such a moment: "I would like to have no other
privilege than to go before the pope, bishops and cardinals to unburden my soul, and, if I have erred, even if they should kill me, I could
not feel a more welcome thing."[16] This astute, enterprising miller
wanted to disclose the truth as he saw it to the inquisitors, but there is
no reason to suppose that his everyday interlocutors, peasants, artisans,
and priests, had not heard many of the ideas which concerned his
strange cosmogony, God, Jesus Christ, the Madonna, the angels, the
Bible, the nature of man, salvation, the sacraments and religious
practices, or the ecclesiastical hierarchy.

Menocchio spoke with everyone and the town let him talk. Once

---

[13] See S. Seidel Menchi, *Erasmo in Italia 1520–1580* (Turin: Bollati Boringhieri, 1987),
122–42.

[14] See 7, 14–15, 16–17, 19–20.

[15] See I. Mereu, *Storia dell'intolleranza in Europa. Sorvegliare e punire. Il sospetto e
l'Inquisizione romana nell'epoca di Galilei* (Milan: Mondadori, 1979); J. P. Dedieu, "L'Inquisition et le droit. Analyse formelle de la procedure inquisitoriale en cause de foi," *Mélanges
de la Casa de Velázquez* 23 (1987): 227–51. See, as an example, the manual by U. Locati,
Praxis iudiciaria inquisitorum . . ., Venetiis, apud Damianum Zenarium, 1583, 50–61.

[16] See 20, but also 5, 18.

in a while someone reproached him and cautioned him to utter fewer crazy things (*bagliate*), but did not denounce him to the authorities. Such questions were traditionally resolved within the community itself, jealous of its values and the solidarity of its members, who were reluctant to accept outside influences.[17] We know the names of fifteen or so of these interlocutors, who are witnesses at the trial, or other persons named by them, several of whom are Menocchio's relatives. A few were from Grizzo: Francesco Fassetta and his brother Antonio, who was related to the miller, Daniele Fassetta, Bernardo del Ceta, Melchiorre Sgiarbas, Nico; others were from Montereale: Giovanni Povoledo, Giovanni Antonio Melchiori and his brother Domenico, Giuliano, son of Stefano, deceased, who is a cousin of Menocchio and of Melchiorre Sgiarbas, Bartolomeo, son of Andrea, deceased, a cousin of Menocchio's wife, Pellegrino, son of Francesco, deceased, Pellegrino de Zanin, the tavern keeper Piccin, the chaplain and the priest. It appears that only one, Melchiorre Sgiarbas or Gerbas, thirty-six years of age, married with children, an armchair maker, shared in some way in the miller's heresies (God is nothing if not air, Christ was not born from the Holy Spirit and is simply a man; Mary is not a virgin), blasphemed God and the Madonna in the taverns, and did not observe Lent.[18] Some, Giuliano Stefanut and Domenico Melchiori, had reproached Menocchio; Sgiarbas's father had threatened his son. The others said nothing. The priest was the only person who regularly stood up to the miller.

According to Menocchio, even though before the judges he admits having spoken to many people, besides the priest and the chaplain, his real listeners were actually only four: Zulian Stefanut, Melchiorre Gerbas, Francesco Fassetta, and Nicolò, a painter of Porcia. Others lent him books, namely his uncle, Domenico Gerbas, and persons from Barcis and Arba.[19] He claimed he never discussed his ideas with his wife and children and spoke with almost no one. Actually, the circle of Menocchio's interlocutors and his social contacts in the village and even outside it were not so restricted. But there is a very good reason for the extreme reticence of the accused: the tribunal, faithful to its

---

[17] The reference is at 15. On the attitude of the community towards heretics, see J. Martin, "L'Inquisizione romana e la criminalizzazione del dissenso religioso a Venezia all'inizio dell'età moderna," *Quaderni storici*, n.s., 22 (1987): 777–802.

[18] On Melchiorre Gerbas see also AAUd, *S. Officio*, b. 8, fasc. 132.

[19] See 24–26, 30–31, 33–34, 37, 41–42.

stated obligation, is trying to ferret out the accomplices, and Menocchio, reluctant to harm anyone and violate village solidarity, does not reveal their names. In fact, his calling of miller placed him in contact with everyone, not just peasants, but also tradesmen, lumber merchants, weavers, because mills served not only for the grinding of grain, but also to full cloth and saw up the logs which were floated downstream from the mountains above Montereale. Even if a certain traditional hostility existed between peasants and miller in the stratified society of the village, the mill, just like the tavern, the general store, and the churchyard on feast days, was the preferred place for meetings, for transacting business, for trading ideas, and for just talk.[20]

The priest and the village.

Menocchio had been voicing his views for some twenty-five or thirty years and nothing had changed, as far as we know, until the new priest arrived at Santa Lucia in 1574, on the 13th of December. The parish of Santa Maria of Montereale was an episcopal benefice and the priest Odorico Vorai had obtained it through regular competition after the departure of the previous incumbent, Stefano Decano of Grizzo. Vorai, a cleric with some education, liked to discuss his ministry with other priests and read manuals on pastoral counseling. He was very serious about his mission and from the beginning had busied himself with the task of leading his parishioners back to Christian practices and orthodoxy in accordance with the decrees of the Council of Trent, which were then beginning to be applied to help heal the grave crisis within Catholicism, especially in rural areas.[21] Besides the ignorance and

---

[20] See Ginzburg, 97–98, 119–21.

[21] In large part the information on the priest and the parish is taken from AVPd, *Biblioteca capitolare, Visite*, bb. 6 e 7, "Visitatio apostolica . . . Concordiensis . . . ," unnumbered leaves, the sections dealing with Montereale. A partial, but reliable, copy of b. 6 is in AVPn, *Visite pastorali*, b. 3, reg. "Sacrarum visitationum Nores ab anno 1582 usque ad annum 1584," made from the original by Don Antonio Maria Podestà in 1693 and authenticated by the chief episcopal notary of Padua, Giovanni Fabris. Vorai said he had read the book by Pietro Palude, *Scorteno sacerdotale*, but the reference seems to be incorrect since there is no such title among the works of Pierre de la Palu (ca.1280–1342) in J. F. Michaud, *Biographie universelle ancienne et moderne*, vol. 32 (Graz: Akademische Druck-u. Verlagsanstalt, 1968), 56–57. There is a vast bibliography on the application of the Council of Trent. The most comprehensive recent contributions are: G. Alberigo, "Studi e problemi relativi all'applicazione del concilio di Trento in Italia, 1945–1958," *Rivista storica italiana*

decadent religious life of the faithful, he had to face the challenge of Menocchio's utterances. At first he tried to deal with this annoying impediment to his priestly authority by gentle manners, by conversing and discussing, but when he saw that he could not convince the miller through his own efforts alone, at the beginning of the 80's he brought him before monsignor Maro at Concordia: "These fancies of yours are heresies, and to get you straightened out we are going to monsignor the vicar, who will explain that this is all heresy."[22] But not even the reasoning of the vicar general changed anything. Menocchio and the priest each continued on his separate way.

Father Odorico was conscientious in the exercise of his liturgical duties and his devotion seemed to have an inspired quality to it when he celebrated the Mass ("at the altar, he looks like a saint").[23] His pastoral activity was directed at two essential aspects of renewal mandated by the Council of Trent: on the one hand, the reorganization and regularization of the physical church and of its property; on the other, the imposition of key elements in the religious practice, particularly the observance of Lent and the obligation to receive confession and communion yearly from one's own priest, precepts that were widely neglected by the people.[24]

Montereale was not a large parish. It numbered about 650 souls, of whom 520 perhaps were of communion age, grouped around three

---

70 (1958): 239–98; M. Rosa, *Religione e società nel Mezzogiorno tra Cinquecento e Seicento* (Bari: De Donato, 1976), 74–144; A. Prosperi, "La figura del vescovo fra Quattro e Cinquecento: persistenze, disagi e novità," in *Storia d'Italia. Annali 9*, (Turin: Einaudi, 1986), 221–62; A. Biondi, "Aspetti della cultura cattolica post-tridentina: Religione e controllo sociale," in *Storia d'Italia. Annali 4*, 253–302.

[22] See 20. Melchiorre Gerbas stated instead that the trip to Concordia occurred ca. 1574: see AAUd, *S. Officio*, b. 8, fasc. 132, session of 18 February 1584. The vicar general was then Camillo Cauzio, who definitely held the office from March 1573 to June 1576: see AVPn, *Visite*, b. 1, reg. "1573. Visite Querini," fols. 1r–46v; ASVe, *Santo Uffizio*, b. 44, fasc. "De Melchiori don Daniele," proceedings from 26 May to 6 June 1576. A native of Cittadella and a nephew of the archpriest, he had undergone a trial as a relapsed heretic in Venice between January 1549 and 1550. We do not know how it concluded because the records are incomplete, but at any rate it did not prevent him from pursuing an ecclesiastical career: ibid., b. 8, fasc. "Cautio pre Camillo."

[23] The words are Antonio Spel's: see n. 166.

[24] The obligation to confess and take communion with one's own priest was laid down by Lateran Council IV in 1215: see *Conciliorum oecumenicorum decreta*, curantibus J. Alberigo, J. A. Dossetti, P. P. Joannou, C. Leonardi, P. Prodi (Bologna: Istituto per le scienze religiose, 1973), 245.

population centers, Montereale, Grizzo, and Malnisio, each with its own church (there were two in Grizzo). The religious services performed were the customary ones for the time: Sunday and holiday Masses were celebrated in the parish of Santa Maria and on the first Sunday of the month also at Grizzo, in the church of the confraternity dedicated to the Madonna. The parish church also was served by a chaplain who was supposed to say Mass at the altar of Saints Rocco, Sebastiano and Francesco on feast days and twice weekly. The income from the benefices was not sumptuous, but adequate: a hundred or so ducats yearly for the priest, forty or so for the chaplain, plus sundry fees. The chaplain, Andrea Ionima, left much to be desired: he almost never wore the clerical habit, he was ignorant—he did not really know how to celebrate Mass, rarely recited the office, and enjoyed dancing and playing cards. He kept a woman servant, provoking suspicious gossip by the townspeople. He had not even managed to obtain title to the benefice of the altar of San Rocco, and was passed over in favor of a deacon from Montereale, Father Curzio Cellina, who pocketed much of the income, leaving only twenty or twenty-five ducats for Andrea. The latter scraped along as best he could and kept a flock of sheep, with the result that his hands were frequently soiled and smelly. In sum, he was a priest from the lower classes who had little of the religious about him, but he was not very different from most of the lower clergy throughout Italy before the Tridentine reforms.[25] He had come to Montereale, in fact, after the bishop of the neighboring diocese of Ceneda had expelled him in 1566 from his parish of Mareno di Piave because of his ignorance and undignified ways.

Odorico Vorai, the new priest of Montereale, busied himself with the consecration of the church, and with putting the baptistry in order, caring for the hangings, and replacing window panes. He also attempted to recover the revenues from the entirety of the properties of the church, which totaled several hundred ducats annually and were meant to cover expenses, but which, in the priest's own words, had been

---

[25] On the clergy, in addition to the bibliography indicated at n. 21, see especially: L. Allegra, "Il parroco: un mediatore fra alta e bassa cultura," in *Storia d'Italia. Annali 4*, 895–947; X. Toscani, "Il reclutamento del clero (secoli XVI–XIX)," in *Storia d'Italia. Annali 9*, 575–628; M. Guasco, "La formazione del clero: i seminari," ibid., 634–715; G. Miccoli, " 'Vescovo e re del suo popolo:' La figura del prete curato tra modello tridentino e risposta controrivoluzionaria," ibid., 885–928.

"badly managed, in fact usurped by the village of Montereale itself."[26] These holdings, generally land which had been bequeathed and was rented out, were administered by two officials, *camerari*, elected yearly by the community, and at that time seemed to be handled more for the benefit of parishioners than of the church. Rents were paid late,[27] and often in cash, rather than in kind, at a rate obviously much lower than market prices.[28] Father Odorico had wanted to be present at the yearly reckoning, but gave it up after 1581. He may have felt that his presence would be useless because the inhabitants of Montereale were determined to preserve their freedom in administering the proceeds of the church properties, even though in other villages the *camerari* usually answered to the priest or, more rarely, to the lords of the place.

The town's ability to manage the collective properties would be greatly reduced and finally lost in succeeding centuries, but at this time was still in full force. Agriculture consisted not only of the cultivation of private land, immediately adjacent to inhabited centers, but of the use of communal property, generally fields and woods, for which the communities laid down the norms for their exploitation, and then watched over their application. In the foothills of the western part of the Friuli communal property and communal grazing land covered

---

[26] See AVPd, *Biblioteca capitolare, Visite,* b. 7, Montereale, defense articles for the priest Odorico; the quotation is from article 1.

[27] In the pastoral visit of 26 September 1535 there were seventy odd debtors to the parish owing 653 ducats; Santa Maria di Grizzo had two dozen owing 33 ducats; San Giovanni Battista di Malnisio had about twenty owing 51 ducats. In the visit of 29 November 1552 the debtors of Montereale were about seventy for a total of 84 ducats, those of San Bartolomeo di Grizzo twenty or so owing 23 ducats. In the visit of 26 September 1555 the debtors of the parish church numbered over sixty and owed 257 ducats, Grizzo's about forty owing 75 ducats. In the visit of 22 August 1558 the debts of Montereale for only the three preceding years amounted to 102 ducats, Grizzo's to 35 ducats: AVPn, *Visite pastorali,* b. 1, reg. "Liber visitationum incipit anno 1535," fols. 82r–97v; reg. "Ab anno 1550 usque ad annum 1561," fols. 108v–110v, 191v–195r, 298v–299v. In 1552 the episcopal visitor ordered that in the entire diocese it should be the church administrators (*camerari*) who must answer for all debts, with the right of exacting what was owed from the insolvent.

[28] See AVPd, *Biblioteca capitolare, Visite,* b. 7, Montereale, dispositions of 31 October 1584. A bushel of wheat was calculated by the debtors of Montereale at l. 8, as opposed to l. 10 s. 10 in the visitor's calculations. The then current price in Udine was l. 9–10 per bushel, namely l. 12–13 in relation to the measurement for a bushel in use at Montereale: see G. Stainero, *Patria del Friuli restaurata,* In Venetia MDXCV, fol. 37v.

two-thirds of the territory, but less in the economically richer and more developed central plain.[29]

The income from the benefices and church property of Montereale suggest an economic situation of relative ease, compared with the poverty of the mountain areas and with the wealth of the central lowlands, especially around Pordenone.[30] Despite many contemporary laments, the second half of the sixteenth century was, on the whole, a time of prosperity in Friuli and in the Republic of Venice, in whose jurisdiction Friuli lay. Of course, we need to take into account social stratification, periodic fluctuations and the broad spectrum of economic conditions among the various classes and groups, as well as the poverty of a good part of the population. But, in general, this was a period of agricultural expansion, of demographic growth (interrupted by the plague of 1575), of rapid urbanization and commercial development, of a large money supply (but with a relative slide in buying power), not a time of economic decline or widespread poverty.[31]

Father Odorico's attempts to improve the religious life of the faithful achieved modest results: people went to Mass on holy days, even if some among them, either out of disinterest or lack of respect,

---

[29] See A. Guaitoli, *Comunità rurale e territorio. Per una storia delle forme del popolamento in Friuli* (Udine: Cooperativa editoriale il Campo, 1983), 68–89, especially the map at 77. On the organization of rural communities in Friuli, see F. Bianco, *Comunità di Carnia. Le comunità di villaggio della Carnia (secoli XVII–XIX)* (Udine: Casamassima, 1985); idem, *La comunità di villaggio tra conservazione e rivolta. La Valcellina e la Valcolvera (secoli XVII–XVIII)* (Pordenone: Biblioteca dell'Immagine, 1990).

[30] From the surveys of the apostolic visitation conducted in 1584, cited at n. 21, the income from the benefices in the mountain country varies from 60 to 160 ducats annually, those in the foothills from 50 to 200 ducats, with revenue similar to the church administrations (except for Spilimbergo, whose property has a revenue of 800 ducats), but there are only a few dependent endowed altars and churches with income between 2 and 40 ducats. In Pordenone the benefice of the parish of San Marco amounts to 100 ducats each for the two assistant curates, the church administration has revenue of 400 ducats and in this church alone there are two altars with income of 100 ducats, nine altars earning between 40 and 60 ducats, five altars with 20–25 ducats, for a total of sixteen altars with an income of 740 ducats.

[31] There is an abundant bibliography; see, among others, R. Romano *L'Europa tra due crisi* (Turin: Einaudi, 1980), 76–156; A. Tagliaferri, *Struttura e politica sociale in una comunità veneta del '500 (Udine)* (Milan: Giuffrè, 1969); G. Corazzol, *Fitti e livelli a grano: Un aspetto del credito rurale nel Veneto del '500* (Milan: Angeli, 1979). On ecclesiastical property, see E. Stumpo, "Il consolidamento della grande proprietà ecclesiastica nell'età della Controriforma," in *Storia d'Italia. Annali 9*, 265–89.

ate and drank before the service. The obligatory day of rest was observed, although not always. But it was a religion of externals. In the
words of the priest: "the populace feels little devotion, and there are
very few among them who come to Mass willingly." Moreover, there
was resistance in some quarters, such as an attempt to rob the taberna-
cle with its most holy sacrament, while others counselled the priest "to
just keep on eating and drinking and not bother himself about their
souls, let them go to the Devil, if that is where they want to go." Some
of the young men, Zanut Bezzin, Bastian Sebenico, and Francesco
Fusat, even had threatened and tried to thrash the priest because in a
sermon he had pointed them out by name as being among those who
did not go to confession.[32]

The rites connected to the life of the fields, such as rogations,
were felt more deeply. Not long before, in 1566, there had been a
bequest to distribute seventy-two loaves of bread, worth two pennies
each, among the participants. These ceremonies, which were capped
off with a hearty meal, were still being performed, as they had been in
the Middle Ages, with the participation of the neighboring parishes
which were once the chapels of the ancient parish of Montereale: on
the first day the procession wended its way from Montereale through
the fields, reaching San Leonardo. The following day the priests and
townspeople of San Leonardo, San Martino di Campagna, San Foca
and Sedrano all finished up at Montereale.[33]

The decadent religious life of Montereale was not peculiar to it,
but reflected a prevalent situation. The anonymous author of a denunciation dating from 1580, for example, penned a description of the
behavior of the people of Fanna, just a few kilometers away, which
would have been just as appropriate for Menocchio's own village:

If these individuals [i.e., the eight accused persons] attend Mass,
they do so out of habit, not from devotion, and that brief mo-

---

[32] See AVPd, *Biblioteca capitolare, Visite*, b. 7, Montereale, deposition of priest Odorico
on 18 September 1584, articles 2 and 11 in his defense, and the depositions of the priests
Martino de Hernostis and Alvise Varmo made on 2 and 8 November 1584. On the threats
to Odorico, see the deposition of Bernardo del Cotta dated 2 November 1584; AAUd, *S.
Officio*, b. 8, fasc, 132, session of 25 April 1584; fasc. 136: on 29 April 1584 Vorai
denounced Giacomo, nicknamed Matho, because he had not received communion for
several years. See also Vorai's denunciation against the Margnani, 20 below.

[33] See AVPd, *Biblioteca capitolare, Visite*, b. 7, Montereale, orders by the visitor on 2
November 1584.

ment while they stand listening to the priest they are half outside the door so that they can the more readily go to play cards,
or play *morra,* in that holy place in the sacrosanct cemetery, all
the while cursing with cruel and horrible blasphemies [...]
Usurpers of church property, now of this poor church, now of
that one, persecutors of priests, monks, and every other type of
cleric, always bad-mouthing them and harassing them, because
they would like to live just as they please [...] They say that
priests gobble up the dead and do even worse to the living and,
to put it in their words, use the living [*usano con li vivi*]. In
Fanna there are more than a thousand souls: there are not
twenty among them who know the Pater Noster, the Ave Maria
and the Credo, or who care to learn them.[34]

Menocchio was among those not touched by the priest's reforming
ministry. Not only did he hold his own against him, sticking to his
ideas, but after 1580 stopped going to him for confession. There was
a personal antagonism between the two, evidently, because Menocchio
fulfilled his religious obligation by confessing himself to priests in
neighboring villages, Maniago Libero and Barcis. However, he did
receive communion in his own parish. On Holy Saturday in 1583 he
explicitly asked Father Odorico for permission to confess himself to
another priest, and was turned down.[35] The hostility between them
was undoubtedly caused by the sharp differences in their ideas and by
the miller's harsh criticism of priests and religion in general; but there
was probably something more purely personal. Odorico may have been
conscientious in the performance of his ministry, but he was no saint.
True, he did not keep a steady woman, a concubine, in the parlance of
the day, a common practice of the clergy which had found acceptance
among the people since it did not affect relations within the community. However, his sexual license was a source of preoccupation, because
he chased after women to obtain their favors. His audacity reached the
point of actually asking for them, especially the young ones, from their
friends and relatives, offering gifts and money in return. Once, he even
had dared make such a request of Menocchio, at least according to
Giovanni, the latter's eldest son, in a deposition he made at a trial:

---

[34] ASVe, *Santo Uffizio,* b. 46, fasc. "Da Re Salvatore, Dalla Puppa Giacomo ...,"
denunciation dated 16 June 1580 by the tribunal; cf. note 1 of the denunciation.
[35] See 26; AAUd, *S. Officio,* b. 8, fasc. 136, interrogation of Vorai, 19 May 1584.

As for how the priest lives, the first thing he does is ask for a woman to have relations with, and this is public knowledge and he has done it to many, and, among others, the priest once said to my father: "Ser Domenico, I would like a favor from you, but I want it kept secret." And when this was promised the priest told him that he wanted Menica, his daughter, my sister, and would he be kind enough to do him this service. And my father answered, "Nothing doing" and stomped off. We did not make more of a fuss because my father is poor and tries to mind his own business. He [the priest] did not succeed either with Iseppia, but I know that many times he tried, offering her money, and doing her favors, and she never accepted anything from him. And once the priest threw some money wrapped in a cloth over the balcony of my house, so that my sister would find it. She did find it and not knowing who had left it, she gave it to an aunt [...]. And he courts my sister and others publicly, but I do not know if anything happened with them.[36]

Obviously, according to the priest, this was all slander, but a witness also speaks of attempts made with another of Menocchio's daughters, Maria, and several people mention women's names as proof of the priest's immoral habits, so that this gossip is at least plausible. The bell ringer's wife, a part-time servant in the rectory, goes so far as to report: "And that priest Odorico said to me more than once, 'If Menocchio had given me his daughter, he would not be where he is now, a prisoner of the Inquisition.'"[37] The statement may reflect more the woman's malicious version of the encounter than what Vorai actually said, but at any rate it presupposes that he really made the request. The conflict between Menocchio and the cleric thus takes on a different coloring, and can be viewed against the backdrop of a sharp antagonism between priest and parishioners.

---

[36] AVPd, *Biblioteca Capitolare, Visite,* b. 7, Montereale, deposition of G. Scandella, 16 September 1584.

[37] Ibid., deposition of Antonia, wife of Giacomo de Benedetto, 14 November 1584.

The first trial.

The start of the inquisitorial trial in Concordia shattered the unstable equilibrium which had existed within the community for years, and moved the conflict to a higher, institutional plane. The village itself becomes directly involved: thirteen witnesses provide evidence against Menocchio before he is even arrested. The priest from a neighboring village and still more witnesses are questioned later. The dispute now has as a participant the Holy Office, an institution whose history in Italy is relatively obscure and whose name still evokes images of pyres, torture, and secret proceedings. Recent scholarship, however, especially that part devoted to the Spanish Inquisition, offers a more nuanced view, liberated from the myth of the "Black Legend." Based on a thorough appraisal of the sources, this newer historiography tends to view the Holy Office as a tribunal which proceeded rationally and mercifully compared to other law courts of the time. The dark colors in the older picture of the repression of religious dissent drawn by earlier writers have been notably softened. There are no comprehensive studies on the Roman Inquisition which operated in Italy and whose organization, jurisdiction and procedures in some respects resembled the Spanish, but with specific features of its own.[38] A few brief remarks of a historical and legal nature will suffice to understand Menocchio's story, the means by which the documents preserved in the

---

[38] For the bibliography on the Inquisition, see E. van der Vekene, *Bibliotheca bibliographica Historiae Sanctae Inquisitionis,* 3 vols., (Vaduz, 1982–1992). On the Spanish tribunal, see B. Bennassar, *L'Inquisition espagnole, XVe–XIXe siècles* (Paris, 1979); *Historia de la Inquisicion en Espana y America,* eds. J. Pérez Villanueva & B. Escandell Bonet, vol. 1, (Madrid, 1984); H. Kamen, *Inquisition and Society in Spain in the Sixteenth and Seventeenth Centuries* (London, 1985). On the Roman Inquisition, see E. W. Monter & J. Tedeschi, "Toward a Statistical Profile of the Italian Inquisitions, Sixteenth to Eighteenth Centuries," in *The Inquisition in Early Modern Europe,* edited by G. Henningsen and J. Tedeschi in Association with Charles Amiel (DeKalb: Northern Illinois Univ. Press, 1986), 130–57, with bibliography, now revised in Tedeschi's *The Prosecution of Heresy: Collected Studies on the Inquisition in Early Modern Italy* (Binghamton: Medieval and Renaissance Texts and Studies, 1991), 89–126; A. Prosperi, "L'Inquisizione: verso una nuova immagine?" *Critica storica* 25 (1988): 119–45; *L'Inquisizione romana in Italia nell'età moderna: Archivi, problemi di metodo e nuove ricerche. Atti del seminario internazionale, Trieste, 18–20 maggio 1988,* eds. A. Del Col & G. Paolin (Rome: Ministero per i Beni Culturali e Ambientali, 1991). For an analysis of the history and myth of the institution from the Middle Ages to modern times, see E. Peters, *Inquisition* (New York & London, 1988).

archives of the institution were generated, and their reliability as historical sources.

The judges were two, the episcopal vicar and the inquisitor: this was the rule in the courts of the Roman Inquisition, especially in the Republic of Venice. Juridically their authority differed: the bishop acted by his ordinary prerogative, in virtue of his faculty to govern a diocese; the inquisitor acted by the authority delegated to him by the pope. In the Middle Ages inquisitors had been named according to the special needs of a time and place, but after the creation in 1542 of a permanent commission of cardinals, the Congregation of the Holy Office, in practice every important diocese had an inquisitor in residence. Each of the two judges had full authority to proceed without the other, but according to the pontifical constitution *Multorum querela* of 1317, a key pronouncement in defining their relations, they had to act in concert at three crucial and delicate stages of the trial: when the conditions of a prisoner's incarceration had to be made more stringent, to authorize the use of judicial torture, and at sentencing. In theory, the office of inquisitor, since he was the representative of the pope, the highest authority in the Church, prevailed over that of the bishop, but in fact, from roughly 1540–1560 it was the bishops and their vicars who exercised preeminence in the Republic of Venice.[39] In the period that interests us here there was a gradual ascendancy of the inquisitor, as the result of the centralization of authority exercised by the Congregation of the Holy Office.

In the diocese of Concordia the activity of the Inquisition had commenced in 1550 with a trial under Bishop Pietro Quirini. The first judge with delegated authority from the Holy Office had been Fra Francesco Pinzino, in 1558, who was vicar to the inquisitor general of Venice for the diocese of Concordia. He was succeeded by a series of relatively inactive diocesan inquisitors. In January 1575, following episcopal complaints about the chronic absenteeism of inquisitors, the Holy See entrusted the jurisdiction of Concordia to the inquisitor of

---

[39] See N. Davidson, "Rome and the Venetian Inquisition in the Sixteenth Century," *Journal of Ecclesiastical History* 39 (1988): 16–36; A. Del Col, "Organizzazione, composizione e giurisdizione dei tribunali dell'Inquisizione romana nella repubblica di Venezia (1500–1550)," *Critica storica* 25 (1988): 244–94.

Aquileia, residing in Udine, Fra Giulio Columberto da Assisi.[40] In December 1579, the office of apostolic inquisitor general for the patriarchy and diocese of Aquileia and diocese of Concordia was entrusted to Fra Felice da Montefalco, doctor of theology, prior and lecturer in the Convent of San Francesco in Udine, and a minor conventual as were all inquisitors who occupied that position. Unlike his predecessors, who were nominated by a superior of the order, probably the minister of the province of Sant'Antonio, he was the first to be appointed directly by the Congregation.

The four-and-a-half years in which Fra Felice filled the position were marked by feverish activity: sixty-eight persons tried, thirty-six investigated, seventy-odd denunciations received but not followed up, fourteen trials from the previous administration renewed and for the most part completed. At least thirty-eight sentences were promulgated resulting in one condemnation to capital punishment (performed posthumously) against a *relapsus* recaptured after a prison break, three other capital condemnations against contumacious offenders, two condemnations to *carcere perpetuo* against recidivists and one for grave heresies (against Menocchio), eleven sentences of reconciliation accompanied by abjurations and various penalties, seven canonical purgations, six sentences imposing salutary penances, five orders to remain at the call of the tribunal, and two admonitions. There were four inquisitorial courts, each with its archive: Udine and Cividale in the diocese of Aquileia, Concordia-Portogruaro, and, for a brief period, Pordenone in the neighboring diocese.

At Cividale, the bishop's representative on the court was the dean of the chapter, commissioned by the patriarch himself. At first the patriarch and his vicar were displeased by this proliferation of inquisitorial seats, since this meant the required presence in the tribunal of the secular official who had jurisdiction over the apposite territory, a provision resulting from agreements between the Republic of Venice and the Holy See. In practice, over the long run, this worked to the advantage of the ecclesiastical administration because it led to a greater

---

[40] See A. Del Col, "La storia religiosa del Friuli nel Cinquecento. Orientamenti e fonti," *Metodi e ricerche*, n.s., 1, (1982), no. 1: 72. For a general survey of the operation of the Inquisition in Friuli, see now idem, "Shifting Attitudes in the Social Environment toward Heretics: The Inquisition in Friuli in the Sixteenth Century," in *Ketzerverfolgung im 16. und frühen 17. Jahrhundert*, eds. B. Moeller, H. R. Guggisberg & S. Seidel Menchi. Wolfenbütteler Forschungen, 51 (Wiesbaden: Harrassowitz, 1992), 65–86.

penetration and broader jurisdiction for the Holy Office.[41]

Relations between the inquisitor and the episcopal vicars of the two dioceses were frequently strained. In fact, with Paolo Bisanti, former Bishop of Cattaro and now coadjutor and vicar general of the patriarch, as well as apostolic commissioner of the Holy Office, there was almost constant discord. Disguised at first, it may have been occasioned by personality differences (Bisanti considered Fra Felice "a man of poor judgment, although quite literate"), but it was more likely connected to problems of jurisdiction. The inquisitor claimed every case involving superstition and prohibited foods for the sphere of authority of the Holy Office. Bisanti, on the other hand, considered these categories to fall within episcopal purview when they were not accompanied by the suspicion of heresy, and he deemed the inquisitor's pretensions an untoward encroachment. Among other proceedings, Fra Felice reopened and brought to a conclusion the first trial against *benandanti*, which had been suspended in 1575 by the judge of that day. Bisanti was highly irritated by the fact that the inquisitor had appointed a notary of his own in August 1581, with the assent of the patriarch, and was now keeping an archive independently of officials in the patriarch's court. Even though he had both ordinary and delegated authority similar to Iacopo Maracco, the preceding vicar who had directed the administration of the tribunal, Bisanti found himself obliged to follow the lead of the inquisitor.[42]

Another bone of contention was Bisanti's ongoing attempt to downplay the significance of Holy Office activity, and the number of

---

[41] See AAUd, *S. Officio*, bb. 5–8, fasc. 85–138. From the inventory cited at note 152, the accused appear to total 69, while from a first-hand reading of the documents I count 108: 68 tried, 36 investigated, 4 accused, to which should be added another 66 accused who were not further prosecuted, recorded in b. 73, fasc. "Liber denuntiarum officii sanctissimae Inquisitionis Aquileiensis et Concordiensis," fols. 9v–18r. The resumed trials are in fasc. 47, 52, 60, 64, 65, 67a, 70, 71, 74–76, 83, 84 e ASVe, *Santo Uffizio*, b. 44, fasc. "De Melchiori don Daniele." The sentences preserved in b. 58, fasc. "Sententiarum contra reos S. Officii liber I," fols. 80r–144r, "Sententiarum . . . liber II," fols. 1r–56v, total 23, while the others are preserved in fasc. 96, 103, 108–10, 123, 128, 132–34, 136–38. The complaints of Giovanni Grimani and Paolo Bisanti are contained in letters to the inquisitors of Venice, dated respectively 25 February and 8 March 1581, in ASVe, *Santo Uffizio*, b. 162.

[42] See *Le lettere di Paolo Bisanti, vicario generale del patriarca di Aquileia (1577–1587)*, a cura di F. Salimbeni (Rome: Edizioni di storia e letteratura, 1977), 95, 233, 237, 279, 296, 349, 383–84, 484–85. The notary, from early August 1581, was the priest Giovanni dei Negri: AAUd, *S. Officio*, b. 73, reg. "Liber denuntiarum officii . . . ," fol. 1r.

heretics and suspects in the Venetian portion of the diocese of Aquileia, while Fra Felice's febrile activity was demonstrating just the opposite. The latter, in fact, twice officially requested, on 18 December 1581 and 5 November 1582, in plenary sessions of the tribunal, that trials which had been suspended be reopened and brought to a conclusion. Since the vicar's opinion was that "here there is little to do for the Inquisition, nothing in fact,"[43] one suspects that his interest in minimizing the impact of heresy was inspired by the understandable desire to cast his patriarch, Giovanni Grimani, in a favorable light. Although Grimani, who had been under suspicion of espousing false doctrines, was subsequently acquitted, nevertheless he was still without a cardinal's cap and a metropolitan's *pallium,* thanks to the firm opposition of the cardinal inquisitors, who were making him pay for his past sympathies towards the Reformation.[44]

The situation was not so complex in the diocese of Concordia, nor the discord permanent, but here too Fra Felice tried to impose his will from the start. In fact, in an inquest which he found in process at the time of his arrival, he became convinced that the two accused must indeed be guilty. Accordingly, on 4 February 1580, he requested the government representative (*provveditore*) in Pordenone to arrest them. But the vicar general, Scipione Bonaverio, considered this unjust, as far as one of the two was concerned, Giovanni Daniele Melchiori, parish priest of Polcenigo, and opposed it. The latter was thus simply cited, but did not appear; an order for his arrest was then issued but not executed because the inquisitor in Venice transferred the case to his own jurisdiction on 14 April 1580, following appeal by the defendant. At any rate, the activity of the Holy Office in the diocese of Concordia was extremely limited: three cases in 1580, one in 1581, two of which were concluded by Fra Felice only years later.[45]

---

[43] See *Le lettere di Paolo Bisanti,* 231, 240, 272, 326, 409, 448, 508. The quote is at 59–60.

[44] See A. Del Col, "La riforma cattolica in Friuli vista dal Paschini," in *Atti del convegno di studio su Pio Paschini nel centenario della nascita, 1878–1978* (Udine: Deputazione di storia patria, 1979), 135–39; P. Simoncelli, "Inquisizione romana e Riforma in Italia," *Rivista storica italiana* 100 (1988): 56, 64, 83.

[45] See ASVe, *Santo Uffizio,* b. 44, fasc. "De Melchiori don Daniele," unnumbered leaves; in Udine only two folios have survived from this large trial which ended up being appealed to Venice: AAUd, *S. Officio,* b. 73, fasc. 12. The four cases from the diocese of Concordia are *ibid.,* b. 5, fasc. 85, 86, 90; b. 6, fasc. 97.

This state of affairs was not merely the result of quarrels between episcopal vicars and inquisitors, but should be viewed rather in the context of the papacy's general policy of reform and centralization in this period. The more direct control of the diocese through apostolic visitations and the greater intervention by the Congregation of the Holy Office inaugurated by Pius V (1566–1572) was broadened by Gregory XIII (1572–1585) and continued by Sixtus V (1585–1590), who reorganized the entire Roman Curia for this purpose.[46] Even the custody of Holy Office archives on the part of local inquisitors in the Republic of Venice stemmed from an order of the Holy See in 1568, opposed in vain by the Council of Ten, which viewed the measure as an increase in Roman influence over the tribunals and the end to its own ready access to documents deposited in the episcopal archives. A limited correspondence between inquisitors in Udine and the Congregation had commenced in 1558, but only became regularized, receiving its own archival classification, from 1588 on.[47]

When the first extrajudicial denunciation against Domenico Scandella was made in September 1583, and the first interrogations began in October, the inquisitor was occupied with litigation in Udine

---

[46] Cf. L. von Pastor, *The History of the Popes from the Close of the Middle Ages,* 40 vols., (St. Louis, 1898–1953), 12: 503–13; 13: 210–24; 14: 259–318; 16: 305–52, 478–82; 17: 288–343, 400–4; 19: 296–322; 21: 192–97; 24: 198–219. For the patriarchate of Aquileia, cf. C. Socol, *La visita apostolica del 1584–85 alla diocesi di Aquileia e la riforma dei Regolari* (Udine: Casamassima, 1986).

[47] On 15 January 1569 the Council of Ten ordered the *rettori* of Brescia, Padova, Vicenza, Verona, Bergamo, Treviso, Udine, Rovigo, Feltre and Belluno to inform the bishops in secret of the government's opposition to the transfer of the archives into inquisitorial hands: ASVe, *Consiglio dei dieci, Secreto,* reg. 8, fols. 139r–v. The decision was taken following the consignment of his archive by the bishop of Brescia: see C. Cairns, *Domenico Bollani, Bishop of Brescia. Devotion to Church and State in the Republic of Venice in the Sixteenth Century* (Nieuwkoop: De Graaf, 1976), 209–11. For the Udine archive see ASVe, *Santo Uffizio,* b. 160, letter of the government representative Francesco Venier to the heads of the Council of Ten, Udine, 18 January 1569: the *rettore* states that he has communicated the order to the episcopal vicar Maracco, who had declared that he would obey. Maracco's request for an opinion from the Holy Office in Rome, without date but made on 23 May 1561, is preserved in AAUd, *S. Officio,* b. 1, fasc. 23. The letters from the Congregation are at bb. 59–63 and extend to 1766; b. 64 contains a register of the copies of these letters; bb. 66–68 includes some letters from Rome on financial matters (16th century), letters to the Inquisition of Concordia from Venice, from Rome, and from local commissioners and vicars; and letters from the inquisitor and vicars in Portogruaro (1635–1685 c.).

and Cividale.[48] Thus the preliminary inquest against Menocchio had to be initiated by the vicar general, Giovanni Battista Maro. Maro, doctor in canon and civil law, a canon of Concordia, had served as vicar in 1570, acting vicar general in 1579, and vicar general from 1581–1582 to 1585. His experience as a judge in inquisitorial proceedings was limited to presiding at a session of the Holy Office in 1570 and again in October 1579. On the latter occasion he earned for himself a solemn rebuke from the Bishop Pietro Quirini for having let himself be overshadowed by the inquisitor Columberto. He had conducted interrogations personally only in August and September 1583 in a trial which he initiated against a certain Orlando Burigana during a visitation to the parish of Vigonovo.[49] It is probably lack of expertise that causes Maro, on 29 and 30 October, in the presence of the commissioner of the inquisitor, Fra Andrea da Sant'Erasmo, guardian of the convent of San Francesco in Portogruaro, to ask the witnesses virtually identical questions. Meanwhile, the inquisitor, Fra Felice, even though heavily occupied in the other diocese, pays a brief visit to Portogruaro on the 9th of December to question a witness, and, on the 2nd of February, interrogates another dozen or so at Montereale. These rapid movements by the inquisitor outside the official seats of the tribunal, not limited to this occasion, quickened the pace of the investigations and saved witnesses from journeying outside their village. Fra Felice was an experienced judge and did not repeat the same questions. Since the evidence was of sufficient weight, he was able to cite the defendant to appear at once, order an inspection of the books found in his home, and make an arrest the next day. On 4 February Menocchio is escorted to the episcopal prison at Concordia. The inquisitor returns to Udine and the first four interrogation sessions are conducted by the vicar general alone, who limits himself to rehashing the evidence and posing a few general and not overly taxing questions.

---

[48] Ibid., b. 7, fasc. 116, 117, 118, 121, 123.

[49] See note 1 of the first trial. As for his activity in the capacity of inquisitorial judge, see ASVe, *Santo Uffizio*, b. 29, fasc. "Marcolino Antonio"; b. 44, fasc. "De Melchiori don Daniele," dated 10–29 October 1579; AAUd, *S. Officio*, b. 7, fasc. 119. For the pastoral visit, see AVPn, *Visite pastorali*, b. 1, reg. "Visite Querini," dated 15 August 1583, where one finds recorded only the visitor's customary invitation to present themselves spontaneously to people who were not living as faithful Catholics, or who had matrimonial litigation or reserved cases to resolve.

If the procedure followed here was correct from the canonical point of view, it did not, however, respect the Venetian statutes that required the presence of the Republic's provincial governors (*rettori*) at all trials, from the first depositions and interrogations through the final sentencing. The *podestà* Francesco Maria Minio had participated only at the session held on 29 October, but the new incumbent in the office, Pietro Zorzi, who had just arrived in Portogruaro, on his own initiative requested that the law be respected in full.[50]

These were not new regulations; they dated back to decrees for the entire dominion issued by the Council of Ten on 30 October 1550. They provided for the presence of the provincial governors at trials, for the participation of two jurists, doctors of law, and for the transfer of the most important cases to Venice. The Council of Ten, the highest Venetian organ of penal justice and state security, and in that period also the chief magistracy for the conduct of both internal and foreign affairs, now extended to the peripheral tribunals of the Inquisition directives which had been limited since 1547 to the Venetian court. The Council intended thereby to formalize its control over these provincial Inquisitions, as well as to exercise a closer vigilance over heresy, as it had done from time immemorial over all serious crimes. The Holy See strenuously opposed this serious encroachment on canon law, which absolutely excluded the presence of laymen in inquisitorial trials and limited the role of civil authorities to that of lending assistance in the execution of sentences. Nonetheless, an agreement was struck on 15 September 1551 between the Council of Ten and the papacy, after almost a year of angry contention. In exchange for the Republic's firm support in the work of the Holy Office, the Church accepted the most important of the provisions demanded by the Venetians, and thus conferred canonical legitimacy on them. The Republic, which wanted religious dissidence repressed, but desired to maintain a direct and continuous control over the work of the Holy Office, succeeded in imposing a lay presence at trials under the pretext that it conferred greater prestige on the Inquisition. For its part, the

---

[50] See 4, 40. That the new governor was acting autonomously is deduced from the fact that the central authorities took no action on the matter that year: ASVe, *Consiglio dei dieci, Comune*, reg. 37; *Secreto*, reg. 13; *Roma*, reg. 3; *Criminale*, reg. 14; *Capi del Consiglio dei dieci, Lettere*, file 84; *Lettere secrete*, file 10; *Lettere dei rettori*, b. 190 (Portogruaro); *Senato, Secreta*, reg. 84; *Deliberazioni Roma ordinaria*, reg. 5; *Terra*, reg. 55; *Santo Uffizio*, b. 162 (original letters from ambassadors and *rettori* to the Council of Ten).

state abandoned its demand for the participation of the two lay jurists and that certain serious trials be transferred to Venice. In reality, the Council of Ten had deftly succeeded in circumventing the official accord, and on 25 September, together with the agreed-upon dispositions, sent a secret order which reiterated the obligation of transferring important trials to the Dominion for adjudication, and gave instructions for the selection of laymen as counselors and assistants, with or without the ecclesiastical presence.[51]

In the following decades each of the two powers, which shared the common goal of wanting to see civil and religious order maintained, sought in practice to impose its sway over the other, or at least free itself from subservience to the other, without achieving conclusive results. This tension is apparent even in Menocchio's trial. On 28 April 1584 the two judges are compelled to have the defendant ratify, in the presence of the civil magistrate, the four previous trial sessions which had been held without the participation of the secular authority. But subsequently, as early as 7 and 12 May, they took advantage of the absence of the *podestà*, Zorzi, and continued the trial without him, arguing that the proceedings had already been dragging on too long.[52] Occasionally, the Venetian magistrates would permit the trial to be prosecuted even in their absence, especially during the interrogation of witnesses.[53] Another source of discord, sometimes played out in the open but on other occasions behind the scenes, concerned the

---

[51] See Del Col, "Organizzazione, composizione," especially 269–70, 280–81, 292–94. Previously, the only comprehensive account of Venetian decisions in matters regarding the Holy Office was, despite its gaps, Paolo Sarpi, *Sopra l'officio dell'Inquisizione* (18 November 1613), in Sarpi's *Scritti giurisdizionalistici*, ed. G. Gambarin (Bari: Laterza, 1958), 119–30, with explanatory information on subsequent pages. For the regulations regarding the confiscation of heretics' property, see note 64. On the question of sentences to capital punishment it should be noted, for example, that against Fra Baldo Lupatino the Council of Ten emitted its own sentence to a *carcere perpetuo*, as a substitute for the death sentence promulgated by the Inquisition: see ASVe, *Consiglio dei dieci, Criminale,* reg. 7, fols. 104v–105r; the capital sentence pronounced on 13 October 1562 against Giulio Gerlandi had to be executed by officials of the Holy Office, not the secular arm: ASVe, *Santo Uffizio,* b. 18, fasc. "Gherlandi Giulio," three copies at fols. 32r–33v, 60r–v, 82r–v; the capital sentence emitted by the Inquisition of Brescia against Stefanello Planerio in 1558 was kept in abeyance until December 1566, when the Council decided to place the repentant prisoner in a less harsh prison: ASVe, *Consiglio dei dieci, Secreto,* reg. 8, fols. 66v–67r, 72r–73r.

[52] See 40, 47, 56.

[53] See, for example, AAUd, *S. Officio,* b. 71, reg. "Liber actuum S. Officii," fols. 3r–4v (Udine, 5 November 1582); b. 7, fasc. 125 (Cividale, 16 October 1583).

presence of lay jurists: in the sessions at Udine two are almost always in attendance, but at Cividale and Portogruaro there is no such permanent participation and lawyers are called only to serve as consultors at the end of the trial, although ecclesiastical assistants are frequently on hand during the proceedings.[54] Even in Menocchio's case, the latter are occasionally present—at the deposition on 30 October 1583 and at the trial sessions on 7, 16, 22 February and 8 March 1584, while the secular consultants are convoked on 17 May for their final opinion.[55]

In the overall, everyday operation of the Inquisition, as it was envisioned by both ecclesiastical and secular spheres, the latent discord and ensuing accommodations were just a ripple on the surface of a slowly moving river. A deeply rooted commonality of interests between Church and state resulted in agreement on the principal ends of the Holy Office. Though there were frequent disagreements, they were always confined to specific practical situations, such as questions of procedure. The assistance furnished by the civil authorities in the daily work of the Inquisition and in the execution of capital sentences or of sentences that might provoke popular outbursts, is the most consistent reason given by historians for the Church's acceptance of lay interference in the workings of the Holy Office. But in reality, the participation of the secular arm was not indispensable and the courts frequently used their own officials and ecclesiastical prisons.[56] In Menocchio's trial, for example, the civil authorities played a relatively unimportant role: the summoning of the witnesses and of the accused is performed in Montereale by an emissary of the episcopal court; the inspection of books is carried out by the episcopal notary who accompanies the inquisitor; and the arrest is accomplished by an episcopal functionary backed up by three guards provided by the counts of Maniago. They escort the prisoner as far as Vivaro where they are replaced by four men of the town who escort the prisoner the rest of the way to Concordia. The jail to which he is taken is the bishop's, which later also

---

[54] See, for example, AAUd, *S. Officio*, b. 1, fasc. 3, 22, 23; b. 7, fasc. 107–10, 121–22 for Udine, while for Cividale b. 1, fasc. 8, 9, 18; b. 7, fasc. 118, 123–25 and for Portogruaro b. 5, fasc. 90; b. 7, fasc. 132–41.

[55] See 7–8, 22–23, 30, 32, 36, 64.

[56] P. F. Grendler, *The Roman Inquisition and the Venetian Press, 1540–1605* (Princeton: Princeton Univ. Press, 1977), 39–62; Del Col, "Organizzazione, composizione."

serves to house Menocchio during his sentence to "perpetual imprison-ment."[57]

Inquisitorial judicial procedure was a loosely structured system and offered many possibilities for variations and exceptions. The case of Menocchio illustrates the salient features of an entire trial right through sentencing. We have already noted that it began with the inquest phase (official initiation of the proceedings on the basis of public notoriety or of a denunciation and testimony received from witnesses). If the evidence was weighty enough the trial went on to the prosecutorial phase (a listing of the criminal counts or *inquisitio*, the citation, arrest, arraignment of the accused), without a sharp distinc-tion between the phases and with many variations from case to case. The prosecutorial system of evidence was founded in practice on the presumption of guilt and worked to the disadvantage of the defendant: two first-hand witnesses who agreed in their testimony were enough to prove guilt, but a confession was the crucial element of proof at which the entire procedure aimed.[58] Torture and harsh incarceration, the two most rigorous prosecutorial instruments, were applied at the discretion of the tribunal when the accused refused to divulge fully his crimes or accomplices. The ecclesiastical judges and the Venetian officials could consult with legal experts at various moments in the trial.

After the prosecutorial phase came the turn of the defense, duly offered to the accused, who could refuse it if he wished and throw himself on the mercy of God and his judges. He could either attempt to mount his own defense or entrust the responsibility to a lawyer approved by the tribunal. The accused could obtain a copy of the trial records, but with the deletion of all information which might lead to the identification of the prosecution witnesses. The defense basically consisted in the attempt to demonstrate the unreliability of the prose-cution's witnesses, or their enmity towards the accused, and the latter's

---

[57] See 3, 10–12, 21–22, 100.

[58] There is no comprehensive modern work on the procedures of the Roman Inquisi-tion. See the works cited at notes 15 and 38. On the administration of justice in the Republic, see *Stato, società e giustizia nella repubblica veneta (sec. XV–XVIII)*, ed. G. Cozzi, 2 vols., (Rome: Jouvence, 1980–1985); G. Cozzi, *Repubblica di Venezia e Stati italiani. Politica e giustizia dal secolo XVI al secolo XVII* (Turin: Einaudi, 1982).

good reputation and Christian life.[59] The type of defense adopted by Menocchio reveals a certain familiarity with the law, but also some frankly peculiar aspects. Before his arrest, he had been counselled by his friend, the priest Giovanni Daniele Melchiori, and by the lawyer Alessandro Policreto, to be cautious and restrain himself, avowing that in his heart he did not believe the errors which he had admitted.[60] In the first two sessions he tried to follow this good advice, even if without much conviction, but then he could no longer contain himself and blurted out his ideas in great detail. This made him a confessed criminal and there was little hope for his defense (some jurists even excluded it in such a circumstance), and he did not seriously attempt it with a lawyer but proceeded alone. He drafted a statement with his own hand and submitted it to the judges, who took it as a petition. In the document he followed the usual criteria for a defense: he had always lived as a good Christian, his erroneous ideas had been suggested by a false spirit, he was repentant and implored mercy and pardon. As if in extenuation, he named the causes of his errors: he had believed that it was enough to love God and one's neighbor; the books he had read (especially Mandeville's *Voyages*), the yearning to know, the false spirit counseling him, the hostility between the priest and himself, and the heavy burden of his work had kept him from observing divine and ecclesiastical precepts fully. A third of the defense is made up of a long analogy in which Menocchio compares himself to the patriarch Joseph. Menocchio too had been betrayed by a brother and spiritual father (the priest), sold to the inquisitor and imprisoned for having tried to explain, as had Joseph, things difficult to comprehend. In the end he suggested that the Lord would save him.[61] It was a dangerous line of

---

[59] See, for example, N. Eymeric, *Directorium inquisitorum . . . cum scholiis seu annotationibus . . . Francisci Pegnae . . .* (Venice: Apud Marcum Antonium Zalterium, 1595), 295–98; Locati, *Praxis iudiciaria,* 79–82. For the first of the two manuals there is an abridged, modern translation: N. Eymeric-F. Peña, *Le manuel des inquisiteurs,* Intro., trans., and notes by L. Sala-Molins (Paris-The Hague: Mouton, 1973); on this edition, see A. Borromeo, "A proposito del 'Directorium inquisitorum' di Nicolas Eymerich e delle sue edizioni cinquecentesche," *Critica storica* 20 (1983): 499–547. For a comparison with the stricter practices of the Council of Ten, see G. Cozzi, "La difesa degli imputati nei processi celebrati col rito del Consiglio dei X," in *La "Leopoldina". Criminalità e giustizia criminale nelle riforme del '700 europeo.* Ricerche coordinate da L. Berlinguer (Milan: Giuffrè, 1989), 1–87.

[60] See 37–39, 55.

[61] See 61–63. Scandella states that the writing is a defense document (63) but the judges differ (60–61, 83).

argument, but the judges seemed not to notice, or let it pass, because if they had scrutinized the document carefully they could have deemed it evidence of false repentance, which might have seriously affected the severity of the condemnation.

The definitive conclusion of the trial followed the norm, since sentences could entail, in order of increasing harshness: absolution, salutary penances, canonical purgation, reconciliation for suspicion of heresy or for formal heresy (which included the abjuration of errors and varied penalties: spiritual, corporal, pecuniary), or capital punishment. In the case of Menocchio, who was convicted of reading prohibited books and of formal heresy, he was sentenced to be reconciled. Even though the guilt of the accused had been abundantly proven, for maximum certainty two lay doctors of law were also summoned, Girolamo Pigozzino and Valerio Trapola, on the same day that the defense made its case. The latter was the lawyer to whom Menocchio's son had entrusted his father's fate immediately after the arrest. The entire trial dossier was read to them and, after two days, on 19 May, they gave their opinion: the accused was indeed a formal heretic, in fact, a heresiarch.[62] Menocchio was repentant, and repentance at the first trial meant a sentence of reconciliation and abjuration. The death sentence was reserved exclusively for the impenitent and the relapsed. There was one exception to this provision, however. Even a penitent person was liable to capital punishment, according to two papal bulls of 1556 and 1558, if the heresies included denial of the Trinity, the virginity of Mary, and the divinity of Christ.[63] Since Menocchio's professed beliefs involved these theological points, he might have been dealt with more severely, but his judges in their mercy—to use their words—spared his life.

Menocchio was permitted to make an abjuration, with the severity of the penalties proportionate to the gravity of the crimes. The sanctions imposed had, as their principal purpose, to cut off the heretic—even physically—from the religious community of believers. They were also intended to administer a punishment to him personally and, finally, to save his soul through spiritual penances. The sentence in this trial lists them in order: first of all Menocchio is condemned to wear in perpetuity a gray vestment emblazoned, front and back, with yellow

---

[62] See 64.

[63] See Monter-Tedeschi, "Toward a Statistical Profile," 156.

crosses, and on five feast days and on the day of the patron, St. Stephen, stand before the door of the cathedral in Concordia, head bared, lighted candle in his hand, and a rope hanging from his neck. He is also condemned to "perpetual" imprisonment, to fast every Friday on bread and water, to go to confession twice monthly, and, daily, to read articles of the faith assigned by the tribunal, and recite the seven penitential psalms with the litanies of the saints or the rosary. His property is confiscated, as was required by canon law, but, in accord with Venetian statutes,[64] it is allowed to pass to his children, after deduction of the trial expenses and his maintenance in prison. Before actually coming to the judgment, the sentence records in detail the criminal charges, and is much longer than is customary, running to eleven folios. The same is true of the abjuration. There is another unusual feature: both sentence and abjuration are undated and lack the indication that they were actually carried out. But we do know that they were read in the principal church of Portogruaro, Sant'Andrea, and from another document that this occurred at the end of May.[65] The texts that have come down to us, as we shall see, are preliminary drafts: the final, official versions have been lost.

It is possible, nevertheless, to deduce how Menocchio's own sentence might have been promulgated from others issued in Concordia. This rite was frequently performed privately in a church before only a few witnesses, in the inquisitor's own chambers, perhaps even under the arcade of the vicar general's residence, or in the audience hall of the episcopal palace.[66] At other times the reading of the sen-

---

[64] The yellow crosses were twice as large as those used in the Middle Ages. Each of Scandella's stripes had to be two spans in length and a half span in width, while in Piedmont in the fourteenth century it was one in length and three fingers in width: G. Amati, "Processus contra valdenses in Lombardia superiori, anno 1387," *Archivio storico italiano*, ser. 3, 1 (1865): 26. On the confiscation of property, see Sarpi, *Sopra l'officio dell'Inquisizione*, 127; L. Priori, *Prattica criminale secondo il ritto delle leggi della Serenissima Repubblica di Venetia* ... (Venice: Giovanni Pietro Pinelli, 1644), 132, who cites laws of 1547 and 1568.

[65] AVPn, *Processi*, reg. "Nonnulli processus ab anno 1584 usque ad annum 1586," fasc. 1 fols. 1r–2r: the first inventory made of the archive of the Holy Office of Concordia, dated 1 June 1584, in which the trial against Scandella is listed among those completed.

[66] See AAUd, *S. Officio*, b. 58, fasc. "Sententiarum contra reos S. Officii liber II," fols. 55r (7 May 1584), 57r (3 June 1579), 58v (1 February 1589), 63r (1 May 1590), 65r (5 August 1591), 66r–v (25 September 1593), 69r (26 October 1593), 70v (29 October 1593), 73v–74r, 84r–v (6 and 17 September, 3 October 1596), 13v [24 March 1597].

tence was a public and well-attended ceremony[67] and this, given the gravity of his case, is what must have taken place for the miller. The ceremony probably resembled one performed a short time earlier, on 7 December 1583, in connection with the heretic Orlando Burigana: on a feast day during a solemn Mass in a church overflowing with spectators, nobles and citizens alike, and in the presence of the authorities (the *provveditore,* the chief of the militia, the priest, the four guardians and priors of the city's convents), the inquisitor preached a sermon on the faith on a platform especially erected for the occasion. At its conclusion the convicted person recited his abjuration and a clerk read the sentence.[68] For Menocchio, the apposite feast day might have been either the Sunday of Pentecost, 20 May, or one of the two following holidays, the 21st and the 22nd, or Trinity Sunday, the 27th, all festivals which could have had a bearing on his specific heresies. At the end the condemned man was incarcerated in the episcopal prison of Concordia.

Inquisitorial documents as a historical source.

The judicial operations of the Holy Office have produced rich documentation of exceptional interest, not only for reconstructing its procedures, activities and influence in the religious and cultural life of the modern era, but also for uncovering important historical phenomena which have left unique traces of religious dissent, magic and witchcraft, and popular culture in these records. Unfortunately, even today, although a dozen or more local inquisitorial archives are accessible, the central repository of the Congregation of the Holy Office in Rome, now known as the Congregation for the Doctrine of the Faith, remains closed. The archives of the Spanish and Portuguese Inquisitions, instead, including the central archives, are open to scholars. The documentation preserved in the Italian inquisitorial collections is of a varied nature: in addition to the principal series of trial dossiers, there are long series of acts, denunciations, letters from the supreme Congregation, inventories, account books, and miscellaneous papers. Their

---

[67] Ibid., fols. 58v (2 February 1589), 88r (7 August 1599), 94v (14 February 1601).
[68] Ibid., fols. 40r–v.

state of preservation varies depending on events experienced by the individual archives over the centuries.[69]

The trial dossier is not a homogeneous aggregate: it contains a mass of disparate documents, the reliability of which needs to be weighed critically, as with all historical sources. The essence of the trial is found in the transcripts of the interrogations, written by notaries attached to the episcopal courts, sometimes augmented in this period by notaries of the Holy Office, who would later supplant them. The norms called for recording word for word what transpired at each session. There are no studies to tell us how this requirement was observed; in other words, we do not know to what extent the transcripts correspond to the actually spoken words. Although this basic methodological question remains unanswered, we assume that the reliability of these records is generally of a high order. It should be kept in mind that it is not always possible to follow the dialogue between judges and accused, because occasionally the questions were not recorded. The real interest of the court was in the responses which provided information on the crime. We also must assume that most of the transcripts were written down during the actual sessions and that these files are what have come down to us, but we cannot be certain that this is always the case. Some of these transcripts, even though they may be the only surviving document and be fully valid judicially, are certainly copies and may require emendation.[70]

In the present trial the depositions of the first thirteen witnesses, with the exception of the fifth, are copies. Even Menocchio's interrogations which appear at first glance to have been written down during the actual sessions and are signed by him at the conclusion of each, present paleographical peculiarities which lead to two sets of conclusions: the sessions of 7 and 16 February, 28 April, and 12 May 1584 show signs of corrections and variants which permit no other explanation than that they are a direct transcription. In addition, they have

---

[69] See J. Tedeschi, "The Dispersed Archives of the Roman Inquisition," in *The Inquisition in Early Modern Europe*, 13–32. Cf. 27–28 for a survey of local archives. (The essay is reprinted in revised form in Tedeschi's *The Prosecution of Heresy*, cited at n. 38).

[70] A. Del Col, "I processi dell'inquisizione come fonte: considerazioni diplomatiche e storiche," *Annuario dell'Istituto storico italiano per l'età moderna e contemporanea* 35–36 (1983–84): 31–49; N. Davidson, "The Inquisition in Venice and its Documents: some Problems of Method and Analysis," in *L'Inquisizione romana in Italia nell'età moderna*, 117–31 (cited at n. 38). On the duties of the notary, see Eymeric, *Directorium inquisitorum*, 288.

two questions crossed out, for which answers are not recorded. The sessions of 22 February, 8 March, 7 May, on the other hand, only show typical copying errors. These final transcripts, in other words, have been copied from previously written down texts or simple notes, executed at the end of the trial or at the close of each session. Menocchio's autograph signature does not raise a problem. It could have been affixed at any time after he was already in prison. It is worth mentioning that the last set of transcripts was drawn up by less experienced notaries, the coadjutor Terenzio Placentino (22 February) and Valerio Canipa (8 March, 7 May), while the first set of records, instead, were all prepared by the chief notary Giovanni Ghibellino, except the one for 12 May written by Canipa. Even during the second trial, the transcripts of the session held on 12 July 1599, wholly in the hand of Orazio Crasso who served as notary for both the bishop and inquisitor, have some textual corrections made during the actual writing, while in the second part there are copying errors made by Crasso himself.[71] It is reasonable to conjecture that the act of copying was faithful to the original text, without modifying or embellishing it, or having to reconstruct it from notes hastily jotted down in short hand.

Philological analysis of the documents is based upon corrections, additions and variants in the text which generally are passed over in an archival reading, but which are indispensable for a good critical edition. Two of the proposed emendations thus permit us to reestablish the original text which had been corrupted by the copyist with errors which radically affect the meaning. For example, in one place the notary writes "Christ" in the place of "God" and creates an absurd thought: "... because Christ willed that his Son should die."[72] Another classic lapse in copying occurs when "angels" is changed into "men." The latter term at first seems less odd in connection to the worms in the words of a witness reported earlier: "I heard him say that in the beginning this world was nothing [...] and it coagulated like a cheese, from which then were born a great number of worms, and these worms became angels [the copyist writes 'men'], of which the most powerful and wise was God [...]. And there was an evil one with

---

[71] See the "Philological Note" at xciv–xcvi.

[72] I have made the emendation in the text (see 51 of the first trial). On the difference between the language in the transcription and the language of Menocchio, see Ginzburg, 89–90.

his legions, Satan, who tried to fight against this God but he was beaten."[73]

The substitution of "men" for "angels" could in theory have been made by the witness who repeated the words at third hand, or by someone who had heard Menocchio personally and then put the words into circulation. But this hypothesis would suggest that these people thought that God and Satan were men (*not* that they had heard it, because Menocchio surely had said angels), an absurd, illogical concept for any Christian, even if only repeating the words of a heretic.[74]

But there is clearer evidence that the act of recording verbal testimony on paper might significantly modify words spoken at the trial or cause the omission of key sentences. At the start of the session of 8 March, at the very first question, which is not recorded explicitly, Menocchio replies:

> As I already said, I believe that when man is born he is like an ox and a beast and that God then gives him an angel and I believe that when we are in the mother's womb, we are just a pulp and dead flesh, but as soon as we are born, God sends us this angel, but before that, as I said, we are dead flesh [...] And when man grows up, whether it comes from God or from the Devil, another spirit comes into us which fights with that angel. And when man dies, both spirits go where it pleases God.

Menocchio is referring to testimony he gave earlier, but in his reflections on man and the soul only a few allusions to them surface: "And as for the souls, they came from the spirit of God and thus they must return to the spirit of God"; "I believe that soul is one thing, spirit another. The spirit comes from God [...]. I believe that they are two spirits, one opposed to the other and that when the body dies, they return to God."[75] The miller can always remember clearly ideas he has already expressed to the judges: if they are not found in the transcripts, it is because the notary leaves out things which, in his

---

[73] Cf. 9.

[74] For this particular type of error, see F. Brambilla Ageno, *L'edizione critica dei testi volgari* (Padua: Antenore, 1975), 49–52. I owe the reference to the courtesy of Laura Casarsa.

[75] The first citation is at 36, the others at 31, 33. Scandella speaks of man also at 25–27, 31–32. For evidence that the opening sentence in the reply refers precisely to statements made in the trial, see similar remarks at 24–25, 31, 33, 47, 50.

opinion, seem confused or unimportant. We can demonstrate such an omission in the second trial. The following question is asked at the beginning of the session held on 19 July 1599: "The last time that you were before us, at the end of the session you stated you thought you were a philosopher, astrologer, and prophet, but that even prophets erred. How do you understand this matter about being a prophet and prophets err?" But there is not a word of these remarks to be found in the 12 July interrogation. The next question also alludes to a statement in the first session, but this one is indeed recorded in the document.[76]

Inquisitorial sources need to be evaluated critically for more than questions concerning the relationship of the transcripts to the spoken words and the material condition of their production; they need especially to be studied in relationship to the legal machinery and functioning of the institution. The transcripts of the interrogations were not compiled primarily to record ideas and facts about the life of the accused, or even the reactions of his listeners, but rather to establish judicial evidence. The trial records, thus, reflect the requirements of the judges. We have briefly noted the different interests revealed by the testimony of both witnesses and accused, and the separate methods of interrogation followed by the vicar general and the inquisitor when each acted alone.[77] In the instances when both are present, it is not specified which of the two is asking the question, but with luck the historian can identify the voice of the actual interrogator. The replies often begin with "Yes sir, no sir," or with "Yes father, no father." In the latter case, the response has to be to the inquisitor, in the first it can be to either.[78] In reading the sections that can be attributed definitely to Fra Felice, it can be seen that his questions are almost always tough and astute, often linked by a logical thread so that he frequently is able to catch the accused contradicting what he has said in previous sessions (showing that these questions were conceived in advance), or even earlier the same day. He presses hard on precise, clearly defined themes, but still avoiding, it appears, crossing that thin and subtle boundary which would have made his questioning obviously suggestive. Monsignor Maro, instead, asks simpler questions, generally intended

---

[76] See 136. The assertion in the first session to which the second question refers is at 133.

[77] See above at xv–xvi.

[78] See 42, 44–45, 51, 53–54 for "Yes, sir" and 51, 55, 58–60 for "Yes, Father".

to confront Menocchio with things said earlier by witnesses or by the accused himself. Only rarely does he pose questions aimed at obtaining more precise details about a certain heresy.[79] His method of interrogation is certainly not suggestive and leaves the defendant more leeway to express himself as he wishes, while Fra Felice's generally is more incisive. In light of these observations and the prefacing of replies with "Yes father, no father," we may conclude that in the session of 28 April and at the beginning of the first session on 7 May it is Maro, whose education is more juridical than theological, himself more prone to conciliation, who is doing the questioning. The second half of the morning session on 7 May, the one on the afternoon of the same day, and the entire hearing on the 12th are conducted by the inquisitor, more expert in the matter, and endowed with greater training in theology and philosophy.

The doctrinal range of the proceedings is thus left to the judges, intent on piecing together the evidence, and in this trial it almost never departs from topics raised by witnesses at the preliminary inquest or by Menocchio at his own initiative.[80] The investigation is conducted in more depth than breadth: the court is not interested in reconstructing the accused's religion in its totality, but rather in weighing the evidence against him. One extraordinary moment does occur at the interrogation of 28 April when the vicar general asks Menocchio to talk freely about his ideas. The latter has just admitted saying that "if he were not afraid of the law, he would say a lot of things that would shock" and now he is offered an occasion: "... to tell everything that was on his mind and that he wanted to say." He then reveals things that we otherwise would not have known (his complaints about poor people being addressed in Latin, his criticism directed against the wealth of princes and of the Church). He then moves on to subjects he had discussed previously which perhaps meant more to him (the simplification of Christian doctrine to the love of God and of one's neighbor, the salvation of all men and not just of Catholics, the uselessness of the Church's laws). But of his own volition he immediately returns to the realm of theology, illustrating his theories on the

---

[79] See also Ginzburg, 54–56, 70–77.

[80] There are only three questions which definitely cannot be connected to the preceding themes: the one on the holy water (59), which perhaps concerns the validity of sacramentals and the power of priests and of the laity (27); the one on processions (59), which may concern the cult of saints; the one on the earthly paradise (59).

sacraments, and mentions the seven in turn (he sees all these as human inventions and merchandise, and offers a few specific observations on each one). He concludes with the falsity of hell and the human inventions in the Bible.[81] Even though absolutely no suggestive question is asked, it seems as though the very trial itself draws the discussion inevitably in a certain direction, unless we should suppose, as seems reasonable, that a benevolent suggestion by the vicar general lay behind the mention of the sacraments.

Transcripts are thus preconditioned by the trial situation and by the interrogation of the judges, affected by the intelligence and cultural background of the inquisitors, modified by the skill and capacity to comprehend of the notaries. But lack of objectivity is not an exclusive characteristic of these documents. All sources need to be carefully analyzed so as to disclose both the way in which they were put together and the intent, whether expressed or unconscious, of their authors, as well as the facts they contain and their connection to historical reality. In reading the transcripts of this trial, despite the danger of misrepresentations, two primary voices will stand out, that of the judge and that of the accused. There is a large cultural gulf separating Menocchio and his two examiners, vicar and inquisitor, who often do not seem to understand exactly what he is trying to say and have to probe further. This is the case especially when it is the turn of the inquisitor to conduct the interrogation.[82]

To appreciate the richness of Menocchio's ideas as they emerge from these proceedings, let us first attempt a brief comparison with a case built upon suggestive questioning and, second, with a highly stylized inquisitorial document. During the prosecution of some citizens of Cividale conducted alone by the inquisitor Fra Bonaventura Manento in 1559, the majority of replies on doctrinal matters are so lackluster and stereotyped that they virtually repeat the question, or give a mere yes or no. The defendants are so careful not to add something of their own that the result in one instance is this curious exchange:

When one was asked "What is your opinion about the authority of the supreme pontiff?," he replied, "Father, please tell me exactly

---

[81] See 42–44.

[82] See C. Ginzburg, *Ecstasies: Deciphering the Witches' Sabbath.* Translated by Raymond Rosenthal (New York: Pantheon, 1991), 13–14, 208.

what you mean." Asked whether he believed that the supreme pontiff
is the vicar of Christ on earth, he replied, "Yes sir."[83]

The comparison with formal documents, Menocchio's own sentence and abjuration, is even more illuminating. The two texts were
always prepared by the court and in this case we can even observe
precisely the manner in which they were compiled, because the documents that have come down to us are a first draft, not the final version. The sentence is an official summary of the trial because, before
coming to the words of judgment, it explains the procedure followed
in the case, and lists in detail the heresies and other crimes of the
offender. The primary scribe is the episcopal notary, Giovanni Ghibillino; the judge entrusted with drawing up the document is the inquisitor, who has already marked up the entire trial record with marginal
notes highlighting the matters discussed, and then groups them by
subject arranged in a sort of ascending order of importance according
to a precise theological scheme. The frame of reference is Catholic
scholastic theology and the ideas of the accused are organized according to these themes and to this scheme: prohibited books, conversations with the simple faithful and persistence in heresy, pope and
clergy, the laws of the Church, priests and the religious; saints, images,
indulgences, prayers and Masses for the dead, fasting, preaching, the
Bible, divine precepts, holy water, earthly paradise; creation of the
world, angels, human nature, the soul; original sin, mortal sins, individual predestination, the call to salvation, justification, the sacraments
(baptism, confirmation, matrimony, confession, the Eucharist, holy
orders, extreme unction), the resurrection of the faithful, the Last
Judgment, eternal bliss; finally, ending up with the Madonna, the
attributes of God (eternity, immateriality, absolute perfection), the
Trinity, and its individual members: Father, Son and Holy Ghost. Fra
Felice is preoccupied, even stunned, and interjects among these themes
expressions which reveal his repugnance and horror, not his curiosity
about Menocchio's heresies. Each topic is accompanied by the doctrinal evaluation of the theological concepts voiced by the defendant and
formalized by the judge; only a few phrases are reproduced in the
vernacular or in Latin.[84] Menocchio's own words and ideas have not
totally disappeared, but only a conceptual skeleton remains and his

---

[83] The trial is preserved in AAUd, *S. Officio*, b. 1, fasc. 18; the quotation is at fols. 7v–8r.
[84] The sentences in the vernacular are at 85–86, 91.

small cultural world has been broken up and reassembled on a different design. Even statements that seemed untainted by heresy or suspicion are squeezed in this judicial vise. For example, an imprecation to kill ecclesiastics is considered evidence of Menocchio's hostile animus towards them. It strikes us, instead, as an understandable, spontaneous outburst of desperation and frustration at the moment of his arrest when he shouted out that he would burn down churches and their priests with them.[85] Similarly, the miller's ironic and sacrilegious quip when his friend the priest Melchiori was preparing the host—"By the Virgin Mary, these are big beasts,"— becomes, in the mind of the inquisitor, a heretical expression directed at the image of the crucifix that was impressed on the unconsecrated host.[86]

The same theological construction, thematic arrangement and recomposition, is found also in the abjuration. The first part of the document is a confession of faith which reverses the heresies of the accused and turns them into positive statements, the second expresses detestation and the actual recantation of the heresies themselves (with the section on matrimony lacking). The entire text is translated directly from the Latin of the sentence with some simplification and slight modifications. A paragraph has dropped out of both parts, one referring to monks and nuns and to priests, likened by Menocchio to devils who wanted to be adored on earth more than God, who wanted to know more than God, and a statement that he would not give a penny for the lot of them (this is the inquisitor's summary of the last sentence, which in Menocchio's own words runs: "I wouldn't give a red cent [bezzo] either for priests or Masses.")[87] The disappearance of this section is not unintentional, unlike the accidental omission of the statement on marriage. Rather, it is a conscious act of censorship on Fra Felice's part, thus preventing the public from hearing this slanderous opinion about priests, which would be read in Italian, at the solemn ceremony of abjuration. In any case, the prevailing voice in these texts is no longer the miller's of Montereale, but the inquisitor's, a graduate in theology.

---

[85] See 84–85, 37.

[86] See 91, 11, 38.

[87] See cxv. The paragraph on ecclesiastics is in the sentence (84–85). The quotation is at 19.

The ideas of Menocchio: Analogies with the Reformation, Anabaptism, Antitrinitarianism.

What did Domenico Scandella really believe, what were his ideas? Not those reported by his fellow villagers, not those summed up by Fra Felice da Montefalco, but his own? These ideas have been admirably elucidated by Carlo Ginzburg and are amply documented to the slightest detail in the trial records published below. To draw a composite picture, despite points that are uncertain and difficult to clarify fully, it is necessary to identify the various co-existing cultural threads which make up this personal amalgam.

First of all, we are not dealing with a conglomerate of several disconnected ideas, as might appear from a superficial reading of the records and from the reconstruction of these ideas contained in the sentence. Menocchio's religious world has a definite structure, a logic of its very own, even if not always discernible in all its ramifications, but nevertheless not imposed from outside or by design. It can be found in the cosmogonical account described by the fourth witness on 30 October, in the clarification of this same account furnished by the accused to the vicar general on 7 February, in a more elaborate version on 7 May, and in the clarifications requested by the inquisitor at the completion of the proceedings.[88]

Menocchio's theory about the origin of the cosmos is intertwined with a schematic account of salvation and is a function of it. It is primarily a religious explanation, not a philosophical or scientific one; about faith, not about the knowledge of reality. At the beginning there was chaos, composed of the four primordial elements mixed together—earth, air, water, fire. God (or the spirit of God, the most holy majesty) was co-eternal with chaos and began to proceed from imperfect to perfect, thereby developing intellect and knowledge, until he gave order and understanding to chaos, drawing from it the most perfect light or the most perfect substance, just as the best part is taken out of milk to make cheese. From this light or substance worms were born, spirits who were the angels and among these the most important was God (or better yet the Holy Spirit), he too created from the primordial mass. God was the Father, the most perfect light who elected the Holy Spirit, who was inferior to him and was his assistant, and who in turn

---

[88] See 9, 25–26, 47–59.

chose four captains or stewards, Lucifer, Michael, Gabriel, Raphael, and by means of them, as if they were craftsmen, created the world, namely the seven skies, corresponding to the days of the week, which we call the seven planets, and then the earth, trees, animals and man. God's place was near the sun: in fact, it is not the sun which illuminates but God, who is true light and the sun is like a mirror which reflects the divine light. Lucifer wanted to be equal to God (or more properly to the Holy Spirit), but he was vanquished and chased away with all his angels. God, always through the Holy Spirit and his craftsmen, then made Adam and Eve and human beings to fill up the places left vacant. In the end, when men no longer followed the commandments, God, after having taken as his sons Abel, Noah, Abraham, Isaac, Jacob and Moses, also elected Christ as his son, who was of the same nature as other men, not conceived by the Holy Spirit but by St. Joseph and born from Mary, a woman like others, not a virgin. Christ was the greatest of the prophets, who was then seized and hanged (or trussed up) like a beast, and died, but did not bodily rise again; he did not save mankind through his death, but was only an example and a model of conduct. This cosmogony is both materialistic and spiritualistic, articulated by means of a remarkable metaphor based on milk and connected through radically heretical statements about God, the Trinity, and Christ in an attempt to find an explanation and a religious purpose to reality and to life.

Menocchio's concept of man is just as heretical as his cosmogony and also closely linked to it. In his pantheistic vision there is an intimate correspondence between the world and man, between macrocosm and microcosm, since all are composed of the four primordial elements. Thus the soul is made of matter, is not immortal and dies with the body, reverting to the four elements, while the spirit remains which returns to God. Life's purpose is to comport oneself well morally for the sake of paradise, a place surrounding the world from which everything can be seen, full of light, a perpetual feast where after the Last Judgment, there will only be disembodied spirits who will be able to see God, who is pure spirit. The Christian can attain salvation through love of God and his fellow; all morality and religion are reduced to this. In fact, loving one's neighbor is more important than loving God: for example, to blaspheme is not a sin because it does not harm one's fellow man. The seven sacraments, the precepts of the Church, prayers, purgatory serve no purpose and are considered useless since they are human inventions and used by the clergy to exploit the

faithful. All men have the Holy Spirit from birth "because God baptizes us, who has blessed all things." Only the sacrament of the Eucharist
survives, in part, but it contains and communicates not Christ but the
Holy Spirit (or the Trinity itself) and brings happiness to the spirit
which receives it. The religious authority and competence of the pope,
bishops and priests are no different than those of other mortals. The
meaning of the sacred, the function and mediatory role of the clergy
and the conditions of salvation are thus radically altered. The ecclesiastical hierarchy, official religious places and practices have no more
importance than other men and all places. The Church is not governed
by the Holy Spirit more than is every man. Salvation is attainable by
all who comport themselves well: Christians, heretics, Turks, Jews, all
can be saved equally because God has sent into all the Holy Spirit to
illuminate them.

This reconstruction is limited to the essentials, leaving aside many
secondary themes, details and explanations which might have enriched
the structure but blurred the basic configuration. What strikes us right
off is the complexity and expressiveness of the Friulan miller's religion.
The inquisitors were horrified at the gravity of the heresies, but we are
astounded at the richness and daring of his thought. Menocchio does
seem to be aware on occasion of his intellectual prowess, but no matter
how perceptive and original, he lived in his own time, he breathed the
oral culture of a peasant world and of his village and the culture which
he could attain through the reading of books in the vernacular and
conversations with educated persons. The rapid spread of printing in
the sixteenth century had quickened the circulation of ideas and
offered to a broad public new conceptual instruments and possibilities
of expression. How then was the culture of this literate miller constructed? What currents can be discerned, and how are they connected
within his mental world?

Many of Menocchio's ideas are traceable to the common patrimony of the Reformation, as it was known in Italy among the dissident
groups dispersed around the peninsula and especially in the Republic
of Venice: denial of the virginity of the Madonna, the rejection as
human inventions of ceremonies, sacred images, Lenten obligations,
purgatory, the pope, prelates and priests, sacred localities, objects, and
events. These and other evangelical ideas were widely diffused until the
1550's, more cautiously in succeeding decades, and Menocchio could
have heard them in Portogruaro, Pordenone, Porcia, Spilimbergo,
Udine and elsewhere. A sole vague allusion surviving in the documents

connects the miller to the town of Porcia by way of a certain Nicolò, a painter. The ideas of the Reformation had spread there during the 1540's and 1550's among a group of artisans, of whom the most dedicated and active was a weaver known as Antonio "de l'oio," but also among priests, the local nobility and a physician, Orazio Brunetto, who in various ways was in touch with other dissidents in Venice, Oderzo, Portobuffolè, Pordenone, Serravalle, and the castle of the Frattina family near Portogruaro. The group of artisans did not confine its activities to its own town: Zan Hieronimo, the brother of the weaver who had enthusiastically espoused the new doctrines, peddled his wares all along the foothills, from Polcenigo to Tramonti, meeting people along the way. The participation in this circle of Nicolò the painter is not verified, but we know that he gathered with groups in Pordenone in the house of Orazio Brunetto.[89]

Other statements of Menocchio's resemble Anabaptist and Antitrinitarian doctrines: denial of the divinity of Christ and of the Trinity, reduction of religion to morality, rejection of the sacraments (the Anabaptists denied the utility of infant baptism, but in some cases endowed even adult baptism with a purely symbolic and spiritualistic significance), championing of religious toleration, condemnation of the Church's wealth and the authority of the hierarchy. Such doctrines circulated throughout the Friuli. There was one place in particular, Cinto, between Portogruaro and Pordenone, from which many people emigrated to the Anabaptist communities in Moravia during the 1550's and 1560's; itinerant Anabaptist preachers, such as Giulio Gerlandi and Alessandro Iechil, were still going about in the latter decade.[90]

In addition to occasional contacts and conversations, Menocchio could have found many of his ideas in books. Carlo Ginzburg has skillfully reconstructed his relationship to the printed page, underlining

---

[89] See Ginzburg, 18–27; A. Del Col, "Eterodossia e cultura fra gli artigiani di Porcia nel secolo XVI," *Il Noncello*, no. 46 (1978): 9–76. Nicolò, a painter, was actually denounced to the Holy Office in Concordia in 1606 by a cousin of the children of Orazio Brunetto, by now deceased, and on another occasion by one of Brunetto's children. On the ideas of the Reformation in Italy, see S. Seidel Menchi, *Erasmo in Italia*, with bibliography.

[90] On Anabaptism in the area, see G. Paolin, "Dell'ultimo tentativo compiuto in Friuli di formare una comunità anabattista. Note e documenti," *Nuova rivista storica* 62 (1978): 3–28; idem., "L'eterodossia nel monastero delle clarisse di Udine nella seconda metà del '500," *Collectanea Franciscana* 50 (1980): 107–66; idem., "I contadini anabattisti di Cinto," *Il Noncello*, no. 50 (1980): 91–124.

not only the fragmentary and partial quality of the list, consisting mostly of borrowed books, but even a manner of reading which unconsciously filtered the words through a selective and distorting mental grid which continually harked back to an underlying stratum of oral culture.

What interests us most in Ginzburg's study is not so much the way Menocchio read the books, but what he extracted from them. The ideas which the miller could find, deduce, or rediscover in the printed texts almost all pertain to the current of the Reformation and to that of Antitrinitarianism. The works he read were books of piety, a travel account, a chronicle, the *Decameron* in an unexpurgated edition, but only one emanated from the circle of Italians who had espoused the new theological doctrines. It was one of the least widely diffused then and largely ignored by scholars today. In *Il Sogno dil Caravia,* the book in question, by the Venetian Alessandro Caravia, we can discern between the lines the doctrine of justification by faith alone, the concept of a religion reduced to a few essential scriptural precepts, the denial of purgatory, the condemnation of the use of Latin, the rejection of "sumptuous churches," the notion of confession made to God from the heart, the vision of saints as exemplars rather than intercessors. Menocchio probably took his idea that Mary was not a virgin indirectly from the *Rosario della gloriosa vergine Maria* by Fra Alberto da Castello, and from the *Leggendario de le vite de tutti li santi* by Iacopo da Varazze with an analogous deductive process, that homage was never paid to the Madonna while she was on earth (and therefore could be said to have been inferior to the empress Mary of Austria, who instead received many honors). From the *Historia del Giudicio,* in the verses that paraphrase Mt 25: 41–46, he found the idea that it was more important to love one's neighbor than to love God. In Mandeville's *Travels* he discovered pages that devaluated auricular confession and said Jesus Christ was the greatest of the prophets, that he was not crucified, but ascended to the heavens alive to judge the world, and that it was Judas Iscariot who was crucified in his stead. Menocchio also deduced from it, according to his own statement, that when the body dies the soul also dies, making an astounding intellectual leap in terms of what actually is in the text. The legend of the three rings in the *Decameron* suggested to Menocchio the idea of religious toleration and that man can be saved each in his own faith, Christian, Muslim, or Jew. In the *Fioretto della Bibbia* he found indirectly the denial of Christ's conception through the Holy Spirit, because St. Joseph addressed Jesus as "my son"; in other pages of this work he read about the creation of the world from the four elements and the correspondence between microcosm and macrocosm. Finally, in the *Supplementum supplementi delle croniche* by Fra Iacopo Filippo Foresti Menocchio encountered the concept of chaos, conceived as matter created by God, in a passage which reads: "Before earth, sea, and the sky, which covers everything, existed, nature had an appearance throughout its expanse that the philosophers called Chaos, a great and inchoate matter."[91]

This glance at Menocchio's literary sources may permit us to discern the roots of several disparate elements in his thought, but despite everything, the logic, the structure that links them remains beyond reach. This is so even if we consider two other writings added tentatively to the list by Ginzburg, since they were mediated by persons from the world of elite culture and would show the plausible influence of this culture on the thought of a worldly miller receptive to the most varied stimuli. First of all we have a faded and distorted echo of Michael Servetus's *De Trinitatis erroribus:* Christ's humanity is deified through the Holy Spirit, and the Holy Spirit is conceived as the energy, intellect, and inspiration of the Father (not a person separate from him) and as a presence operating in man and in nature. As for the distinction between mortal soul and immortal spirit, this could have derived from Averroistic circles at the University of Padua, specifically from the thought of Pietro Pomponazzi, revised and simplified with religious overtones by Girolamo Galateo (the sleep of souls until Judgment Day) and by Camillo Renato (the distinction between mortal *anima* and immortal *animus)* and subsequently diffused in the form of the doctrine of the sleep of the soul among Venetian Anabaptists. The only plausible intermediary who might have carried this idea to Menocchio was the parish priest of Polcenigo, Giovanni Daniele Melchiori, his childhood friend.[92]

The heretical ideas then in circulation and the miller's literary sources, direct or indirect, in themselves do not completely explain the fullness of his thought, which seems, in Ginzburg's interpretation, to harken back to an oral, peasant culture and suggests a centuries-old stratum of beliefs. The only fragment really identifiable with an ancient cosmogonic myth is the metaphor of the cheese and the worms. On

---

[91] See Ginzburg, 31–54.
[92] Idem, 65–74.

closer view, however, this metaphor wavers between being an image used to illustrate the cosmogony more completely and a cosmogonic myth: the witness who talks about it refers first to the image of the froth beaten by the sea and then to that of the cheese; Menocchio asserts that God creates angels from the most perfect light, just as cheese is made from the most perfect coagulated milk, using it as an image, while on two other occasions he uses it to express the myth, suggesting the notion of spontaneous generation.[93]

The milk metaphor is surprising because it is foreign to our imagery and to the most familiar myths. But the myth of a cosmogony in terms of milk, comprehensible where pastoral cultures are concerned, had a certain diffusion in antiquity, and fragments of it linger in Indian and Altaic myths. Traces and partly disguised hints of these myths can be encountered in western culture. One of these mythological accounts of an Altaic people, the Buriati, has entered our own lexicon, even if it only survives today as a name: Milky Way, Galaxy (from the Greek *galaksìas*, from *gala*, milk). Terms which connect the processing of milk with the beginnings of life can be found in Aristotle, Clement of Alexandria, and the Bible (Job 10:10), while elements of this cosmogonic tradition are scattered in European folklore and alchemical thought.[94] Thus the traces of a faint network survive which perhaps link these fragments to the Indo-European area.

Ginzburg's analysis of Menocchio's culture, has, with the exception of references to the lactic metaphor or cosmogony, for the most part limited itself to and strangely enough accepted and credited the explanations and frame of reference adopted by the judges: Menocchio's ideas came either from people or from books. I do not mean to suggest that many other channels for their transmission exist besides the oral and the written; images are not a factor here. I wish to point out that this frame of reference was a procedural instrument intended to establish the guilt of the accused. In fact, the inquisitors concluded that Menocchio, without accomplices and with very few books, was a heresiarch. In other words, that he himself had created his heresies, borrowing only a very few points from contemporary and ancient heresies. Menocchio, for his part, sought to maneuver within this

---

[93] See the trial at 9, 25, 47, 57.

[94] See Ginzburg, 56–58; R. Lionetti, "Menocchio, la storia, il sogno. Studio sulla cosmogonia lattea," *Metodi e ricerche*, n.s. 2, no. 1 (1981): 35–55.

framework (accomplices-books-personal creativity), avoiding at all costs the disclosure of peoples' names for fear of incriminating them. He could certainly have mentioned the dead without risk, but he did not even do this. He credited his errors to his brains and to his readings. He told the judges, who wanted the names of accomplices, that he had thought up his own ideas, but did mention the titles of a few books to lessen his own responsibility. He stuck to this line during the second trial, and did not falter even in the torture chamber: "Most illustrious sir, I told you, even the other day, that I did not learn my errors from anyone, but got them out of my own head or read them in books."[95]

Some of the things that Menocchio claimed to have taken from books hardly seem to fit their contexts and suggest that he projected opinions he already possessed upon his readings. He cited the books in part to ease his conscience, and in part as an ingenuous, if pathetic and confused, defense strategy. The inquisitor was certainly not about to check the texts, and even if they had been readily available, the truthfulness of the miller's statements would have had no relevance for him. If a few comparisons with the originals stand up, others give the impression of having been concocted by Menocchio on the spot or in his prison cell. It is virtually impossible to extract the doctrine of the mortality of the soul from Mandeville's *Travels,* or that of the uniquely human nature of Christ from the *Fioretto della Bibbia,* or the rejection of Mary's virginity from the *Rosario della gloriosa vergine Maria,* in the way that Menocchio articulated these concepts. Such examples could conceivably be taken as defective recollections of his readings, but in other instances the aspect of self-preservation is out in the open: contrary to Menocchio, the *Fioretto della Bibbia* never uses the word "chaos," but rather speaks in orthodox terms of God's creation of matter.[96] As for the allusion to "a Simon Magus who took the form of an angel," which the accused thought he had read in Mandeville's *Travels,* there is no mention of this figure in the book. All these assertions came in response to questions intended to uncover the sources of Menocchio's ideas. In fact, he thought up the last reply precisely to ward off the vicar general's insinuations that he had been a heretic for more or less thirty years, long before the readings which,

---

[95] See for example 24, 30–31, 34–35, 42. The quote is at 154.
[96] See the trial at 35; Ginzburg, 52–54.

according to Menocchio, went back only five or six years.[97]

Although judge and accused stand at opposite poles in the trial, they refer to a virtually identical scheme for the origin of Menocchio's ideas: oral transmission, reading, creation out of one's own intelligence. Menocchio eliminates the factor of oral transmission for reasons that we have already mentioned. Only the other two approaches remain viable for him: he talks about books, alludes to his own mental agility, casts blame on an evil spirit for inculcating ideas as true which the inquisitor now defines as heretical. Only rarely does he claim to be proud of his intellectual prowess ("because I have a keen mind"), and it is almost always to deflect questions about accomplices.[98]

In evaluating the evidence the historian may feel at times that he is taking the place of the inquisitor, linking facts, weighing ideas, almost as if he is reexamining events through his own eyes. But mediation and interpretation are inevitable; there is no such thing as an antiseptically objective document, and every reader will use a text in his own way. The historian's job requires a critical awareness of these risks.[99] Even the analogy between inquisitor and anthropologist made by recent writers, while stimulating and appealing in some respects, is misleading when it attributes to the judge qualities and interests that he probably lacked, such as a scholar's curiosity, a learned interest in reconstructing the cultural world of the accused, or when it is forgotten that the culture and mentality of the inquisitor were usually closely founded on scholastic theology and canon law, not on history. Even taking into account the distance of centuries, there are great differences between inquisitor and anthropologist or historian in regard to cultural tools and goals, and these must remain uppermost in our minds if we are to avoid being trapped in the web of designs and procedures of the inquisitors themselves.[100]

---

[97] Ginzburg, 157; the trial at 41.

[98] For the questions on the books, see 31, 33–35, 41; on the accomplices, see n. 95; the quote is at 128.

[99] See Prosperi, "L'Inquisizione: verso una nuova immagine," 144–45.

[100] See Del Col, "I processi dell'Inquisizione," 44; R. Rosaldo, "From the Door of his Tent: the Fieldworker and the Inquisitor," in *Writing Culture: The Poetics and Politics of Ethnography,* edited by J. Clifford and G. E. Marcus (Berkeley & Los Angeles: Univ. of California Press, 1986), 77–97; Ginzburg, *Ecstasies: Deciphering the Witches' Sabbath,* 95–96.

Menocchio's ideas: Cathar influences.

As a way around the quagmire of accomplices-books-personal creativity, attention should be given to the intuition and crucial theological
qualification introduced by Fra Felice: it provides still another key to
the ideas of the Friulan miller. Domenico Scandella has a strictly
dualistic conception of man, one that at first glance would appear to be
merely a curious and eccentric construct, combining intelligent but
randomly heterogeneous and disconnected elements. On closer examination it has links to dualistic concepts of the origin of spirit and
matter, of good and evil, to the cosmic battle between God and the
Devil, to a resulting morality which envisions men battling to secure
victory for light, spirit and God against the shadows and the Devil,
and in the end occupy the places left vacant in paradise by the fallen
angels. Replying to questions about the Last Judgment, Menocchio
states: "God is the author of good, but does no evil, and the Devil is
the author of what is evil and does no good; and if man takes the part
of the Devil he does not go to heaven and his light is extinguished, but
if he does good works he goes to heaven and his light is not extinguished."[101]

The inquisitor notes in the margin: *principium boni, principium
mali* and in the sentence at the conclusion of the trial writes that this
is the twofold principle of good, namely God, and of evil (the Devil),
according to the opinion of the Manichees.[102] On the lookout for
analogies and precedents in the heresies he has studied in the manuals,
he could be mistaken here because, in fact, Menocchio does not
explicitly identify the good with spirit and evil with matter, in the
Manichean sense, but speaks of good and evil principally on a moral
plane. But if the inquisitor may have been mistaken on the individual
point of doctrine, he does know his theology, and, endowed with a
good logical instinct, has perceived something that smacks of the
Manichean, of the dualistic. To be sure, the antitheses God/Devil,
good/evil, spirit/ matter, light/dark, divine inspiration/diabolic temptation, are themes which exist through the entire course of Christian
history and in themselves are not unusual or heretical. What is peculiar, instead, is the manner in which these juxtapositions are connected

---

[101] See 52.
[102] See ibid. and 87.

in Menocchio's cosmogony and account of salvation: there is an unquestionable dependence on Cathar doctrines, even if a few essential points are missing, and some variations and accretions have crept in. Actually, it would be preferable to speak of Catharisms in the plural since there were differences of doctrine and discipline among the various Cathar churches. The movement was especially widespread in southern France and in north central Italy. Its organization was crushed in the thirteenth century by the Albigensian crusade, the Inquisition, and the preaching of the mendicant orders, but residues could still be found in Piedmont at the end of the fourteenth century. Cathars never possessed a single exclusive doctrine, a *corpus* of established beliefs. On the contrary, alongside a few common elements, there was great diversity, division, fluctuation, and internal disagreement over myths and ideas, and in the institutional relations among the churches and territorial organizations.[103] What interests us here is the Italian phenomenon and its sources.

The Cathar movement, gnostic in character, whose turbulent origin and history have been variously interpreted by scholars, was differentiated doctrinally between an absolute and a moderate form of dualism. The former admitted two coeternal divinities, one good, the other evil, each able to create its own angels, the first ruler over the heavens, the second over the material world. The latter, more moderate in conception, held that there was only one God, from whom originated good and all the angels, while Lucifer or Satan was the organizer of matter and the cause of evil. The only Italian Cathar church to adopt the more radical form of dualism was at Desenzano on Lake Garda. The other four or five followed a more moderate version, including the conventicle in Vicenza, in the Mark of Treviso, which at first adhered to the moderate doctrines and Slavic rite of the church of Bagnolo, but from the mid-thirteenth century, when it totaled over a hundred

---

[103] There is a vast bibliography on Catharism. I shall limit myself to citing: *Historiographie du catharisme* (Toulouse: Privat, 1979); R. Manselli, *L'eresia del male* (Naples: Morano, 1963; 2nd bibliographically updated ed. 1980); G. Miccoli, "La storia religiosa," in *Storia d'Italia, II: Dalla caduta dell'Impero romano al secolo XVIII* (Turin: Einaudi, 1974), 609–734; G. Rottenwohrer, *Der Katharismus* (Bad Honnef: Bock-Herchen, 1982); G. Zanella, *Itinerari ereticali: Patari e Catari tra Rimini e Verona* (Rome, 1986). The analysis of sources is discussed in G. Zanella, "L'eresia catara fra XIII e XIV secolo: in margine al disagio di una storiografia," *Bullettino dell'Istituto storico italiano per il medioevo e archivio muratoriano* 88 (1979): 239–58.

"perfected," adopted to some extent the radical doctrines of the group in Desenzano. About 1214–1215 there was a flourishing Cathar community in Gemona, to which the bishop of the Treviso Mark, Pietro Gallo, had transferred. This is our only piece of information for the Friuli.[104] The historical and theological evidence is too vague, fragmentary and chronologically isolated—even though we have reports about inquisitorial trials against Cathars at Treviso in 1262–1263 and in 1280[105]—to permit a really conclusive comparative analysis. In this unexplored terrain, it is necessary to stick closely to the available sources.

The transmission of dualistic concepts and myths took place orally for the most part, since of the very few texts circulating among Cathars or written by them, only two have actually come down to us, the *Interrogatio Iohannis* of Bogomil origin and the *Liber de duobus principiis*. Manuals and compends written by inquisitors, works which presumably did not contribute to the spread of Cathar doctrines, are other available sources. All the texts are in Latin, thus accessible only to persons of a certain culture, while the majority of believers and "perfected" were initially of lower status and largely uneducated; only later were there members from higher cultural and social levels. Moreover, there is ample documentation of the continual peregrinations of the perfected among the various church groups for the purpose of the oral dissemination of the Cathar teachings. Thus, we can reasonably suppose oral transmission in the case of Menocchio as well. We can proceed by looking closely first at his views on man and salvation, and finally at his cosmogony.

Menocchio's concept of man is precisely that of moderate Catharism: man is composed of a material side, mortal body and soul (in fact, several souls corresponding to the operations of the mind: intellect, memory, will, thought, belief, faith and hope) and of the spirit, which is immortal. The spirit is separate from man, has the same will as man, and "sustains and governs" him. The spirits are in fact two, one good

---

[104] On the Church of the Marca trevigiana, see Manselli, *L'eresia del male*, 216–17, 318; A. Dondaine, "La hiérarchie cathare en Italie," *Archivum fratrum praedicatorum* 19 (1949): 290; 20 (1950): 297–99. For a detailed statistical description of Catharism in northern Italy, see G. Zanella, "Malessere ereticale in Valle Padana (1260–1308)," *Rivista di storia e letteratura religiosa* 14 (1978): 341–90.

[105] See Ilarino da Milano, "Gli antecedenti inediti di un noto episodio dell'Inquisizione francescana a Treviso (1262–1263)," *Collectanea Franciscana* 5 (1935): 611–20.

and the other evil, each opposed to the other which, at the death of the body and soul, return where God wishes. When man is in the mother's womb, he is like marrow and dead flesh without spirit or breath, and after his birth God puts an angel into him, who is opposed by another spirit introduced by the Devil (or perhaps by God) when the man has grown up.[106] According to the Cathars, both men and angels were made up of three elements: body, soul and spirit, elements obviously to be understood differently in each. For Menocchio, the angels and the Holy Spirit, as well as man, are composed of the same matter. The introduction of an angel in man's material body was a common belief of the Cathars, and the moderate wing believed that the angel could be one who had fallen with Lucifer or one generated by spirits already enclosed in matter.[107] The notion that at the death of the body the soul also dies circulated widely among the Cathars of Piedmont during the second half of the fourteenth century.[108]

Christ too is the equal of all men in birth and nature, and has a body, soul and spirit like theirs. What distinguishes him is his election

---

[106] See 25, 31–33, 36, 50, 53.

[107] Manselli, *L'eresia del male*, 202–6; *Interrogatio Iohannis*, brought from Bulgaria to Concorezzo by Bishop Nazario (1190–1215), in *Le livre secret des cathares. Interrogatio Iohannis. Apocryphe d'origine bogomile*, ed., trans., and with commentary by E. Bozóky (Paris: Beauchesne, 1980), 58, 130–34; *De heresi catharorum in Lombardia* (end of 12th century–beginning of 13th), in Dondaine, "La hiérarchie cathare," 1: 309–11; *Liber supra Stella* (1235 ca.), in Ilarino da Milano, "Il 'Liber supra Stella' del piacentino Salvo Burci contro i catari e altre correnti ereticali," *Aevum* 19 (1945): 313–14, 319, 340 (another edition, the pagination for which will be indicated in parentheses, is in I. von Döllinger, *Beiträge zur Sektengeschichte des Mittelalters* [Münich, 1890], 2: 58, 60, 66, 84); *Summa contra haereticos* by Fra Giacomo de Capellis (1235–1240), in D. Bazzocchi, *L'eresia catara. Appendice. Disputationes nonnullae adversus haereticos* . . . , (Reggio Emilia: Tip. Guidetti, 1920), 38–39; *Summa contra patarenos*, attributed to Peter Martyr (1238–1239), in T. Kaeppeli, "Une somme contre les hérétiques de s. Pierre Martyr (?)," *Archivum fratrum praedicatorum* 17 (1947): 325–27, 329; *Adversus catharos et valdenses libri quinque* by Fra Moneta da Cremona (1241–1244), ed. T. A. Ricchini (Rome: Typographia Palladis, 1743), 3–5, 61–74, 105–7, 129–35; *Liber de duobus principiis* (written before 1250), in *Livre des deux principes*, ed. and trans. by C. Thouzellier (Paris: Les éditions du cerf, 1973), 242–50; *Summa de catharis et leonistis* by Ranieri Sacconi (1250), in A. Dondaine, *Un traité néo-manichéen du XIIIe siècle, le Liber de duobus principiis, suivi d'un fragment de rituel cathare* (Rome: Istituto storico domenicano, 1939), 71, 76; *Tractatus de hereticis* by Fra Anselmo d'Alessandria (second half of 13th century) in Dondaine, "La hiérarchie cathare," 2: 312–13.

[108] See Amati, "Processus contra Valdenses," *Archivio storico italiano*, ser. 3, 2 (1865): 17, 25; G. G. Merlo, *Eretici e inquisitori nella società piemontese del Trecento* (Turin: Claudiana, 1977), 27, 33, 36.

as Son of God. When Menocchio speaks of him, he occasionally seems confused, but this may be due simply to careless transcription of his words. When asked if Christ had a soul, he replied: "I believe he has a spirit like ours, because soul and spirit are the same thing,"[109] meaning that Christ's soul and spirit are the same as ours.

The conflict between God and the Devil is moved to the inner person: according to our Friulan miller, the heart of man is in two parts, one light and the other dark, with the evil spirit dwelling in the dark and the good spirit in the light. Persons who do good works and keep the light lit within themselves go to heaven in the form of purified spirits. They will fill the places left vacant by the fallen celestial spirits, and their bodies never rise up again. As for those who perpetrate evil deeds, at death the light is extinguished within them and they do not attain paradise. On Judgment Day those who performed good deeds are rewarded. There are no bodies in paradise, not even Christ's, which was left behind in the tomb. Only pure spirits see God, and the entire world and all the things of the world are rendered transparent to the eyes of the spirit, like similitudes or bodiless apparitions: even material things will become spiritual. Persons left without the inner light do not ascend to heaven, but will remain behind, unable to see: there is no purgatory, nor hell, the existence of which Menocchio seems not to admit because "it is just a business, an invention of men who know more than others."[110]

The denial of the resurrection of the body, including Christ's (for some he would have regained it on Judgment Day and then laid it off again and been dissolved into the four elements) was characteristic of most Cathars, except for Giovanni di Lugio, and the group at Concorezzo. The rejection of purgatory was also quite common among them. They almost always believed in hell as an eternal punishment, but some of them thought of it as being only in this world.[111]

Seen in this light, there is no longer any reason to attribute contradictions, missteps, and obscurities to Menocchio's view of man,

---

[109] The quote is at 50.

[110] See 24, 31–32, 45, 51–55; on hell, 18, 37, 44; the quote is at 44.

[111] See *Interrogatio Iohannis*, 76–86, 169–74; *De heresi catharorum*, 310–12; *Liber supra Stella*, 313–14, 319, 339 (58, 61, 65, 83–84); *Summa contra haereticos*, 193–206; *Summa contra patarenos*, 327–28; *Adversus catharos et valdenses*, 346–56; *Summa de catharis et leonistis*, 71–72, 75–77; *Tractatus de hereticis*, 311–13, 319. See also Merlo, *Eretici e inquisitori*, 27–29, 32–40 and the trials published there in appendix.

as Ginzburg did on several occasions.[112] The contrast between mortal soul and immortal spirit, and the longing for paradise are normal concepts in Catharism. In the Universal Judgment only pure spirits participate, not humans with resurrected bodies, and so the miller speaks of angels, not of men.[113] He considers prayers for the dead useful, because in this way God draws them closer to the light of paradise, "God will put the dead person a little ahead and will illuminate it a little more": according to some Cathars it was possible to provide a progressive salvation.[114] The allusion to souls as the angels who hover about God in the traditional image of heaven is not an attempt to evade the intensive questioning of the vicar general, and contains no reference to the errant souls of the dead, but should be taken literally in the sense explained above. "Those souls [i.e., ours] are like the painted angels near Our Lord God, who keeps them close by him, depending on their merits, and those who have done evil he disperses around the world:" souls are angels, those who have been good go to paradise, those who have been bad remain matter. The "painted angels near Our Lord God" can be found in many churches, but Menocchio had often gazed upon those frescoes in the choir of the church of Santa Maria in Montereale that can still be admired today in the old edifice, which has survived intact within the cemetery grounds.[115]

Even Menocchio experienced the interior conflict between a good and evil spirit and in the trials dramatically questioned whether his ideas came from the Devil rather than from God. Initially, he considered himself "philosopher, astrologer and prophet" who knew "the nature of the heavens" and the truths that were revealed by the angel within him; and he compared himself to Joseph who disclosed through divine illumination the truths hidden from the masses. But in Menocchio's mind there was a struggle being waged between the two spirits and the first doubts were voiced during the interrogations of 7 February 1584, in terms which wavered between an instinct for self-preserva-

---

[112] Cf. Ginzburg, 37–38, 61, 68–69, 71–72, 76–77, 124–25.

[113] See 36.

[114] See 54; *De heresi catharorum*, 311; *Summa contra haereticos*, 10; Amati, "Processus contra Valdenses," 51.

[115] See 32. The frescoes were executed in 1559 by Giovanni Maria Zaffoni, called il Calderari: I. Furlan, "Il Calderari nel quarto centenario della morte," *Il Noncello* 21 (1963): 3–30. I owe the reference to the courtesy of Paolo Goi.

tion and sincerity: "That which I have said either out of the inspiration of God or the Devil, I do not confirm it is either the truth or a lie, but I ask for mercy and I will do whatever is taught me." After two years in prison, however, he admitted that he had said some crazy things, "into which I stupidly fell blinded by the Devil," while his return to the true faith and his suffering in prison had brought him back to God: "I thus felt great happiness and God comforted me always while I was praying to his divine majesty, that I felt I was in heaven."[116] At the second trial in 1599 the doubts had indeed won out and were no longer merely a defense expedient: "Sometimes the Devil tempts me to say certain words"; "and if I have had evil thoughts, or said some word falsely, I never believed them [...] because Our Lord God has taught me to believe that everything I thought and said was vanity, not wisdom"; "I thought that I was a prophet because the malignant spirit made me see vanities and dreams and was persuading me to see the nature of the heavens and similar things. And I now believe that the prophets spoke what angels dictated to them"; "this opinion the Devil put into my head." In any event the miller conceived of the angel and the evil spirit within him in a real, not mystical sense.[117]

Menocchio's concept of salvation, similarly, has many points of contact with the ideas of the Cathars, who initially believed that the God of the Old Testament was the Devil and that the patriarchs and the prophets were Satan's emissaries. Their text, *Interrogatio Iohannis,* claims only Moses and Elias, with the latter returning in the guise of John the Baptist. But gradually the list grows longer and alters the original concept, because it comes to include Noah, Abraham, Moses, the prophets, and John the Baptist, who all made predictions about Jesus Christ through the Holy Spirit unconsciously as though involuntarily compelled. Other accounts record with variants Abraham, Isaac, Jacob, Moses and the ancient fathers, the prophets, David, Elias, and John the Baptist. In the mid-thirteenth century at Desenzano, Giovanni di Lugio taught instead that Noah, Abraham, Isaac, Jacob and the other patriarchs, Moses, Joshua and all the prophets, as well as John the Baptist were sent by God.[118] Menocchio believed that the will of

---

[116] See 24. The comparison with Joseph is at 61–62; the quotes are at 136, 28, 102.

[117] The quotes are at 131, 135–37; cf. Ginzburg, 106–7.

[118] See *Interrogatio Iohannis,* 68–70, 148–51, 156–58; *De heresi catharorum,* 311–12; *Summa contra haereticos,* 44, 50, 57, 92–93, 104; *Summa contra patarenos,* 323; *Tractatus de hereticis,* 311–12; *Summa de catharis et leonistis,* 75.

God, through the Holy Spirit, had elected as his children Abel, Noah, Abraham, Isaac, Jacob, Moses, John the Baptist or Elias.[119] This list corresponds almost exactly to Giovanni di Lugio's, with the omission of Joshua and the addition of Abel. I do not know how to explain the absence of the former (perhaps because he is a secondary figure compared to Moses), but the figure of Abel, who is never seen as one of God's emissaries in the Bible, can already be found in the *Summa contra haereticos* by Fra Giacomo de Capellis in the thirteenth century, where he is represented as the Church's first martyr and the first just man, who offered himself as a sacrifice to God and not to the Devil.[120] That this polemical writing may be responsible for Abel's appearance, which was later absorbed into the Cathar tradition, is possible but indemonstrable. But the inclusion of this figure in Menocchio's own list may have a more immediate and ascertainable explanation, one that we grasp as soon as we enter the old church of Montereale. On the arch high up on the left Abel is depicted offering a lamb, and an angel is descending to receive the gift. Far up on the right Cain is represented holding up a sheath of wheat or corn, with a devil poised to accept the offering. The juxtaposition between the two, between the angel and the demon, is distinct and is even highlighted by the flame which is rising intact from Abel's altar, while the flame from the altar of Cain is broken up into many tongues of fire. To the miller of Montereale, Abel appears as the first son of God, an exemplar and model of the good.

After the prophets of the Old Testament it is Christ's turn to be sent, the greatest of the prophets, born a man like all others. According to Menocchio the salvation that he brought was not a consequence of the merits of his death, because he did not really die (Simon the Cyrenian was crucified in his stead); Christ represented merely an example to follow.[121] Cathars held various notions on the passion and death of Christ, including Menocchio's, although in his beliefs the original doctrinal coherence which infused them was lost: some of the sect said that Jesus Christ was neither crucified nor died (he had not even assumed human flesh and everything that he did as man was phantasmagoric); others asserted that he had indeed been crucified

---

[119] See 16, 48.

[120] See *Summa contra haereticos*, 43.

[121] See 10, 16–17, 19, 25–26, 51–52.

(and that he had assumed flesh). But none admitted his redemptive merits.[122] Man is saved, according to Menocchio, by following the law of Christ, namely, by loving God and one's neighbor. All of morality and the extent of our religious obligations consist in doing God's works, which means to love, adore, sanctify, revere and thank him, and especially to be charitable, merciful, peaceful, loving, honorable, obedient to one's betters, forgive injuries, and keep promises. These works bring one to God, while those deeds which "displease God and are pleasing to the world and the Devil" are seven in number: stealing, assassination, usury, cruelty, shame, vituperation, and murder.[123] This is basically the moral position of the Cathars: do God's works and shun those of the Devil and of the world. There are also some similarities with the repertoire of what constituted evil actions in Cathar morality: fornication (or adultery), theft, murder, blaspheming God, speaking falsely, breaking promises, and oath taking, all analogies that can be explained in reality through common indebtedness to the Ten Commandments, except for the sin of not keeping one's promise. But there is a discrepancy on some substantial points since all the severe prohibitions against sex and certain foods (cheese, milk, eggs, flesh) have disappeared from Menocchio's views, although among the Cathars only the perfected were expected to observe them. Menocchio, in fact, rejected the fasts and abstinences imposed by the Church, which concerned these very foods. It should be noted that this was a refusal already practiced among the Cathars of Piedmont by the end of the fourteenth century.[124]

Along with the Cathars, Menocchio denies any value to the Church, to the hierarchy, to the sacraments, to ecclesiastical precepts and injunctions. However, he admits their validity, in opposition to classic Catharism, if and when they are vehicles for the Holy Spirit. Thus, the Eucharist communicates not Christ but the Holy Spirit (or the entire Trinity), imparting light, joy and consolation. The other sacraments are valueless because they are a business and because man

---

[122] See *De heresi catharorum,* 311; *Liber supra Stella,* 314, 321, 327, 337 (61, 66–67, 73, 82–83); *Summa contra haereticos,* 18; *Summa contra patarenos,* 321, 324; *Adversus catharos et valdenses,* 243–51; *Summa de catharis et leonistis,* 71, 75–76; *Tractatus de hereticis,* 310–11, 313.

[123] See 52.

[124] See Manselli, *L'eresia del male,* 225–31; Merlo, *Eretici e inquisitori,* 40; Amati, "Processus contra Valdenses," 25.

already has the Holy Spirit: extreme unction is of no avail since it anoints the body, not the spirit; the Eucharist and the Mass were suggested or devised by the Holy Spirit so that men would not be like beasts, probably intending that they thus raise themselves over matter through the spirit. Free will is the Holy Spirit, the will of God, which man has received. Indulgences are good because they come from the Holy Spirit and are given by one of God's stewards, the pope.[125] Such assertions not only contradict the original ideas of the Cathars, but also those of the Reformation, and have nothing in common with Catholic theology.

It is difficult to see any hint of such Cathar rites as the greeting, the *consolamentum*, the breaking of the bread (but perhaps the importance Menocchio attributes to the Eucharist is a distant echo of it), the *servitium* or *apparellamentum*, a species of public confession (probably from this stemmed his rejection of auricular confession).[126] Even the *Pater noster* is used by Menocchio in the Christian version ("Panem nostrum cotidianum da nobis hodie [...] sed libera nos a malo") and not in the Cathar ("Panem nostrum suprasubstantialem da nobis hodie [...] sed libera nos a malo. Quoniam tuum est regnum et virtus et gloria in secula. Amen"). However, Menocchio shows his originality even where the *Pater noster* is concerned: in his supplication of 12 July 1599 he includes in his own hand the second part of the prayer (thus there is no problem of faulty transcription here) and he sets it down in inverse order in respect to the canonical version: "Set libera nos a malo et ne nos inducas in tentazionem et demite nobis debita nostra, sicut ne nos dimitimus debitoribus nostris; panem nostrum cotidianum da nobis hodie."

The transposition may have been unintentional, but it may also be that the articles have been listed in order of decreasing importance, going from spirit to matter, from the freeing of one from evil to the daily bread.[127] On the other hand, Menocchio was a vigorous critic of the Bible itself: only a small part of the Holy Book is actually inspired by God, the rest is the invention of priests and monks. Cath-

---

[125] See 43–45, 49; *Liber supra Stella*, 323, 336 (68–69, 82); *Summa contra haereticos*, 136–38; *Summa contra patarenos*, 329; *Adversus catharos et valdenses*, 277–346; *Summa de catharis et leonistis*, 64; *Tractatus de hereticis*, 319.

[126] Manselli, *L'eresia del male*, 231–41.

[127] Ibid, 233; *Rituel cathare*, ed. and trans., C. Thouzellier (Paris: Les éditions du cerf, 1977), 198–216 and appendix 20, after 285. See the second half of the *Pater noster* at 135.

ars had the most disparate ideas on the subject, from the attribution to the Devil of all or of part of the Bible, to the acceptance of some or all of the books in the Vulgate version.[128]

What makes Menocchio believe that all people—Christians, heretics, Turks, Jews—are saved equally is precisely the uselessness of ecclesiastical mediation and his belief that the Holy Spirit dwells in all people.[129] This is not an idea that can be traced to the original Cathars, who only admitted salvation was possible within their own churches, in line with their different obediences and orders. Granted, the *Liber de duobus principiis* upholds a doctrine of the universal salvation of souls, on the assumption, however, that they are creatures of the good God and must return to him. This is something that a segment of the Cathars had always believed, at least those who adhered to the notion of the origin or creation of all spirits at the beginning of the universe. And at the end of the thirteenth century, Bolognese Cathars maintained that "sicut sunt LXXII lingue, ita sunt LXXII fides," meaning that all the faiths were equally good.[130] In his second trial Menocchio traced the idea back to the tale of the three rings in the *Decameron* (there is an allusion to it in the first trial also), where there is no mention of the Holy Spirit, which is the usual reason given by the miller as proof of universal salvation. The centrality of the Holy Spirit in Menocchio's doctrine of salvation and cosmogony perhaps best explains his idea of toleration, or more exactly, of the equivalency of religions, which he also discovered in Boccaccio.[131]

---

[128] See 17–18, 44. For Cathar ideas on the Bible, see, for example, *Summa contra patarenos*, 322–23; *Summa de catharis et leonistis*, 75.

[129] See 43, 58, 132–33.

[130] Manselli, *L'eresia del male*, 190–92, 223–24; *De heresi catharorum*, 310–11; *Liber supra Stella*, 330 (77); *Summa de catharis et leonistis*, 65; *Liber de duobus principiis*, 252–58; *Acta S. Officii Bononie ab anno 1291 usque ad annum 1310*, ed. L. Paolini and R. Orioli (Rome: Istituto storico italiano per il medioevo, 1982), 14.

[131] For the inquisitor, Scandella's idea went back to Origen's apocatastasis: cf. 92 and Ginzburg, 49–51, 92–93. The concept of the equivalence of religions circulated in the Friuli with the same formulation, but with a different intent, one corresponding to Reformation doctrines: on 25 May 1580 Giovanni de Honestis was accused of having said that "all are saved, Jews, Turks, Christians and pagans, because Christ died for everyone" ("quod omnes salvantur, Iudei scilicet, Turcae, Christiani et infideles omnes, quia Christus mortuus est pro omnibus"): AAUd, *S. Officio*, b. 73, fasc. "Liber denuntiarum . . . ," fol. 10r; on Honestis see A. Del Col, "Lucio Paolo Rosello e la vita religiosa veneziana verso la metà del secolo XVI," *Rivista di storia della Chiesa in Italia* 32 (1978): 451–55; idem., "Due sonetti inediti di Pier Paolo Vergerio il giovane," *Ce fastu?* 54 (1978): 70–82.

The judges in the first trial misunderstood Menocchio's views on salvation and assumed that they had affinities with Reformation doctrines that were actually totally alien to him. In his questioning of the witnesses, the vicar general quoted the miller as saying: "Without so much preaching and doing, it is enough for salvation not to harm one's neighbor," signifying that it is more important to love one's neighbor than to love God, and that works of piety and ecclesiastical teaching are useless. The statement is thus interpreted by the officials to mean justification by faith alone and is transformed into: "our good acts are of no merit in the sight of God."[132] Menocchio, instead, believes that man must perform good works if he expects to save himself, because God summons all to salvation; these works are done by the grace of God, which is the Holy Spirit sent to illuminate everyone, and not by grace obtained through Christ. So when Fra Felice asks him on 12 May what he thinks of justification, the miller does not understand the term. The inquisitor explains it to him and Menocchio responds with the very words of Fra Felice's explanation, a typical reply to a leading question, but finally returns to his idea that what justifies is "the Holy Spirit, the will of God and the words of Jesus Christ." Fra Felice is also struck by the thought that the defendant, in speaking of the men who are destined to fill the places left vacant by the angels, might be alluding to predestination and asks him if this is so. Again, this term turns out to be incomprehensible to the miller. Once it has been explained to him, he gives his opinion on the subject, which is very different from the inquisitor's: God has not preordained anyone to eternal life; He anticipates that the places will be filled, but He does not know by whom, because He who does God's works and who has a better fate and the planets in his favor will be saved. In the sentencing Fra Felice will condemn with harsh words the exclusion of God from the final destiny of mankind, which is contrary not only to the Protestant doctrine of predestination, but even to the Catholic doctrine of the anticipation of merits.[133]

We have seen the close affinity between Menocchio and the Cathars in their anthropology and the analogies and divergences in their soteriology. If the Cathar doctrines present in general diversity and divergences, their cosmogony emerges as the most obscure and

---

[132] See the original utterance at 5, 6 and the transformation at 7, 9.
[133] See 58, 90.

contradictory aspect of their beliefs. There are a few general lines in common, but also a substantial and irreconcilable difference, between the broad range of ideas in moderate Cathar dualism and the miller's cosmogony.

There is agreement on the eternal existence of spiritual and material reality (although a segment of the Cathars admitted the creation), God as the creator of spirits, with matter set in order by a being inferior to him. The scene of cosmogony/salvation history followed by the Friulan miller is analogous to that contained in the original and most widely circulated text of Catharism, the *Interrogatio Iohannis*, which speaks first of the arrangement of the heavens and of the elements (air, water, earth, fire) by the angels, and then narrates Lucifer's struggle to become like God, his fall and that of his angels from their celestial thrones, the formation of the sea, of the earth, of the celestial bodies from the four elements by means of the demons, and finally, the creation of animals, of plants and of man. After the events in the terrestrial paradise, the struggle between God and the Devil continued in the world, where Satan sent forth Moses and Elias in the form of John the Baptist, and God brought in Mary and Jesus Christ by means of the Holy Spirit. The salvation conveyed by Christ consists of baptism in the Holy Spirit and in fire, the bread of life descended from the seventh heaven and the *Pater noster*. Whoever performs God's works will go with the light and on Judgment Day the Son of Man will chase into hell Satan, demons and sinners, and all the earth will burn, while Christ will send his angels to gather up the just, place them on immovable thrones, bestow on them everlasting crowns, and the Son will reign with the Father in eternity.[134]

The substantial difference concerns the ordering of matter. In the thought of moderate dualism it is the work of Satan, but for Menocchio it is the Holy Spirit, an angel inferior to God, but a good one, who uses the four archangels, among whom is Lucifer; when Lucifer

---

[134] Manselli, *L'eresia del male*, 82–84, 198–203; on the cosmogony of moderate dualism, see *De heresi catharorum*, 310–11; *Liber supra Stella*, 310, 314, 339 (55, 60–61, 84); *Summa contra haereticos*, 17, 26–28; *Summa contra patarenos*, 320; *Adversus catharos et valdenses*, 5–6, 109–16, 124–26; *Summa de catharis et leonistis*, 65, 76; *Tractatus de hereticis*, 319–20. On the eternity of matter, see *Liber supra Stella*, (68 only); *Brevis summula* (c. 1250), in C. Douais, *La Somme des autorités à l'usage des prédicateurs ...*, (Paris, 1896), 115–16; *Summa de catharis*, 73; *Tractatus de hereticis*, 320. See the plan and the text of *Interrogatio Iohannis*, 32–86.

is expelled, the world is completed by the other three. Matter, thus, is no longer evil; spirit and matter develop and then separate from the same primordial elements, from chaos, through the will and under the domination of God. Menocchio has a pantheistic concept of reality: all things, everything that is good, air, earth, water, fire are God. He even established a detailed parallelism between God and the elements: God is fire because fire is everywhere, just like God; the Father is air, the highest element; the Son is earth, because he is produced by the Father; and the Holy Spirit water, because it comes from the air and the earth. The relationships among the persons of the Trinity resemble those of Christianity (the Son is generated by the Father, the Holy Spirit proceeds from the Father and from the Son), but the names are all that remain since the Son and the Holy Spirit are inferior. In fact, Menocchio places the spirits in a descending scale of perfection and of light: first God the Father, then the Holy Spirit, followed by Christ and the angels.[135]

The Friulan miller certainly is no Cathar, nor is his religion, as it is documented in the trials, entirely based on Cathar concepts. This should be obvious, and yet his ideas, as we have seen, appear to be organized in a doctrinal complex which is related to them and shares many developments and adaptations produced by the Cathars in their attempts to accommodate their thought to the culture of the epoch and as a consequence of the active reaction of Christianity. Even the Cathars used the names of the three divine persons and conceived of the latter two as inferior to the Father.[136] Menocchio's concept of the Holy Spirit could have come from them. The *Interrogatio Iohannis* states that Adam and Eve were made by the Devil, not by God as foolish people believe, while God "de spiritu sancto omnes virtutes celorum fecit": through the Holy Spirit he created all the virtues, that is the angels of the heavens. In the *De heresi catharorum in Lombardia* and in the *Liber supra stella*, a good angel is sent by God as an assistant in the division of the elements to Lucifer and to an evil spirit trapped in the chaos, since, unless they were three, they were unable to function; the god who, according to Genesis, created heaven and earth

---

[135] See the witnesses at the first trial, and 24–26, 31–32, 47–49, 56–58, 131–32.

[136] See, for example, *Interrogatio Iohannis*, 42; *Liber supra Stella*, 313 (58); *Summa contra haereticos*, 25; *Adversus catharos et valdenses*, 4; *Summa de catharis et leonistis*, 71; *Tractatus de hereticis*, 314, 316; Dondaine, *Un traité néo-manichéen*, 20–21.

was actually Lucifer.[137] But there is nothing that explains or recalls the parallelism between God, the persons of the Trinity and the four elements that we have noted in Menocchio's pantheistic concepts.

Evil entered the world, according to the miller, at the time of the rebellion of Lucifer, who was expelled into matter with all his angels. The battle between good angels and fallen angels thus remains within man, but also within matter. Menocchio does not speak of the latter explicitly, but his conviction can be deduced from certain statements. At one point, interrogated on the subject of holy water, he asserted: "The Devil enters things and injects his poison into them, but when they are blessed by the priest, that poison is removed, and also with holy water the priest chases away the Devil." The water can be sanctified even by a lay person who knows the ritual words. Thus, the clash between God and the Devil occurs within things. In the second trial Menocchio speaks of a battle among spirits which takes place in the air. Asked: "When you hear thunder and lightning, what do you usually say?" he replied: "I believe that God made all things, that is earth, water and air," as though trying to avoid replying. But after alluding to the parallelism between God and the elements, he added: "I believe that those spirits which are in the air fight among themselves, and that the lightning is their artillery." A few days later questioned by the judge about these spirits, he explained: "I believe that they are spirits created by God, who are in the air."[138] All spirits, in fact, had been created by God and presumably the battle was not occurring among the good, but between the good and the bad. It is not surprising that even this notion is encountered in the mythical patrimony of the Cathars, expressed in both the *Interrogatio Iohannis*, where the Devil makes thunder, rain, hail and snow and places his angels as ministers over them, and in the *Tractatus de haereticis*, where the Devil causes rain and snow, thunder and storms, and the swirling of the wind.[139]

Menocchio's ideas are mostly extraneous both to the Reformation and to Catholicism, as has already been noted in connection with the Trinity, Christ, the Eucharist and the Mass, free will, indulgences,

---

[137] *Interrogatio Iohannis*, 62; *De heresi catharorum*, 310; *Liber supra Stella*, 314 (60). The cosmogony was, at any rate, the most obscure aspect of Cathar doctrines: cf. *Medioevo ereticale*, ed. O. Capitani (Bologna, 1977), 21.

[138] See 59, 131–32, 138.

[139] See *Interrogatio Iohannis*, 56, 127–28; *Tractatus de hereticis*, 313.

predestination, justification, the final resurrection, and the Bible. The same is true of original sin: man can do evil only after having received the two spirits, thus before birth he cannot have sinned.[140] Even Menocchio's notions which might seem traceable to Anabaptism, Antitrinitarianism, and rationalist spiritualism can be found among the early Cathars: the rejection of the Church and of all its sacraments, the thesis that the sacraments have been conjured up by ecclesiastics out of pure greed, the irrelevancy of priests, the sharing of sacred powers among laymen, the mortality of the soul, the denial of the resurrection of all bodies and of the virginity of Mary, the conception of Christ by Joseph and not the Holy Spirit, as well as such statements as: if Christ had been God, he would not have died as he did, and the cross should not be adored.

Some of these concepts do not go back to the classic Cathar positions of mid-thirteenth century, but are later developments documented roughly from the end of that century for the next hundred years, and are sometimes considered corruptions of typical doctrines or concoctions and revisions by individuals or small groups. Personal variations and modifications occur, sometimes resembling Cathar ideas precisely, sometimes further elaborated, articulated and inserted in an integral complex such as the one that emerges in Menocchio's trials centuries later. In Bologna, for example, at the close of the thirteenth century a full-fledged member of the Cathar sect would have held that the pope and other ecclesiastics are good and have authority if they observe Christ's commandments; and he would have also acknowledged the validity of the Mass and confession, if the priest was an upright person and in a penitent state, and might also assert that all faithful Christians could say Mass and hear confession. He would no longer state that the human body is created by the Devil, and even though he would have condemned sex and matrimony, he is and remains married.[141] Even Menocchio recognizes the pope as a "steward" of God and priests as ministers of the good. He ascribes to the faithful the same powers as priests in the matters of confession and the

---

[140] See 53.

[141] L. Paolini, *L'eresia a Bologna fra XIII e XIV secolo. I. L'eresia catara alla fine del Duecento* (Rome: Istituto storico italiano per il medioevo, 1975), 101–7, where such ideas are defined as "a mixture between a clear Cathar position and suggestions of pseudo-orthodoxy." Cf. Merlo, *Eretici e inquisitori*, 40, 279.

blessing of water, and he does not consider matter or sex intrinsically evil.[142]

But Menocchio is not a Cathar. He reads the Bible in a medieval Italian version and books of medieval provenance, with the exception of two that were contemporary. His culture was actually broader than what was unearthed by the judges. In fact, he calls himself a philosopher, astrologer and prophet: philosopher because he reflects on the nature of things, prophet because of his teachings, astrologer because he knows this art and applies it in life, to the point of believing that man can be saved through the influence of the stars.[143] His ideas, nevertheless, seem to have no connection to the *fraticelli*, the Béguines and Beghards, or the movement of the Free Spirit.[144] In fact, the Cathar notions documented in Menocchio's trials are more organic and better articulated than those encountered in the fourteenth-century documents: he represents a case of a conspicuous body of Cathar doctrines surviving well into the sixteenth century together with, as we have noted, differences and variants on a few specific points. This seems to reopen the question of the continuity between medieval and sixteenth-century heresies, a phenomenon that previously lacked documentary support.

In regard to the complex problems of transmission, it seems absurd to think that Menocchio constructed alone, juxtaposing and uniting scattered elements he had casually encountered, an association of ideas that bears so many similarities to the dualism of the Middle Ages. If many coincidences exist between two literary texts, no one for a moment believes that two independent origins are possible: some sort of dependence is always postulated. The same principle should be applied to the ideas documented in the trials, while bearing in mind the fact that they are to a certain extent oral sources.

We have excluded the possibility that Menocchio borrowed from the few Cathar texts in circulation, not just because of their rarity, but because they were in Latin, and thus beyond the reach of the semi-

---

[142] See 44–45, 58–59.

[143] For astrology, see 48, 53, 58.

[144] Miccoli, "La storia religiosa," 875–975. For a limited case of the survival of the doctrines of the Free Spirit at the end of the fifteenth century, see C. Dionisotti, "Resoconto di una ricerca interrotta," *Annali della Scuola Normale Superiore di Pisa*, ser. 2, 37 (1968): 259–69.

literate miller.[145] We do not know of any books in the vernacular that adequately illustrate dualistic concepts, even partially, or that can be related to what Menocchio knew of them. Granted, a few ideas can be found in the early chapters of a work that he knew, the *Fioretto della Bibbia,* but they are almost buried among the lines of an orthodox exposition of the Christian doctrine on creation, God, the Trinity, and the nature of man. First-hand examination of this late medieval biblical popularization makes it highly unlikely that it could have served as one of Menocchio's major sources. At the beginning God "made a large mass of matter, which had neither form nor manner," and then created man from the four elements, to which he will revert. The *Fioretto* argues against the Cathar explanation for the origin of evil:

> Know that evil was found and not created, and the Devil was its inventor and therefore it is called nothing, because in itself it does not have any substance. And therefore you should know that any thing which is without God is nothing, since God did not make evil. There are some who say that God made the good and demons made the bad, but it is not so because if it was so they would be two natures, one good and the other wicked and whoever believed this would be a heretic, because evil does not have a nature, it did not exist naturally, in fact it was found by the Devil and this occurred when Lucifer sinned and was driven from paradise by God. Then sin was discovered anew and Lucifer was made into Satan and from angel was made into the Devil.[146]

Going on to speak about the nature of man, the *Fioretto* repeats the doctrine of the Church according to which the soul is infused into the body, forty days after conception for the male, eighty days after for the female (the book comments "it is true that God has given more grace to man than to woman") and lists the errors of the heretics:

> Now many philosophers have been deceived and have fallen into grievous error about the creation of souls. Some have said that

---

[145] Scandella only knows the Latin used in the liturgy. He cites, in particular, the *Pater noster,* the *Ave Maria,* the *Credo,* the *Confiteor,* and not even correctly: cf. 11, 23–24, 61–62, 135.

[146] *El fiore de tutta la Bibbia hystoriato et di novo in lingua tosca correcto . . .* , [colophon:] Stampato in Venetia per Francesco Bindoni nel anno 1523, adi. 18. del mese di Novembre, fols. A3r, [A5]v.

souls have all been made from eternity. Others say that all souls are one and that the elements are five: the four that have been mentioned above and one other, called *orbis*. And it is said that from this *orbis* God made the soul in Adam and all the others, and for this reason they say that the world will never finish, because dying man returns to his elements. Others say that the souls are those evil spirits who have fallen and are said to enter into human bodies, and, as one dies, it enters into another body and does this until he is saved. And they say that at the end of the world these will be saved. Others say that the world will never be dissolved and that at the end of thirty-four thousand years new life will begin again and every soul will return to its body. And all these are errors and those who have uttered them were pagans, heretics and enemies of the truth and of the faith, who did not know divine things.

The *Fioretto* even offers an explanation for Lucifer's fall: envy of the man made in God's likeness and the refusal to adore him as the image of God according to the divine order imparted to all the angels through Michael. From this followed the expulsion of Satan to earth and his revenge against Adam and Eve, who were in turn driven from the terrestrial paradise because of the first sin.[147]

Concerning the transmission of Cathar ideas to the eastern zones of Italy, it is possible that texts no longer extant circulated. But there is no evidence to support this. Oral transmission remains the most plausible solution in the end. At a certain point in the second trial Menocchio made an unequivocal reference to teachings that he had received from someone whom he did not want to name: "I may have had this opinion for fifteen or sixteen years, when we began to reason, and the Devil put it into my head." And when asked, "With whom did you begin to reason?" after a long pause he replied: "I do not know."[148]

If this hypothesis has merit, we have to face, nonetheless, the obvious problems posed by the gap of two centuries for the evidence of syncretic Piedmontese Waldensianism or Catharism, and the differences in geography and doctrine. The means of transmission and when and where the changes evidenced in Menocchio's trials occurred

---

[147] Ibid., fols. [A7]v, B4r; on the fall of Lucifer, see chapters 39–41, fols. [B6]v ff.

[148] The quote is at 137.

remain a mystery. It is impossible to imagine the persistence of actual, true Cathar communities over such a long period, but there are some vague hints: certainly Menocchio practiced two levels of communication, following the pattern of esotericism-exotericism as pursued by the perfected. He acted as a teacher of knowledge and morality in the village, and the village supported him fully after the condemnation of the first trial. The miller of Montereale is a link in a chain, but for the moment the other links are not apparent; it is impossible to know how many and who were those who developed and transmitted the doctrinal variants and transformations in Catharism.

As for the theory that ideas were passed on orally, it is unlikely that Menocchio is an isolated case and that no other evidence, either medieval or modern, should exist. In this regard, it is disappointing that some preliminary soundings made in the inquisitorial sources have been fruitless. But by adopting a different perspective, the ideas of a monk tried in 1550, who had earlier appeared as one of the many sympathizers of the Reformation, take on new significance. Fra Lorenzo da Spilimbergo, in addition to espousing justification by faith, had also rejected the belief that the Madonna, the prophets, and the saints had ascended to heaven where only God with Christ and the angels dwelt (quoting from a passage in Jn 27:34: "Nemo ascendit ad coelum, nisi qui descendit de coelo, filius hominis"). He also believed that the Madonna was in the terrestrial paradise, that the soul was mortal and that there was no purgatory; only this life existed which he was trying to enjoy. These few statements, most of them of Cathar origin, were reported by witnesses.[149]

At this point how can we characterize the heretic Domenico Scandella? The inquisitor provides a purely juridical definition: he declares him a formal heretic and heresiarch in the first trial, a relapsed in the second, and enumerates the individual errors. If we consider only the sentences with which the two trials conclude, we will almost inevitably end up ascribing Protestant, Anabaptist, and Antitrinitarian ideas to Menocchio. If, instead, we should include the entire trial

---

[149] See ASVe, *Santo Uffizio*, b. 8, fasc. "Fra Lorenzo da Spilimbergo"; A. Del Col, "Discordanze e lotte tra conti e abitanti di Spilimbergo per la gestione dei beni della chiesa e per le nuove idee religiose," in *Spilimberc*, ed. N. Cantarutti and G. Bergamini (Udine: Società filologica friulana, 1984), 109–14; *Tractatus de hereticis*, 314; Amati, "Processus contra Valdenses," 40.

testimony, we would find Cathar doctrines, with some significant modifications. The court is interested in defining the crimes so that it can determine the punishment; theological and canonistic formulae employed by the inquisitors may not suffice for the historian who wants to reconstruct and understand the larger picture. Other questions than those of the judges must be asked.

The anthropology and soteriology of the Cathars survived in Menocchio's system; only the cosmogonic dualism on which they were based is missing. The confrontation between spirit and matter, between angels and demons, remains within man and within physical reality, but for Menocchio it is now derived only from Lucifer's rebellion, no longer from the dualistic origin of the cosmos, and thus approaches and can more easily be reconciled with Catholic doctrine, inasmuch as it serves to explain moral evil. Menocchio is not thinking as a dualist but as a pantheist. This pantheism, however, is singular and contradictory: God is all things and at the same time does not have contact with matter, since he has given order to the cosmos by means of lesser spirits; he does not exercise providence over the world; and he provides for human salvation only in a general, not particular way. The true God of human experience and of the earth is the Holy Spirit, the greatest of the angels, who assumes part of the operations that belong to God and to Jesus Christ in regard to humanity, and inherits all the functions performed by Lucifer in the organization of matter and in the history of salvation of the Old Testament. In addition, Menocchio holds that the personage with whom Jacob wrestles (Gn 32: 23–33) is neither the Christian God, nor the Devil of the Cathars, but rather the Holy Spirit. One of the miller's utterances perfectly encapsulates his conception of the Spirit: "The greatest faith that I have in the world is my belief that there is a Holy Spirit and that he is the word of the most high God that lights up the whole world."

The important role attributed by Menocchio to this representative and mediator of God is traceable, at least in part, to a fundamental device which he uses for interpreting reality: the concept of the indispensability of intermediary cause in the operation of things. Men do not act alone, but by means of implements ("just as a carpenter with a hatchet and saw, wood and other instruments does his work, so God has given something to man so that he can also do his work"), and thus God too acts in this way ("where there is will there must also be the power to do a thing. For example, the carpenter wants to make a bench and needs tools to do it, and if he does not have the wood, his will is useless. Thus we say about God, that in addition to will, power also is needed," that is "to operate by means of skilled workmen"). The Trinity itself is reduced to this way of operating and to the necessity of plurality, of sharing: "things cannot be done well if they are not three, and thus God, since he had given knowledge, will and power to the Holy Spirit, thus gave it to Christ so that they could then console each other."

Menocchio's corrosive critique not only touches Catholic religious life in such key aspects as the sacraments, ecclesiastical mediation, the intercession of saints, but also deprives it of its vertical dimension: precepts about God do not count, it is enough to have good relations with one's neighbor. The function of religions in salvation is also devalued: they are all the same, they serve merely for social control. Menocchio actually reaches the point of questioning the very *raison d'être* of religion, the actual existence of God, with a logical deduction from pantheism: if God is all things, all things are God ("everything that we see is God, and we are gods"). The miller's statements leave no doubt on the matter: God is in man's imagination ("a bit of air and whatever man imagines"); it is a deception concocted by priests who wrote the Bible because, if God existed he would show himself ("It is a fraud on the part of Scripture to deceive people, and if there were a God he would let himself be seen"). These statements are a true measure of Menocchio's thought, since he uttered them in the village and they were repeated by the witnesses. During the trial the judges did not question him on this point.[150]

All these radical ideas, namely Antitrinitarianism, pantheism, the non-necessity of God's existence, the equivalence of all religions, the denial of their function in salvation, and morality reduced to ethical human relations, are not only original thoughts emanating from a popular milieu; they are also the consequences of the most daring

---

[150] For Jacob's struggle, see 48; the quotes are respectively at 38, 50, 57, 49–50, 4, 13, 17. The role played by the Holy Spirit in Cathar doctrines is more limited and quite different: see *Interrogatio Iohannis*, 70, 159–61; *Liber supra Stella*, 314–15 (61–2); *Summa contra haereticos*, 23; *Summa contra patarenos*, 320, 329; *Adversus catharos et valdenses*, 264–75; *Summa de catharis et leonistis*, 65. The concept of instrumental cause is a component of medieval philosophy. Cathars applied it to the body of man: the soul was understood as artificer and the body as the instrument of the soul: cf. *Summa contra haereticos*, 193.

speculation produced by European elite culture. This raises anew, but from another perspective, the question of the relationship between popular culture and learned culture: to what extent are Menocc hio's ideas taken from and a transformation of beliefs occurring in subordinate strata of society, to what extent are they borrowings from above? We can certainly reject the notion that ideas only travel from high to low, but it is not a simple matter to explain how reciprocal exchanges might have taken place. The problem is rendered more difficult by the state of the evidence, which is abundant and direct for high culture, but meager and indirect for popular culture. This gap can be reduced somewhat by searching for new sources, such as the trials of Menocchio. It is not so easy to remedy as effectively the other notable disparity between the two cultures, that connected to their conceptual processes and modes of expression, and to the inadequacy of historical and philological methods for the analysis of popular culture, a discrepancy that remains the most difficult obstacle in the entire question.

The comparison between syncretistic Piedmontese Catharism and Menocchio's doctrinal world permits a few final observations regarding aspects of popular culture connected to witchcraft. Carlo Ginzburg has argued that the concept of the Sabbat emerged in the area of the western Alps in the second half of the fourteenth century "from a convergence of heterodox, dualistic and folkloric motifs." Possibly contributing to it was "a thread of beliefs tied to Cathar dualism," beliefs in God the creator of the heavens and in the Devil the creator of visible things. Witchcraft spread widely in Europe at the beginning of the fifteenth century, although the Sabbat long remained associated with the areas in which it was first practiced. Its diffusion proceeded unequally geographically and was diversified over time. In the eastern Alps, a zone of contact and exchange between Celtic and Slavic regions, the Benandanti, an agrarian cult of the mid-sixteenth to the mid-seventeenth centuries, was transformed by inquisitors into the cult of the Sabbat.[151] Classic witchcraft, in fact, never appears in six-

---

[151] C. Ginzburg, "Présomptions sur le sabbat," *Annales: E. S. C.* 39 (1984): 349; idem, *Ecstasies: Deciphering the Witches' Sabbath,* 13, 76–80, 296 on the origins; 66, 93–97, 297–300 on the diffusion. For the *benandanti,* see also, by the same author, *The Night Battles: Witchcraft and Agrarian Cults in the Sixteenth and Seventeenth Centuries,* trans. John and Anne Tedeschi (Baltimore: The Johns Hopkins Univ. Press, 1983).

teenth-century Friulan trials, although there are many cases of various types of magic, malefice and sortilege.[152]

The absence of witchcraft from the Friuli and the diffusion in its place of the Benandanti, with their night battles to protect harvests from warlocks, strangely coincide with absence of the Devil from the cosmogonic concepts described by Menocchio, with the absence, in other words, of the idea of the dualistic origin of matter. In the western Alps dualism is already present at the origin of the Sabbat; in the east this cosmogonic dualism has disappeared and the Sabbat does not exist at all. This is a negative counter-proof of the influence of cosmogonic dualism on the origins of witchcraft. Menocchio also speaks of battles between angels in the heavens. The Benandanti are summoned "by an angel in the heavens" "beautiful and white," who "directs the company" and "remains in person by our banner," while the warlocks are commanded by a "black angel who is the Devil," or the two captains may be men in spirit like the other combatants.[153] These may be simple casual coincidences, but we can also conjecture a common, distant origin in the mythical angels of medieval heresy. The struggle between angels and devils has become transformed into the battle between Benandanti and warlocks, and it has been transported from the cosmic plane to the plane of material survival, over good and bad harvests.

The presence of witchcraft in the Lombard Alps in the early fifteenth century and in the Trentino at mid-century, and the information available for the Republic of Venice and for the Friuli contribute to better knowledge of some aspects of its diffusion. Evidence of witchcraft has been documented for the western mountainous regions of the Republic, in Valcamonica and in the environs of *monte* Tonale, in the second half of the fifteenth century, roughly in the 1460's. The first inquisitorial trials took place in Valcamonica in 1485 and in 1499 with the sanction of the central Venetian authorities. The accused were few in number. Between 1518–1521, instead, a massive and violent persecution of witches and warlocks was set in motion resulting in more than sixty executions and almost two hundred trials, causing the

---

[152] See *1000 processi dell'Inquisizione in Friuli (1551–1647)*, a cura di L. De Biasio (Villa Manin di Passariano Udine: Centro regionale di catalogazione, 1976), 19–79; M. Sarra Di Bert, "Distribuzione statistica dei dati processuali dell'inquisizione in Friuli dal 1557 al 1786: Tecniche di ricerca e risultati," *Metodi e ricerche*, n.s., 7, no. 1 (1988): 5–31, especially 20 and the appendices.

[153] Ginzburg, *The Night Battles*, 6–8, 9–11, 25–26, 87, 153–54, 157–59.

Council of Ten to intervene peremptorily. After heated dispute with the inquisitors and with the Holy See it succeeded in halting the prosecutions. It is possible that belief in witchcraft was growing in the valleys around Brescia, even if no trace of it can be found in the Venetian Holy Office trials, not even in the twenty-odd cases that came before the tribunal between 1516–1519. Thus it would appear that in northern Italy the Sabbat spread gradually from west to east and that it did not reach the most easterly area spontaneously, but was transplanted by inquisitors between the end of the sixteenth and first half of the seventeenth century.

Two other unusual elements can be noted: the change of attitude on the part of Venetian patricians towards the prosecution of witch-craft and the reality of the Sabbat. At first the government of the Serenissima supported the inquisitorial activity, obviously accepting the existence and danger of witchcraft, but, as we noted, between 1518–1521 it intervened forcefully against the prosecutions. Venice was at war, so one might have expected that the authorities would permit inquisitorial operations to continue that might allow the tensions and fears of the moment to be discharged against marginal groups. Instead, just the opposite took place, explained in the laconic official records of the Council of Ten, on the basis of jurisdiction, public order, and judicial fairness. But in Sanudo's *Diari* one can read unambiguously that the most influential members of the nobility did not believe in the physical reality of the Sabbat and considered it an illusion, a "mad-ness," despite the repeated attempts made by the ecclesiastical authori-ties to convince them otherwise.[154] In this the Council of Ten dis-tinguished itself from many other secular governments, demonstrating that in the higher strata of society, especially as a result of information permeating upwards from the judicial records, skepticism towards witchcraft was more prevalent than is currently believed.

The accomplices and supporters of the heretic.

The work of the Inquisition did not end with the conclusion of Me-nocchio's trial and the attempts to obtain and destroy the prohibited

---

[154] See Del Col, "Organizzazione, composizione," 250–59 and the *Diari* of Sanudo cited there. M. Bernardelli Curuz, *Streghe bresciane* (Desenzano del Garda: Ermione, 1988), does not use new sources.

books he had named.[155] In this period the tribunal no longer glossed over the pieces of evidence that had surfaced against other individuals in the course of an investigation, as had often happened in the early years of its activity, but proceeded diligently against the accomplices and supporters of the accused.

On 3 February 1584 Fra Felice himself gathered information at Montereale against the elder Noto and his son Bartolomeo, accused by the priest of never observing Lent. They were Swiss in origin and their family, originally known as Margnani, had made a fortune in the commerce of grains, wines and animal production at Maniago. The more affluent members had moved to Montereale but also kept their house in the former place. The accusation is not corroborated by the ten witnesses who are interrogated. Instead they accuse of heresy a steward of the Margnani from the Grisons, a certain Tuffo or Toffo. He is constantly swearing and does not believe in God, the saints, the pope, indulgences; he does not attend Mass, go to confession or receive communion, nor does he observe Lent despite the priest's cajoling. Two other Swiss, Luca and Tommaso, cobblers perhaps, read the Gospels with him in their own language and believe that only Christ saves. They have even converted some people of Vivaro to their ideas, one of whom possesses a prohibited book described as *De maestro con discipulo*, a heretical edition of the *Dyalogo del maestro e del discepolo* by Fra Antonio da Pinerolo. Tuffo is summoned to appear in Concordia and on 19 May obtains a delay of twenty days to travel to Bologna after presenting a personal security put up by Noto Margnano for the amount of 300 ducats. The case is interrupted here and not until 1590 does another inquisitor decide that the three sons of Noto Margnano and their steward Tuffo are living in Montereale as good Christians.[156]

Initiatives to check heterodoxy come not only from the Inquisition, but also from simple priests: Giovanni Missalico, the curate of

---

[155] For the books, see especially 39–40, 46–47, 64.

[156] See 20; the trial is in AAUd, *S. Officio*, b. 8, fasc. 130; on the Margnani, cf. A. Stefanutti, "Maniago nell'età moderna e contemporanea: linee e temi di una ricerca storica," in *Maniago: pieve, feudo, comune* (Maniago, 1981), 77, 81; on the *Dyalogo*, see C. Ginzburg & A. Prosperi, *Giochi di pazienza. Un seminario sul 'Beneficio di Cristo'* (Turin: Einaudi, 1975), 153–55; M. Turrini, " 'Riformare il mondo a vera vita christiana': le scuole di catechismo nell'Italia del Cinquecento," *Annali dell'Istituto storico italo-germanico in Trento* 8 (1982): 418, 472–73.

Fanna, "having heard that in Montereale someone had been arrested by the Holy Office, and seeing how things were going for the faith, zealously took action and issued an admonition in writing" against some local heretics. When Fra Felice came into possession of the document, he questioned the priest on 24 March 1584, and the latter named Salvador de Re, already tried in Venice, Zorzi Zussit, previously denounced to the Holy Office in Concordia, and Menego Vorrai. The inquisitor, however, did not proceed against them.[157]

The motions against the accomplices and supporters of Domenico Scandella, instead, all come to a formal juridical conclusion. The only one to be convicted of sharing some of his ideas, Marchiò Sgiarbasso, accused by several witnesses, is summoned and appears before the vicar general in Concordia, bearing a letter from the priest, who describes him as a good Catholic but "a person of poor judgment." After holding sessions on 18 February and 25 April the two judges, considering Sgiarbasso not to be of sound mind, impose an admonition and a few salutary penances on him: he must visit the church of the Santissima Trinità during the feast day of the Trinity, fast without drinking wine for three consecutive Fridays, and attend Mass daily for an entire year.[158]

The case against another supporter, the priest Giovanni Daniele Melchiori, is brought to a hasty conclusion. He had already been heard as a witness on 16 March in the trial against Menocchio, and after the latter's statements about Melchiori's advice had been weighed, he is himself accused and interrogated on 14 May at Portogruaro. Melchiori firmly denies having counseled Menocchio to remain silent, and the next day he is dismissed under obligation to keep himself at the disposal of the court. This is a surprising turn of events: the charges against Melchiori were not substantially different from those against Alessandro Policreto and Vorai, and yet they were dealt with much more severely. Actually the judicial situation of the priest of Polcenigo was extremely delicate, because in 1576 he had been tried by Fra Giulio Columberto and by the vicar general Camillo Cauzio for heretical utterances, magical arts and giving comfort to heretics. The

---

[157] AAUd, *S. Officio*, b. 8, fasc. 135. For the Venetian trial, see note 1 of the denunciation. The denunciation itself is at 1–2.

[158] For the witnesses, see 12, 14, 16–17, 19–20; the trial is in AAUd, *S. Officio*, b. 8, fasc. 132.

case had been reopened in 1579 by the same inquisitor and by the acting vicar Maro, continued by Fra Felice and the vicar general Scipione Bonaverio and concluded upon appeal at Venice on 29 November 1580 with a sentence reconciling him to the Church based on a light suspicion of heresy. The dossier was massive, over a hundred pages, and the two judges of 1584 remembered the affair well, if only for the judicial altercations that accompanied it.[159] During the present appearance if they had considered the evidence convincing, it could have become a case of recidivity, liable to capital punishment. They opted instead for suspension.

The trial against Alessandro Policreto, who had been a lawyer in Aviano until a year before, but was then a simple inhabitant of Pordenone, ended with a canonical purgation for suspicion of complicity. Arraigned at Portogruaro on 14 May by both judges in the presence of the government's representative, on the 23rd Policreto presented testimonials in his favor, and a defense brief consisting of nine articles. Eleven witnesses on his behalf were also examined in Pordenone, a few of whom were from Montereale, the others from the city, including the nobleman Giovanni Battista Mantica, Ascanio Amalteo, the chief notary of the community, and the two priestly vicars. The canonical purgation occurred on 29 May, decreed by the inquisitor alone on the preceding day, but acting also in the name of the vicar general: five members of the highest nobility of Pordenone swore each in turn in support of Policreto's upright Christian conduct and of the good intention behind his advice to Menocchio. The deponents were the *podestà* of the town Hieronimo de Gregoriis, doctor Ettore Ricchieri and Hieronimo Popaite, judges, Pompeo Ricchieri and the doctor Domenico Brunetto. No penances were added. This type of sentence was a conditional absolution issued where the evidence was inconclusive, but if a conviction followed in a second trial it was equivalent to a first condemnation and the accused was then deemed to be relapsed.

On the same day, 29 May, the painter Nicolò appeared before Fra Felice da Montefalco with testimonials issued by two priests of Porcia on the goodness of his life and reputation. He was dismissed for insufficient evidence. The notary recorded the decision on the margin

---

[159] See 38–39; AAUd, *S. Officio*, b. 8, fasc. 134; ASVe, *Santo Uffizio*, b. 44, fasc. "De Melchiori don Daniele."

of a leaf of Menocchio's trial where the miller had given information about him.[160]

Even the priest of Montereale, Odorico Vorai, was summoned to the Holy Office by letter. He presented himself at the convent of San Francesco in Portogruaro on 19 May, convinced that he would be testifying as a witness against Menocchio, but somewhat apprehensive that he might be accused for his own actions. The judges asked him why in February he had written a letter to the miller in prison in which he tried to give him heart, promising him the assistance of relatives and friends and counseling him to full repentance, to speak and believe according to the teachings of the Church and to ask for mercy. Odorico replied that he had written it at the request of Menocchio's children, who at first had been threatening towards him and frightened him, but one day became friendly and asked for his help. And he, to keep on good terms, had hastily written the letter. Asked why there had been discord between the miller and himself, he attributed it to his denial of permission to the latter to be confessed by another priest. The tribunal then reproached him for having absolved and given communion to a heretic, and the priest justified himself saying that he had found Menocchio in a state sufficient for confession. At this point Odorico recognized clearly that he was the accused and to prove his innocence presented five testimonials of the good qualities he had demonstrated in the five places in which he had as priest exercised the care of souls. But the court had one further, very specific accusation in reserve: the priest had maintained in public, to the scandal of those present, that the Church militant, governed by the Holy Spirit, could err. This was nothing less than heresy. With difficulty Vorai succeeded in demonstrating that this was not exactly what he had said: in a conversation with Nicolò and Sebastiano, counts of Montereale, he had stated that if a person who had committed a mortal sin died without having confessed himself, he could be pardoned by God if he was inwardly contrite; the Church militant thus was not in a position to know the entire truth *de occultis* and in this case might have considered impenitent a person who instead was saved

---

[160] On Policreto, see 37–38, 55; AAUd, *S. Officio*, b. 8, fasc. 137. The notary's marginal comment on Nicolò reads: "Die 29 maii 1584. Reverendus pater inquisitor vocavit dictum Nicolaum et cum non haberet aliunde fidem de infamia istius Nicolai et habita fide a reverendo domino Antonio, vicario Purliliarum et presbitero de Bernardinis de bona vita et fama antedicti Nicolai, eum licentiavit et dimisit."

with God, as had been affirmed by St. Augustine: "multa corpora venerantur in terris, quorum animae cruciantur in inferno."

Since the inquisitor had to leave for Udine the next day he delegated his own authority to the vicar general, but the latter was unwilling to accept it and beseeched Fra Felice to remain until the conclusion of the trial. The accused again defended himself from the charge of heresy and acknowledged his error in not having immediately denounced Menocchio to the Holy Office. He claimed that he had not been convinced of the miller's heresy, and thus out of ignorance had let him partake of communion. Under suspicion of having abetted heresy he was condemned to perform a canonical purgation in which his orthodoxy and veracity were sustained under oath by three canons, Papirio Falcetta, Ottavio Collucci, and Giovanni Battista Crescendolo. The penances imposed on Odorico Vorai consisted of the daily recitation of the seven penitential psalms, fasting each Friday for the period of a year, and the purchase within a year's time of a silver paten for the use of the church at Montereale.[161] This was a sobering conclusion for someone who had himself tried to correct Menocchio and convert him. The vicar general lacked the confidence to decide such a delicate case alone, which ended favorably for the defendant only because he agreed to swear that for a period of ten years he had not been wholly convinced that Menocchio was a heretic or even a suspect. Monsignor Maro and the court undoubtedly had realized that priest Odorico had been duped by the sons and friends of the miller. Nevertheless they persisted in applying the provisions of canon law rigorously against him.

The trial against Vorai was in fact the concluding act in a maneuver specifically mounted to ruin him. The priest had begun to fear for his safety even before Menocchio's arrest, because in the town it was being said that it was he who had denounced him; but his apprehension continued to grow because of the "strange signs" and threatening attitudes of the miller's sons. One of Menocchio's friends, Sebastiano Sebenico, had even suggested "a sound thrashing" for the priest, but, instead, Giovanni and Stefano Scandella with the help of Bartolomeo di Andrea, and certainly with the advice of others, chose a different route. When Odorico attempted to explain away the situation and soothe the ruffled feelings, they told him that they no longer believed the denunciation had come from him, they wanted to be his friends

---

[161] AAUd, *S. Officio*, b. 8, fasc. 136.

and hoped they could count on his help and advice. Vorai, with a sense of liberation, then wrote his letter to seal the accord, convinced that he was performing an act of pious mercy. However, he had not signed the letter brought by Giovanni to the prison which ended up in the hands of the vicar general. Giovanni had told his father that the letter had come from his friend, Domenego Femenussa, a lumber merchant, and this is what Menocchio and the tribunal believed until the 14th of May when the miller's son disclosed to the judges that its author was the priest Odorico Vorai himself.[162] And it was once again Giovanni, or someone else close to him, who informed the Holy Office extrajudicially of the heretical utterance imputed to the priest. What followed was the formal trial for heresy and abetting heresy, which ended up damaging his reputation but not much more.

Fra Felice's activity in the Friuli closes with these trials.[163] In fact, on 14 June 1584 a new inquisitor, Fra Evangelista Pelleo da Force, made his appearance in Udine armed with a letter from the Congregation of the Holy Office dated 26 April and another from Cardinal Savelli to the patriarch Grimani dated 5 May. Fra Evangelista asked his predecessor to cease all activity on cases before the tribunal and transfer its archive to him. Fra Felice, visibly upset, accepted these provisions only out of a spirit of obedience. He did let it be known, however, that, according to the law, the injunction to abandon his post had no juridical force because it was not accompanied by an explicit revocation of his mandate; according to the authoritative manual, the *Directorium inquisitorum* by Eymeric and Peña, two inquisitors could both serve in a diocese with equal authority. Fra Felice asked the notary to draw up an inventory of the two archives and consigned it to his successor, but with the proviso that everything would revert to the prior state if the cardinal inquisitors should declare that they did not intend to remove him.[164]

We can only guess at the reasons for this drastic intervention on the part of the Congregation. One explanation may lie in the discord between inquisitor and the patriarchal vicar Bisanti. The latter in fact hastened to write to the patriarch on 18 June that given the atmos-

---

[162] Ibid., fols. 2r–v, 3v–4v; see also 35, 59–60.

[163] Chronologically, the first proceeding following these trials is the initiation of a case on the part of the inquisitor Pelleo on 19 September 1584: AAUd, *S. Officio*, b. 8, fasc. 139.

[164] Ibid., b. 71, reg. "Liber actuum S. O. ab anno 1580 usque ad 1644," fols. 3v–4r.

phere of Fra Felice's departure, the latter would certainly lose no opportunity to denigrate him in Rome, being convinced, in his anger, that he, the vicar, had been behind his removal. And this is, in fact, what happened. The vicar general had to defend himself a few months later in a letter to Cardinal Savelli from the accusations that the deposed inquisitor had made against him.[165]

The village against the priest.

The priest of Montereale, Odorico Vorai, returned to the village. He was worried, deeply worried, in fact feared for his very life, and had stated as much to the court on 19 May. It almost seemed an exaggerated fear, a touch of paranoia. Menocchio had scarcely been condemned and Odorico was already going around with a dagger under his cloak. He laid it aside only in the sacristy, preparing for Mass. Actually he had been carrying it for a few years and occasionally joked about it, as a witness related: when "he leaves his house, first he shouts at this person, and then at that one, puts a hand on his dagger as if he is going to use it, and when people start running, he laughs: 'It is just a joke!'"[166]

He was no longer joking now. Quarrelsome and a womanizer, he had made himself disliked by the villagers of Montereale with his attempts at reforming them and his "haughty and insolent" character. He had not spared them scathing, insolent vituperations and he had often harangued them from the pulpit. For example, on one holiday during the sermon he had exclaimed angrily: "All the people of Montereale are thieves" (almost certainly referring to thefts of wood suffered by the lumber merchants). However, he never attacked the people of Grizzo and Malnisio who, in turn, liked and esteemed him. This was parochialism, a question of likes and dislikes, of differing sensibilities and hostility between neighboring villages rooted in disagreements over the collective use of land. The priest Odorico no longer felt safe in Montereale; the roof of his rectory was made of straw. So he moved to Grizzo to live with a brother-in-law.

---

[165] See *Le lettere di Paolo Bisanti*, 515–16, 530.

[166] The account of the events and the quotations are all taken, unless stated otherwise, from AVPd, *Biblioteca capitolare, Visite,* b. 7, "Examina et processus in visitatione apostolica civitatis et dioecesis Concordiensis ... d. Caesare de Nores ...," unnumbered leaves, section concerning Montereale.

Late on the night of 24 June, the day of St. John the Baptist, while the traditional celebration was being observed in the public square of Malnisio, the priest ran into people from Montereale. They were all in high spirits. He arm-wrestled one of them, and lost. Words began to be exchanged. Antonio Spel, aged fifty, put a hand on his shoulder and tried to convince him that he had been wrong to move away and to persuade him to return, but tempers became heated and there was pushing and shoving. According to some witnesses Vorai was heard exclaiming: "You're all a bunch of cuckolds." That's all that was needed. A fight broke out, rocks flew. Spel grabbed the priest around the waist. Odorico himself must have thought that he was finally in for it, since the details remained engraved in his memory:

And that Antonio grabbed me and squashing me hard against him said: 'We want you back whatever it takes.' And feeling myself being pressed so that I could no longer stand, even though I was yelling 'Let me go messer Antonio, stop this! What insolence is this?' I was forced to resist so that we both fell to the ground. And as soon as we were on our feet again, Venuto del Bianco of Grizzo, Antonio's brother-in-law, showed up and he started shouting, 'What are you doing to my brother-in-law you no-good priest?' and other such things. And then another one came up, called Sagaia da Grizzo, and he too tried to hit me while cursing at me all the while, and I shoved him with my left hand, saying 'Don't lose your head, there's no fight here, we're only joking.' And Sagaia fell to the ground from my push since he was drunk and then I was immediately surrounded by a bunch of people from Montereale carrying various arms, daggers and swords and one had a hatchet.

Odorico unsheathed his dagger and managed to break out where the crowd was thinnest. Nicolò Barisello raised a hatchet to strike him on the head, but the priest ducked. Bastiano Martino, Menocchio's brother-in-law, tried to jab him with a long metal-tipped pole, but succeeded only in ripping his cloak. The priest could have struck back, but instead desperately tried to escape: if he had lingered to fight, his assailants would have overcome him. One of them managed to hook him with an implement and drag him to the ground. The priest immediately sprang to his feet, while bystanders screamed that he was being killed and urged him to escape. Many people of Malnisio now joined the fray, including the priest's brother, who had a sword. A man from Montereale was wounded in the head, Odorico found refuge in a house, and his enemies tried to smash down the doors and drag him out. But by now the fortunes of battle had turned against the partisans of the miller, and the assassination attempt failed.

This episode shows that Menocchio had not only been reaccepted in the community, but actually had friends and supporters: the entire village, not just his relatives, had risen up against the accuser who had violated its unwritten code of solidarity.

In the next three months Vorai went to say Mass in Montereale only twice. He made his chaplain do it in his place and only showed up to baptize and give communion if he was specifically called. His dagger and his small precautions had become indispensable, but they did not suffice. On 18 July he obtained an official letter of protection from the *Quarantia criminal,* the highest Venetian penal tribunal. On 27 July, with the assistance of a lawyer, he presented the document to the governor in Udine, who had it publicly proclaimed in the village. The letter threatened whoever directly or indirectly offended, molested, injured or intimidated the priest and his relatives with a punishment of two hundred ducats and ten years of banishment from the Friuli for oral offenses, and in the case of physical assault a penalty of one thousand ducats, perpetual banishment from the Republic and the confiscation of property.[167] Anyone could grasp the gravity of the threatened sanctions, so that the priest could now occasionally venture back to Montereale, if only to save face a little and pick up the vestment fees from the baptisms.

Such a state of affairs could not go on forever. The villagers' hatred found an outlet with a tactic that was both legal and less dangerous than one of physical assault. On 14 September an apostolic visitation, an exceptional event, got underway in the diocese of Concordia. The papal emissary endowed with full powers was Bishop Cesare de Nores. He started from the foothills and stopped with his retinue in the larger centers, Aviano and Maniago, from which he would then proceed to Spilimbergo. Before the visitor even reached Montereale the mayor of the town and other heads of families, in the name of the entire neighborhood, on 16 September met him at Mani-

---

[167] ASVe, *Luogotenente della patria del Friuli,* b. 287, reg. MM, fol. 66v. I found nothing in *Quarantia criminal,* reg. 23 (1582–1594); b. 58 (containing various decisions, 1499–1662).

ago and presented him with a denunciation against the priest for disorderly conduct, errors and scandals grouped under ten accusations. They encompassed the violation of the secrecy of the sacrament, negligence in having allowed his parishioners to die without the benefit of last rites, attempts to procure women for his purposes, the confessions he heard from several women and girls in the sacristy behind locked doors, the extortion of money from penitents for wood stolen from the river bed of the Cellina, and the wounding of a parishioner on the last feast day of St. John the Baptist.

Testifying against Vorai were Antonio Spel, Giovanni Scandella (who, like Spel, expressed a positive opinion on the priest's pastoral and liturgical activities, but told of his demand to possess his sisters), Giacomo de Benedetto, the bell ringer, the priest Andrea Ionima, and four others from Montereale. Vorai himself was heard and he gave his version of the facts: the woman who had remained with her candle lit during the entire Mass of Holy Thursday because she had borne a child out of wedlock had done so because of his simple advice given outside the confessional, to make amends for the public scandal she had caused. The women he had confessed in the sacristy were hard of hearing. The priest denied having ever solicited girls, although he claimed that in fact, they had been offered to him many times, but he had always refused them. He had collected funds for some thefts, transgressions which came under the bishop's jurisdiction, and he was holding the money at the disposal of his superiors. He admitted the brawl at Maniago, but he angrily explained that it had been an act of legitimate self-defense and he described the assault he had endured. Monsignor de Nores, however, was not convinced and judged these replies suspect and insincere. He suspended Vorai from the practice of divine rites, ordered him not to return to his parish and to present himself at Portogruaro.

The visitation of Montereale thus took the direction set in motion by the concerted strategy of the townspeople. The examination of the buildings and of the sacred furnishings was performed by the bishop on 17 September, and on the 18th members of his entourage questioned, as was the custom, some of the parishioners about the priests. Biasio Caligo, a friend of Menocchio's and two others, came forward and repeated briefly many of the accusations that had already been made against the priest Vorai. They also had some negative things to say about his chaplain. Vorai himself was questioned, and he too attacked the chaplain, denounced Menocchio's friend Sebastiano

Sebenico for abstaining from confession and keeping concubines, and lamented the weak religious faith of the people. The decisions came quickly. On 1 October the chaplain, Andrea Ionima, was suspended from his religious functions for a year, deemed too ignorant to celebrate Mass. On 2 November measures were promulgated to recover lands and credits belonging to the church and the responsibility for carrying them out was assigned to Caligo.

At the end of October Vorai presented himself before the apostolic visitor in Portogruaro and produced, among other things, a long defense composed of 24 articles which explained in detail his activity for the religious renewal of his parishioners, the excellent conduct from which he had never deviated, the treachery of the people of Montereale and the persecutions he had suffered at their hands, the high opinion in which he was held, instead, by the inhabitants of Grizzo and Malnisio, and the hostility against him of certain individuals. In fact, he named all the witnesses who had testified against him in the inquest conducted by the visitor and in the subsequent investigations. He ascribed the villagers' hatred to his attempts to elevate the Christian sentiments of the faithful and his denunciation of Menocchio: "the men of the village, the relatives and sons of the aforesaid Domenego," he said, had immediately begun to threaten him, going so far as to denounce him to the Inquisition. The witnesses who testified in his favor before the tribunal of Monsignor de Nores were a few priests, an itinerant hawker of cakes who had been present at the feast day, an inhabitant of Montereale, four of Malnisio and eight of Grizzo, among whom were the first three witnesses against Menocchio, namely Daniele Fassetta, Francesco Fassetta, and Bernardo del Cotta (or del Ceta).

Meantime Odorico seized upon an ingenious stratagem for setting himself up respectably in the village by exploiting the discord between the people of Montereale and those of Grizzo and Malnisio, conceding nothing to satisfy the former. On 8 November, in fact, the two latter places were empowered by the apostolic visitor to elect their own curate, independently of the parish of Montereale, with the obligation to pay him forty ducats annually, half of which was to come from what the two churches customarily disbursed for the priest of the parish. Father Odorico was present and obviously approved of the clever transaction. This enraged the commune and heads of families of Montereale and on 13 November they submitted a second petition against the priest Odorico, "to prevent that he should ever again have dealings in this parish and with its church," thereby playing the few cards that remained to them: they repeated his heretical statement regarding the possibility that the Church militant might err previously brought to the attention of the Inquisition, and brazenly heightened the charges of sexual misbehavior. The eight witnesses, all from Montereale, included Antonia, the wife of the bell ringer who was a part-time servant of the priest; Florida, a relative of Caligo's; Bartolomeo di Andrea; and the mayor. The women mentioned some racy details and added, to those mentioned earlier, the names of four girls whom the priest had pursued.

The people of Montereale busied themselves countering Odorico's initiatives, even on the institutional plane, and advanced a proposal of their own, which Monsignor de Nores approved, to appoint a stable resident chaplain for the three churches of the parish, with a stipend of fifty ducats, broken down in the following manner: thirty to be paid by the commune of Montereale, ten from the revenue of the properties, and ten from the income of the parish priest. The villages of Grizzo and Malnisio would be able to participate in the selection only after they had contributed half of the thirty ducats offered by Montereale. In the midst of his many preoccupations the visitor did not perceive that the last provision violated the pact agreed on with Odorico Vorai the 8th of November. In the end a compromise was struck with the people of Montereale giving in, losing a few ducats in the process. Grizzo and Malnisio achieved the elevation to the status of parish for the church of San Bartolomeo di Grizzo, which had just been restored. It would have a priest of its own elected by the bishop on the basis of a competition and the villages bound themselves with notarized agreements to provide him with a house and an income of forty ducats annually, in addition to the twenty that they paid to the priest of Montereale for his services in Grizzo. Speaking for Montereale, Biasio Caligo agreed that ten ducats annually would be withdrawn from the properties of the parish. The official justification for the new creation was the usual one, the great distance from the mother church, even though it was only a matter of three kilometers for Grizzo, five for Malnisio, at the most twenty-thirty minutes on foot, perhaps even less, for two to three hundred people. In reality, something else precipitated the creation of the new parish: Vorai's denunciation of Menocchio and the latter's subsequent trial by the Holy Office.

Vorai's ordeal soon ended. The cause initiated by the people of Montereale probably would have concluded in their favor, if it could have been decided by the visitor. But this was not to be. On 14 December Vorai appeared in Udine to defend himself before Monsignor Nores, explained the meaning of his statement which had been deemed heretical, and resolutely denied everything else, imploring God's justice: "I have never said or done anything to favor a heretic so that I could have commerce with a daughter of his, nor for any other reason, and may God strike me down if this is not so." The visitor did not believe him, placed him under house arrest in the city and on 31 December, due to the press of other business and considering further investigation to be necessary, assigned the case to Paolo Bisanti, vicar to the patriarch of Aquileia. Monsignor Bisanti took the priest's side and on 18 January 1585 issued a sentence absolving him from all the charges. A notary informed Odorico, who was being held in the patriarch's jail, and ordered his release.[168]

We do not know where the unfortunate priest ended up. Certainly not in Montereale, where the office was now held by Giovanni Daniele Melchiori, who had gladly left the more onerous and poorer parish of Polcenigo, which consisted of a thousand souls, fifty ducats income plus ten from the chapel of the castle, and quarrels with the monks in the convent of San Giacomo.[169] In 1586 Bishop Matteo Sanudo made a visitation of his entire diocese, but the records for the area of the foothills, which would have provided us with precise information, have not survived.[170] Odorico may have become Grizzo's first parish priest, as he had wished, but perhaps without obtaining the ratification of the bishop, who had the will to reform profoundly both clergy and laity. In 1594 Vorai became the priest of Morsano al Tagliamento, a good sized benefice in the plain, which boasted an income of ninety ducats annually and three hundred souls, but with an impoverished church (reduced to twenty-five ducats in revenue) and parishioners in

---

[168] AAUd, *Processi,* bundle "Sententiarum 1562 usque 1586," unbound leaves, fol. "Sententia ad favorem presbyteri Odorici Varaii, lata die 18 ianuarii '85."

[169] AAUd, *S. Officio,* b. 8, fasc. 130, deposition of Melchiori dated 24 March 1590; AVPd, *Biblioteca capitolare, Visite,* b. 6, "Visitatio apostolica ... Concordiensis ...," fols. 1r–12v, concerning Polcenigo.

[170] AVPn, *Visite,* b. 2, reg. "Sacrarum visitationum sub illustrissimo domino Matthaeo Sanuto episcopo anni 1586": the visitation lasts from 26 May to 14 October, and the two last villages mentioned are in the foothills, Polcenigo and Aviano; b. 3, reg. "Visitationum personalium anni 1593 usque ad annum 1597," 156–59, 160–62, where for Montereale and Grizzo one is referred to the register of the 1586 visit.

reduced circumstances. Here too he persevered in his duty, denouncing to the Inquisition persons he suspected of heresy.[171]

Intermezzo.

Menocchio remained confined in the damp rough prison of the episcopal palace in Concordia. His behavior was exemplary. He prayed, recited the seven penitential psalms, and fasted on Fridays. He became seriously ill during the winter 1585–1586 and almost lost his hearing. But there was hope for him: the court had used the formula of life imprisonment, not of irremissible life imprisonment. After twenty months he beseeched the court to set him free and impose a substitute punishment.[172]

On 18 January 1586 Menocchio's son Zanutto presented to the bishop and to the new inquisitor, Fra Evangelista Pelleo, a petition written by a lawyer in Menocchio's name. The following day the opinion of the jailer was heard, and the condemned man, physically in weakened condition, as the notary recorded, was summoned from his cell. The judges commuted the sentence, assigning to him as prison the village of Montereale, under surety of two hundred ducats to be confiscated if he failed to observe these terms. He was also enjoined never again to utter his evil opinions, wear a penitential garment, give

---

[171] The data on the benefice are drawn from the apostolic visitation indicated at note 21, the part concerning Morsano. P. C. Begotti, "La parrocchia di S. Martino di Morsano e i suoi rettori," in *Morsan al Tilimint,* ed. N. Tracanelli, G. Bergamini, M. G. B. Altan (Udine: Società filologica friulana, 1988), 454, mentions 1592 as the year of the appointment, while it is Vorai himself who speaks of 1594 in the deposition of 19 July 1599: AAUd, *S. Officio,* b. 17, fasc. 384. On this date the priest denounced Domenico Celotto, "l'agna Romana" and the wife of Iacomo Biasutto for practicing magical arts; Francesco Padovano for concubinage and for failing to appear at confession and communion; Panfilo Borgara for concubinage; there are no additional proceedings. On 23 January 1596 he also denounced a gentleman, Orazio di Cordovado, because he had threatened to beat a preacher and for stating that the excommunication would have no effect if he burned the stick; the trial closed with the imposition of salutary penances on 6 September: see b. 14, fasc. 284.

[172] On the formula of *carcere perpetuo,* see J. Tedeschi, "Preliminary Observations on Writing a History of the Roman Inquisition," in *Continuity and Discontinuity in Church History,* edited by F. F. Church & T. George (Leiden: Brill, 1979), 233 (now reprinted in Tedeschi's *The Prosecution of Heresy,* 3–21). The time that had to transpire in prison before grace could be sought ranged from two to three years. Cf. I. Simancas, *Praxis haereseos, sive Enchiridion iudicum violatae religionis . . . ,* (Venice: ex officina Iordani Ziletti, 1568), fols. 81r–v.

alms on Fridays (in place of fasting), go to confession and receive communion six times annually, and forward to the court each year the parish priest's attestations of his good behavior. The security was put up by Daniele di Biasio and Menocchio walked out of prison.

Menocchio easily reinserted himself into the life of the village, and resumed his old relationships. The priest now was his childhood friend Giovanni Daniele Melchiori. In 1590 the community elected Menocchio administrator (*cameraro*); in 1595 he was appointed as an appraiser in a litigation between Count Giovanni Francesco of Montereale and Bastian de Martin, who was Menocchio's brother-in-law and had been among Odorico's assailants. The same year, together with his son Stefano, he rented a mill, taking it over from Fiorito Benedetto, son of the now deceased bell ringer who had supported the charges against Odorico during the apostolic visitation. The Scandellas provided surety on Fiorito's behalf for the debts that he still owed, a demonstration of friendship despite their own difficulties. Still in 1595 Menocchio was chosen as one of the fourteen representatives assigned to prepare Montereale's land valuation for the governor in Udine.[173] But little information emerges from these documents.

In January 1589, roughly three years after the commutation of the sentence, Menocchio briefly came to the notice of the Holy Office again. The inquisitor, Fra Giovanni Battista Angelucci, discovered in the archive at Portogruaro the old anonymous denunciation against some people of Fanna, and he interrogated three of the witnesses named in the document, but did not proceed further. He also read the names of two accused persons of Montereale, the priest Andrea, and Domenico Scandella, but did not find it necessary to question them.[174]

After eleven years of a life made more difficult by the sign of perpetual infamy he had to wear and the restriction of his movements to the village, Menocchio went to Udine to present himself before the inquisitor with a letter of recommendation from the priest. According to the document the miller was leading a Christian and orthodox life, if one could judge the interior by the exterior, as Father Melchiori put

---

[173] Cf. 99–104; Ginzburg, 95–98. The two documents cited there are now printed in the Italian edition of the trials at 229–31.

[174] See AAUd, *S. Officio*, b. 8, fasc. 135: on 17 and 28 January the inquisitor interrogated count Fantussio, son of the deceased Giacomo Antonio, his own son Antonio, and the priest Paolo Paulino.

it. In actual truth Menocchio's behavior had not been so exemplary: he frequently did not wear his penitential garment with its flaming crosses and went outside the town, thus violating the terms of his sentence. The priest knew all this. But the inquisitor, who did not, on 26 January 1597, granted Menocchio full freedom to circulate outside the village, although he did not remove the stigma of the penitential vestment.[175]

For this old man sorely tried by life and the condemnation, this concession provided some relief. But there was one requirement of his sentence that depended entirely upon himself which he could not meet: he was unable to keep silent about his ideas. He occasionally broached them when he was outside Montereale, almost always with people whom he hardly knew. He was well aware what would be the outcome of a second trial, though with the passing of time the realization must have grown dimmer. The fate of recidivists had been clearly explained in the sentence. In reality there had never been a condemnation to death for heresy in the diocese of Concordia; in Udine there had been fifteen or so, but only three had been carried out, one of which had been on the cadaver of a prisoner who had died in prison the night before. According to some older studies, all the other condemned men had managed to escape. Three other suspects, against whom legal proceedings had been initiated in Udine, were extradited to Rome for trial by the Congregation of the Holy Office and executed.

Recent statistical studies concerning sentences pronounced in Venice between 1547 and 1583 against persons residing in the city have identified eleven condemnations to capital punishment, rather than five as previously thought. Though the Venetian Inquisition has been considered moderate in its administration of justice, these figures suggest that it compares in severity with the Spanish tribunals in the same period. News about the execution of heretics at Udine, Venice or in other neighboring dioceses filtered down to the people as remote happenings, their impact diminished by time and distance. Very little real information must have circulated, given the secrecy desired and imposed by Venetian authorities. The Republic permitted the public reading of sentences and abjurations in Venice only after 1566, and never did it authorize a public capital execution. In Udine the first

---

[175] See 109.

death sentence was carried out in 1568 with great secrecy upon the order of the Council of Ten, which had even considered transferring the condemned person to its own prisons in Venice in order to conclude the case with the least possible clamor.[176]

By the end of the sixteenth century it was no longer safe to converse, however quietly and clandestinely, about prohibited subjects. The local Inquisition was now issuing edicts in the vernacular which listed what were crimes against the faith and reiterated the duty of denouncing suspected heretics under pain of immediate excommunication. One of these pronouncements was published by the patriarch of Aquileia Francesco Barbaro and by the inquisitor Angelucci on 3 July 1595. Preachers and parish priests were obliged to read it out in church at least three feast days a year and to remind the faithful of the obligation to denounce suspects of heresy.[177]

While accusations, in the past, had come principally from churchmen and the more zealous among the faithful, this obligation was now accepted by the majority of parishioners. Leonardo Simon, who lived in Roveredo neighboring Porcia, said he had heard "a bull about heresy" and recalled a conversation he had at Udine with Menocchio during the carnival of 1596. They knew one another because they both had played at holiday celebrations in Grizzo and Malnisio; Leonardo, the violin, and Menocchio, the cithara. Menocchio (Leonardo did not know his full name) had criticized monks and the cult of saints, the Gospels, which according to him had been written by priests and monks, and Christianity itself, arguing that even Turks are saved. Furthermore, he had said that Christ did not descend from the cross because he lacked the ability to do so and not because he did not want to. The conversation had been short, consisting of a few such exchanges.

---

[176] For the Friuli, see A. Battistella, *Il S. Officio e la riforma religiosa in Friuli. Appunti storici documentati* (Udine, 1895), 66; L. De Biasio, "L'eresia protestante in Friuli nella seconda metà del secolo XVI," *Memorie storiche forogiuliesi* 52 (1972): 86, 90–95, 104, 109, 111–12; Del Col, "La storia religiosa del Friuli," 71. For Venice, see Grendler, *The Roman Inquisition,* 57–58 in comparison with new data furnished by J. Martin, "Per un'analisi quantitativa dell'Inquisizione veneziana," in *L'Inquisizione romana in Italia,* 143–57; idem., "L'Inquisizione romana e la criminalizzazione," 790 and note 46. The 1568 order of the Council of Ten is in ASVe, *Consiglio dei dieci, Secreto,* reg. 8, fols. 130r–v; the sentence, which appears to have been executed through hanging in the prison during the night, is in AAUd, *S. Officio,* b. 58, fasc. "Sententiarum . . . liber I," fols. 31r–32v, 74r–77v; the trial against Ambrogio Castenario is printed in *1000 processi dell'Inquisizione in Friuli,* 105–30.

[177] The edict is printed ibid., 90.

Simon wrote about it to the inquisitor in Udine, driven by his devotion as well as his conscience: without the absolution which apparently a priest was holding back from him because of his failure to make a denunciation, he could not participate in a jubilee that had just been announced. Father Angelucci asked for information from his vicar in Pordenone, Fra Girolamo Asteo, who obtained it and forwarded it to him promptly at the convent of Portogruaro on 3 April 1596.[178] The denunciation remained suspended. The old inquisitor came infrequently to Portogruaro: the cases there seemed unimportant, mostly concerned with magical practices, and the documents gathered dust. Fra Giovanni Battista was being kept busy in the diocese of Aquileia. In January 1598, while presiding over a trial in Cividale, he became ill, returned to Udine and died shortly thereafter. By the end of February affairs were in the hands of the vicar general of the Inquisition Fra Gabriele Scala of Gubbio.[179]

The second trial and the end.

The Congregation of the Holy Office named the new inquisitor for Aquileia and Concordia on 4 March of the same year.[180] Fra Girolamo Asteo of Pordenone, thirty-six years of age, a doctor in theology, was destined to go far: he held the office until 30 December 1608, contemporaneously serving for a period as provincial minister of his order. He was elected bishop of Veroli 17 November 1608, and died in his episcopal seat in the Lazio some twenty years later. He wrote several works on theological and especially legal subjects, two of which were published while he was bishop.[181]

---

[178] See 105–8. A similar idea on the death of Christ circulated among the Bogomils in the tenth century in the following form: our Lord was not crucified out of his free will, nor for the salvation of mankind, but because he was compelled to it: cf. *Le traité contre les bogomiles de Cosmas le pretre,* ed. and trans. H. C. Puech and A. Vaillant (Paris: Imprimerie nationale, 1945), 60; the cross was not to be revered or adored, as did Catholics, according to the *Liber supra Stella,* 311 (56–57).

[179] AAUd, *S. Officio,* b. 15, fasc. 316, fols. 12v–13r; b. 16, fasc. 317.

[180] See the document of appointment in AAUd, *S. Officio,* b. 71, reg. "Liber actuum . . . ," fols. 19r–20v.

[181] See note 4 to the second trial, 106.

Of the inquisitors who passed through the Friuli in the sixteenth century, he was the second to have a brilliant career. The first had been Fra Evangelista Pelleo, who had concluded his brief term in office to become vicar general of his order, then minister general and finally bishop of Sant'Agata dei Goti.[182] While Fra Evangelista's Friulan activity seems a parenthesis, a passing assignment, Asteo's long and intense period of service there was one of the principal factors in his successful career.

The inquisitorial activity of this monk from Pordenone, measured by the number of trials initiated during his tenure in office, not counting earlier proceedings which he reopened, and without distinguishing between denunciations and actual trials, achieved an extremely high annual rate: twenty-four new proceedings in the diocese of Aquileia, and 10 in the diocese of Concordia. It was the most active period by far in the entire history of the Friulan Inquisition. In the second half of the sixteenth century after the reorganization of a permanent tribunal in 1557, the average for new cases was approximately four per year for Aquileia and one or two for Concordia (1557–1579), climbing to twelve for Aquileia and four for Concordia under Fra Felice (1579–1584) and Fra Giovanni Battista Angelucci (1586–1598), with a slight decrease during the brief period of service of Fra Evangelista.

In the course of the decades the Inquisition prosecuted an increasingly varied number of crimes. At first formal religious heresy connected to Reformation doctrines predominated, but towards the end of the century this form of accusation virtually disappeared to be replaced by proceedings against sundry heretical expressions and propositions, the reading and possession of prohibited books, acts of irreverence and irreligiosity, the use of forbidden foods, and especially magical arts. The repression of this last type of offense grew gradually beginning in the 1570s, until it accounted for fully fifty percent of Fra Girolamo Asteo's time, from then on remaining the most frequently persecuted crime.[183]

The general flow of activity over a long duration is comparable in the four Italian tribunals (Venice, Aquileia-Concordia, Naples, Sicily) that have recently been the object of a quantitative study: a peak

---

[182] See note 76 to the first trial, 99.
[183] See Sarra Di Bert, "Distribuzione statistica," 5–31.

roughly between 1580–1610, with a rapid decline and relative calm during the seventeenth and eighteenth centuries, a development which strongly resembles what was occurring with the Spanish Inquisition. The typology of cases tried by the Italian tribunals is also roughly comparable, but here there are marked differences from Spain due to diverse religious, institutional, political, social and cultural factors.[184]

The quantitative data presently available to us for the Friuli, as for the other Italian tribunals, are necessarily elementary and preliminary, since they are based primarily on archival inventories and only provide an approximate picture of the situation. In the Friuli in absolute numbers 415 persons were denounced or tried between 1557 and 1596 (the corresponding dossiers are collected in 15 bundles); between 1596 and 1606 the figure increases slightly to 426 (7 bundles). During this fifty-year span, half of the accused were tried in the final decade, and a third of the entire documentation was generated in this same ten year period, against the two thirds produced in the preceding forty years. At the same time, the bishops of both dioceses were attempting to put into effect the reforms decreed by the Council of Trent, a bit later than in other north Italian dioceses. Recent studies have shown the importance of the pastoral activity of Francesco Barbaro, first as vicar and then as patriarch (1585–1610), even though he only succeeded in laying sound foundations for the ecclesiastical renewal and did not manage to overcome some of the most serious obstacles due to the poverty of some of the benefices, and the opposition of powerful chapters, women's convents, and lay patrons. Our knowledge of the activity of Bishop Matteo Sanudo (1584–1610) still remains at the stage of tradition and local myth.[185]

The new inquisitor, Asteo, set to work at once and went to the most prestigious and burdensome of his seats, that of Udine, to size up the situation. On 25 April 1598 he commissioned an inventory of the trial dossiers (about three hundred fascicles), sentences (more than a hundred), books (more than a hundred, including a dozen or so inquisitorial manuals), letters and various documents, accounts, property and furniture, and 300 florins in cash, equivalent to 513 ducats, a

---

[184] Monter & Tedeschi, "Toward a Statistical Profile," 130–47.

[185] On the two bishops, see G. Trebbi, *Francesco Barbaro, patrizio veneto e patriarca d'Aquileia* (Udine: Casamassima, 1984); E. Degani, *La diocesi di Concordia,* ristampa con bibliografia aggiornata e indici (Brescia: Paideia, 1977; 1st ed. 1924), 247–48.

considerable sum. The archive was the nerve center of the inquisitorial office: it made possible the continuity of activity, the determination of cases of recidivism, the verification that sentences had been carried out. In this period the archive was the direct responsibility of the inquisitor and was housed in the convent of San Francesco where he lived, testimony that by then this official had become the preeminent figure in the tribunal.[186]

Fra Girolamo Asteo assumed his position in May and on 26 June made a solemn entrance with a fitting ceremony in a hall of the governor's palace. After the chanting of *Veni, creator spiritus,* the apostolic appointment was read, and then the vicar general of the patriarch, the government representative, two lay consultors and the chief notary of the Holy Office took the oath to maintain secrecy and faithfulness to their obligations in the hands of the inquisitor.[187]

The new notary of the Holy Office, Fra Antonio Francesco Sinigardi d'Arezzo, prepared an inventory of the inquisitorial seat at Portogruaro: the archive consisted of over fifty trials, a volume recording various legal acts, fourteen sentences and single denunciations. This inquisitorial office was much less well endowed and its archive in somewhat of a calamitous condition from neglect: some of its records had been kept in Udine, copies of others in Venice; many had been lost. To avoid further dispersals, Fra Felice, on 1 June 1584, had given the order that all the documents should be locked up in the sacristy of the cathedral in Concordia.[188]

Fra Girolamo began his work in the diocese of Concordia in July, 1598. Another ceremony of installation took place on 19 October in the palace of the *provveditore,* in the presence of the episcopal vicar, Valerio Trapola, the local Venetian governor, Giovanni Balbi, an ecclesiastical consultor, and two laymen. On the same day ten interrupted cases, consisting mostly of denunciations, were reopened and it was decided to proceed in almost all, except for one which was suspended and another (a question involving two priests) that was trans-

---

[186] AAUd, *S. Officio,* b. 86, b. internal "S. Spirito . . . ," fasc. B. 2.

[187] Ibid., b. 16, fasc. 321 (16 May), 323–25 (respectively of 10, 12, 16 June); b. 71, reg. "Liber actuum . . . ," fols. 19r–20v.

[188] See AVPn, *Processi,* reg. "Nonnulli processus ab anno 1584 usque ad annum 1586," I fasc., fols. 1r–2r.

ferred to the episcopal court. In the next session, held on 28 October, it was decided to proceed with four other pending cases and to suspend eight. The first case taken under consideration was the denunciation against Menocchio of Montereale, in which the tribunal wanted to determine if this was the same person as Domenico Scandella, also called Menocchio.[189] Once set in motion the judicial machinery would not come to rest again until the final sentence. There was nothing special about the case: it was only one among many for an extremely busy young inquisitor at the beginning of his term in office.

Fra Girolamo stopped off at his residence in Pordenone and there found bits of information that might prove useful: the priest Ottavio of the family of the counts of Montereale, since 1566 chaplain of the Altar of the Most Blessed Sacrament in the richly endowed church of San Marco knew Montereale well. Not only did he confirm that there was only one Menocchio, but added that many years before he too had urged the parish priest to denounce him, and he was now hearing from many sources that Menocchio had resumed his foul utterances. The person who had made the accusation in 1596 confirmed the identification. Asteo then decided to give a hearing to the priest and chaplain of the village. So as not to arouse suspicion or apprehension, or provide cause for retaliation, he had them questioned on 17 December by the priest of Aviano, deputized as his commissioner for the purpose. For greater caution the two were invited to Malnisio. Giovanni Daniele Melchiori and Curzio Cellina related that Menocchio confessed himself and received communion regularly and they considered him a good Christian, adding the qualification "as far as one can judge externally," to the record at the priest's request. Menocchio was everybody's friend and now and then wanted to have his say. Occasionally he failed to wear the penitential garment and even ventured outside the village.[190]

In the tribunal of Concordia there was not much to give cause for concern. In the session held on 2 January 1599 an accused person was absolved with a salutary penance, two other cases were suspended, and two suspects, one of them Menocchio, were to be summoned to

---

[189] AAUd, *S. Officio,* b. 16, fasc. 327 (3 July), 329 (4 August, 11 September), 332–34 (9 September, 18–19 October).

[190] See 109–14; the quote is at 112. For the benefice of the priest Ottavio, see above note 30.

appear. But the inquisitor returned to Udine and the summons was probably not executed.

Four months later Fra Girolamo once again passed through Pordenone and yet another denunciation recalled the case to him. A fellow citizen, worried about incurring excommunication after hearing an edict issued on 20 February and 2 May 1599, related an utterance of the miller that he had heard from others: "If Christ had been God he would have been an ass (*coglione*) to let himself be crucified." The expression was execrable, the denial of Christ's divinity extremely serious. Four days later, on 6 May, the inquisitor questioned the witness, Michele del Turco, and had him explain all the circumstances as prescribed by canon law. On 12 May Fra Girolamo and Monsignor Sanudo, who was making a pastoral visitation of the diocese, decreed the arrest of the suspect and ordered the captain of the castle at Aviano to execute it.

Meanwhile Michele del Turco had returned to the notary of the Holy Office to denounce another utterance of Menocchio's which was going around: "How can you believe that Christ or God Almighty was the Son of the Virgin Mary if this Virgin Mary was a whore?" Michele also related a heretical blasphemy uttered by Giovanni Mellina, an official in Polcenigo, which had nothing to do with the case of Menocchio.[191] By now information was flowing into the Holy Office spontaneously: the obligation to denounce was now broadly accepted, both because it had been inculcated by the edicts and driven home to every witness who appeared before the tribunal.

The case seriously preoccupied Fra Girolamo, who immediately informed the Congregation in Rome with a letter dated 7 May. This had become a common practice in the Friuli for almost the whole of the last decade, with anywhere from two to more than twenty letters written each year. Recourse to Rome served the purpose of clarifying doubts and obtaining advice and instructions. The Holy See thereby kept a moderate but constant control over the provincial tribunals, although the latter retained full authority to act. In addition to reporting information about the trial, the letter posed two questions: should the court proceed even when there was danger to the life of the accuser or prosecution witnesses, and could an arrest be made on the basis of

---

[191] See 115–20; the quotes are at 116, 119. On Mellina see AAUd, *S. Officio*, b. 14, fasc. 285, fols. 13r–18v.

testimony from only a single person? Both doubts were directly pertinent to the trial against Menocchio: the priest Ottavio had briefly recounted the fate of the poor parish priest Vorai, and the dossier contained only one witness for the most serious charge, while the law normally demanded that there be two. The reply, mailed on 5 June, arrived on the 14th. Cardinal Santoro wrote that the pope himself (who presided over the Congregation of the Holy Office) was recommending the greatest diligence in this "extremely serious case." And he specifically recommended the arrest of the heretic and an examination of his books.[192] While the bishop was visiting Aviano on 21 June, for greater security he had the accused arrested by an officer and soldiers of his own court, and had him jailed in the prisons at Concordia. The Congregation was immediately informed by a letter written on 2 July. The inquisitor ordered the confiscation of the suspect's books and papers, and on 5 and 6 July examined them personally. He also asked a specially assigned commissioner to verify the most serious pieces of evidence. The three witnesses were all from Grizzo, one had even testified at the first trial, but they did not provide direct confirmation for the incriminating statement "the Virgin Mary gave birth like other women and not through the Holy Spirit." They had heard it at second hand. One of them, however, Daniele Giacomello, a young man of twenty, recalled some snatches of a conversation with Menocchio from three years before: God is nothing but air; Christ is not God because he let himself be crucified; the inquisitors do not want us to know what they know; "St. Christopher is greater than God since he carried the whole world on his shoulders."

The trial against Giovanni Mellina, who had been denounced at the same time as Menocchio, also concluded in the same month of July. Out of convenience, perhaps, the proceedings against Mellina were recorded on the fascicle of the latter's trial. Popular hearsay had accused the official of having had his wife drowned in the Gorgazzo and he had defended himself by publicly denying the charge and insisting that even Christ himself saying it could not make it true. The sentence against him, pronounced on 7 August, imposed spiritual

---

[192] The letter is printed in appendix, 163–64. In AAUd, *S. Officio*, b. 59, are preserved only the letters received from Rome: eight in 1588, two in 1589, three in 1590, five in 1591, and in the following years, in order: five, two, twelve, six, twelve, three, eleven, fourteen, twenty-two, eight, six in 1602.

penances for the heretical blasphemy he had uttered and confessed.[193]

Menocchio was interrogated on 12 July by the inquisitor and the
vicar general and on 19 July by the inquisitor alone, always in the
presence of the government representative, Pietro Zane. The mecha-
nism in a trial for recidivity is of an astonishing simplicity: it suffices
to demonstrate that the criminal has not observed the penances imposed initially and that he has made heretical statements after the first
sentence. The only possible conclusion is the penalty of death, which
could be commuted at the discretion of the tribunal into *carcere perpetuo*. Repentance on the part of the heretic is a fact of only relative
significance at this point: the penitent *relapsus* has the advantage of
being able to receive the last sacraments and of being hung or decapi-
tated before being burned at the stake, thus suffering a less atrocious
end. The punishment in any case was death because ever since the
Middle Ages the crime of heresy had been equated with *lèse majesté*. If
the latter offense was punishable by death, with far greater reason the
same punishment was deserved by the person who offended the majesty of God.[194]

Menocchio was sixty-seven years old, his hair and beard had
turned white, and he was dressed in a miller's garments. It emerged
from the questioning that he had not faithfully observed the obligations that had been imposed upon him by the first tribunal, in fact, he
could not even remember some of them. Faced by the specific evidence
in the accusations, he denied and equivocated, offered ingenuous
excuses and claimed loss of memory. He was fearful now. He only
permitted himself a few words and these came more in answer to
questions than from the desire to expound his ideas, on such themes as
the Trinity, the relationship between God and his creatures, the
salvation of non-Catholics, and the pure humanity of Christ. In the
eyes of the judges he was not only a recidivist, but a confessed one.

On 14 July the inquisitor wrote to Rome and the cardinals of the
Congregation replied asking for a copy of the trial and advised proceeding to torture to discover accomplices. Such grave heresies had to

---

[193] The quotes are at 122, 127. For Mellina's sentence, ibid., b. 58, file "Sententiarum
contra reos S. Officii liber II," fols. 86r–88v.

[194] See, for example, Locati, *Praxis iudiciaria*, 143–44; for a concise statement on *lèse
majesté*, see G. Miccoli, "La storia religiosa," 677–78.

be extirpated with rigor. But this recommendation had no effect on the course of the trial because it did not arrive until 15 September. By then it was all over.[195]

With the two interrogations of the accused the case was basically concluded and concluded tragically. Only the two final steps remained: to hear the defense and proceed to the sentencing. This time, unlike the first trial, Menocchio, asked for a lawyer: "I do not want to make any other defense except to ask for mercy. Yet, if I could have a lawyer, I would accept one, but I am a poor man." One was selected for him by the court, as was the custom at the time. Dr. Agostino Pisenti was the fiscal procurator of the episcopal curia and he swore, as prescribed by the norms, to defend the man, not the heresies. The document which he presented on 22 July was thoroughly prepared, full of precise citations of the sources from both canon and civil law, and aimed to demolish the soundness of the evidence and to stress the ignorance and simple mindedness of the accused, who thus should be treated with the mercy willed by God. It was a serious effort, but a useless one as far as the proceedings went. On 30 July both Menocchio and his lawyer renounced further defense.[196]

As if the evidence before the court already was not more than sufficient, a third denunciation reached it on 3 August, presented this time by a priest who had recently overheard a Jew named Simon expatiating in a tavern on the subject of the day, the imprisoned heretic, and relating his conversations with him from a year before. The miller had said that the Gospels were written by monks and priests, that the Madonna was not a virgin, and he had alluded to "a most beautiful book," perhaps the Koran. By now denunciations to the Holy Office were becoming habitual, a sort of conditioned reflex.

On 2 August, the tribunal, fully assembled, with the bishop, the inquisitor, the governor, two ecclesiastical and two lay consultors in attendance, decreed that the accused was a relapsed and convicted heretic and ordered that he be submitted to torture so as to extract the

---

[195] The letter is published in appendix, 164–65. The date of arrival is recorded by the inquisitor with a brief summary of the contents on the cover sheet that contains the address.

[196] The quote is at 138. The defense is at 139–51. For Pisenti's appointment, see AAUd, *S. Officio,* b. 14, fasc. 302, dated 21 September 1596. For Pisenti's other defenses, see in fasc. 303, under the dates of 5 April, 21 and 23 September 1596; b. 14, fasc. 285, fols. 17r–v, defense of Giovanni Mellina, July 1599.

names of his companions and accomplices. The norms of the law were being applied without recourse to orders or advice from superiors. Torture, in the form of the strappado, took place in the governor's palace, after the aged defendant had in vain attempted to convince the bishop that he had not learned his heresies from anyone, that he had gotten them out of his own head and from books, and that he had indeed spoken about them with many people, but he could no longer remember with whom specifically. After he was examined to see if he was fit enough to support the ordeal, his wrists were tied behind his back, and he was raised from the floor twice, all the while crying out and invoking Christ, but he named no one. Only after he had been raised one last time did he volunteer the name of an accomplice, or, more accurately, an interlocutor, the count Giovanni Francesco of Montereale, to whom he had said "we did not know what was the true faith." Menocchio also added that the *Decameron* had been loaned to him by Leonardo da Minussa. The interrogation under torture lasted half an hour, the prescribed canonical limit. The next day the accused ratified his testimony, as required by the law for its validation, adding, with a forlorn effort at openness, that the count had reproached him for his words, and also that he had spoken one night with a Jew, with that Simon, in fact, who was already known to the tribunal through that last denunciation.

There are no studies specifically dedicated to the use of torture in the trials of the Roman Inquisition in Italy and it is difficult to have even an approximate idea of its frequency. It is commonly supposed to be inferior to the figures for the Spanish Inquisition, where it was practiced in about ten percent of the cases.[197]

The sentence against Menocchio, emitted jointly by both judges, was announced publicly by the notary on Sunday 8 August 1599 in the principal church of Portogruaro, in the presence, as we can well imagine, of an enormous crowd. The text summarized in a few pages the heresies previously listed in the sentence drawn up fifteen years before, beginning this time with the more heinous ones against the Trinity, and then proceeding in an inverse order from the first one, with a shocked exclamation at the unheard of heresy where the presence of

---

[197] On the standard practice, see, for example, Simancas, *Praxis haereseos*, fols. 65v–73r; Locati, *Praxis iudiciaria*, 386–401. On the usage of the Spanish Inquisition, see B. Bennassar, *L'Inquisition espagnole* (Paris: Hachette, 1979), 108–16.

the Holy Spirit, rather than of Christ is spoken of in the Eucharist ("quod novum penitus ac inauditum est"). The commutation of the sentence, Menocchio's negligence in fulfilling his obligations are next recalled, and the new heresies, as documented in the second trial, are listed. The prisoner, judged to be relapsed, is expelled from the ecclesiastical forum and turned over to the secular arm, which is asked to carry out the sentence without reaching the point of spilling blood or risking death ("citra sanguinis effusionem et mortis periculum"). This is the sinister formula employed to indicate capital punishment.

On 8 August Domenico Scandella was consigned to the civil officials of Portogruaro. The case was now closed as far as the notaries of the Holy Office were concerned. No further record keeping was anticipated. The sentence was immediately executed by the Venetian governor Pietro Zane, in the place and in the manner prescribed by the usage of the most Serene Republic. We do not have direct information and do not know where the pyre was erected. A contemporary Venetian criminal law manual states: "The punishment of the heretic ... is fire, as prescribed in divine, canon, civil, and common law, so that the body while still living should be burned up and be reduced to ashes," while in Venice proper "heretics are sent to be drowned in the canal called *orfano*."[198] The execution certainly took place within a few days. In fact, on 16 August in a notarial act drawn up by the priest Curzio Cellina in Montereale, Stefano's name already appears as the son of the deceased Domenico Scandella.[199]

Menocchio's death did not aggravate his family's financial situa-

---

[198] There are no decisions on the matter by Venetian authorities: cf. ASVe, *Consiglio dei dieci, Comune,* reg. 49; *Secreto,* reg. 14; *Criminale,* reg. 18; *Roma,* reg. 3; *Capi del Consiglio dei dieci, Lettere,* filza 99; *Lettere secrete,* filza 11; *Senato, Deliberazioni (Secreta),* reg. 92; *Deliberazioni (Secreta) Roma ordinaria,* reg. 12; *Terra,* reg. 69; and the files of the rectors' letters cited at note 50. On capital punishment, see L. Priori, *Prattica criminale secondo il ritto delle leggi della Serenissima Repubblica di Venetia ...* , (Venice: Giovanni Pietro Pinelli, 1644; 1st ed. 1622), 130–33, the quote is at 131. It is the same text as the author's *Casi criminali* published in 1599. I owe these references to the kindness of Claudio Povolo. The execution definitely took place in Portogruaro: Donato Serotino, who spoke of it incidentally to the *commissario* of the Inquisition Fra Francesco Cumo at Portogruaro on 6 July 1601, did not recall the date, but stated that "a little before, as I have said, Scandella was executed here in Porto by the Holy Office": AAUd, *S. Officio,* b. 19, fasc, 497; Ginzburg (128) misinterpreted Porto for Pordenone. To say Porto for Portogruaro is still current usage today.

[199] ASPn, *Notarile,* b. 488, n.c. 3786, fols. 20v–21r (notary: Curzio Cellina).

tion. The dowry of his daughter Giovanna, who married the following January, was on the low side, but by no means paltry, coming to a value of 256 *lire*, 9 *soldi*, a little more than forty-one ducats. For purposes of comparison, in April 1599, Maria, the daughter of Biasio Caligo, and perhaps a friend of Giovanna, had also married with a dowry valued at three hundred *lire*, about forty-eight ducats.[200] Life went on.

On 5 September 1599 the inquisitor communicated the outcome of the trial to the Congregation, and on 16 October Cardinal Santoro replied to the letter "in which we learned about the conclusion of the case of Domenico Scandella of the diocese of Concordia, relapsed heretic, and thus consigned to the secular authorities." The terminology itself indicates the end of the trial. There is not a word about the execution that has just transpired. The cardinal also asked Fra Girolamo to attend in person to certain dispositions decreed by the pope concerning another prisoner of the same diocese, accused of formal heresy and heretical blasphemy. The case was considered extremely grave and treated in letters of 30 October and 13 November 1599, and in five others the following year. The subject was a peasant of Arzenutto, in the zone of Valvasone, a certain Antonio Scodellaro, accused of having denied the virginity of the Madonna, the divinity of Christ, and the providence of God. He too was subjected to torture, but to certify his conscious fall into error. In the end he was condemned as one "vehemently" suspected of heresy on 14 February 1601; he abjured and received as punishment a series of spiritual penances.[201] Another trial had concluded, one of some four hundred prosecuted by Fra Girolamo Asteo during his term in office. The work of the Inquisition continued unabated.

---

[200] Giovanna's dowry is published in Ginzburg, 135–36; for Maria's see ASPn, *Notarile*, b. 488, n.c. 3786, fols. 11r–12r.

[201] The pertinent portion of the letter of 16 October is printed in the appendix, 165. My conclusion differs from Ginzburg's (127–28) who erroneously attributed the letters of the Supreme Congregation of the Inquisition, dated 30 October and 13 November 1599, to the case of Menocchio: they pertain instead to the case of Scodellaro. See his trial in AAUd, *S. Officio*, b. 17, fasc. 361, and his sentence in b. 58, filza "Sententiarum . . . liber II," fols. 90r–94v.

Philological Note

The anonymous denunciation and the two trials of Domenico Scandella are housed in the Archivio Arcivescovile, Udine, S. Officio in b. 8, fasc. 135; b. 7, fasc. 126 and b. 14, fasc. 285, respectively. The sentence and abjuration of the first trial and the proceedings for the commutation of the punishment are in b. 58.

In describing the manuscripts I have simplified and adapted common standards for the type of documents being dealt with here. I have alluded only briefly to questions that concern the provenance of the materials.

The English translation omits the textual apparatus of the Italian edition, the numbering of the original folios, and the more technical components of the original philological note.

1. *Description of the Documents.*

Anonymous denunciation in fascicle 135. It consists of two unnumbered leaves of a folio inserted after fol. 4 in the fascicle of the trial, the whole of which includes the title page and 9 additional leaves. It is written by hand *a* (operating perhaps at Fanna, Polcenigo or Maniago). Paleographically, the denunciation is original.

Fascicle 126. The fascicle consists of folios I+50, with a few unnumbered and blank leaves. The writings are in the hands of Valerio Canipa, notary in the episcopal Curia; Giovanni Ghibillino, chief Curial notary; hand *b* (from Portogruaro); Domenico Scandella; Terenzio Placentino, coadjutor in the Curia; the priest Odorico Vorai; hand *c* (from Montereale). Fra Felice da Montefalco adds his marginal notes to many of the pages.

The cover sheet has the date and the title of the fascicle in the hand of G. Ghibillino: "1583, the day 28 October. Trial instituted against Domenico Scandella." In the upper left-hand corner there is a "6," pencilled in the hand of Fra Evangelista Pelleo at the time of the compilation of the first inventory of the archive of the Inquisition of

Aquileia and Concordia, dated 16 June 1584. Fasc. 126, along with several other fascicles, were stored in Concordia in a cabinet in the sacristy of the cathedral and then at the end of the sixteenth century were moved to the convent of San Francesco in Portogruaro, the inquisitor's residence.[1] Immediately below to the left of the "6" there is a "D" written in ink, which is part of a series of capital letters of unknown purpose generally present in the fascicles pertaining to the diocese of Concordia from nn. 16 to 361. Directly over the "6" the number 126 is written in the hand of Fra Antonio Dall'Occhio, who was inquisitor from 1677 to 1692. It was he who reorganized the archive between 1677 and 1679 after the records preserved in Pordenone were transported to Udine.[2]

Paleographically, the trial documents are not all original. The depositions of the first thirteen witnesses, except the one of 9 December, are copies: in fact, the change in the hand between fols. 2v and 3r occurs at the bottom of a page in the middle of a question; that the deposition of 30 October has been erroneously dated the 20th is evinced by the fact that this witness is asked the question on good works in the form used exclusively for the last witness on 29 October and is interrogated about Lent, a subject also only touched upon by the last witness on the latter date. On two occasions a witness is called Bernardo and once is referred to as deceased, while his real name was Bartolomeo and he was certainly alive because he was testifying at the trial. At the bottom of fol. 12 the place where Scandella had been, Concordia, is omitted. In another instance "heri" is written in the place of "hodie" for a summons executed that same day. The records for the sessions held on 7 and 16 February, 28 April and 12 May must have been written down during the actual proceedings, since various changes and corrections in the text are explainable only as alterations decided upon and carried out during the actual setting down of the testimony. Two questions are excised and in their place some sentences from the

---

[1] See notes 164 & 188 of the introduction.

[2] In 1653 the Bishop Benedetto Cappello complained to the pope that the archive of the Holy Office of Concordia had been taken away without his knowledge by the inquisitor. He asked that it be returned to Portogruaro, and furnished a summary inventory of it to the year 1645: see Archivio Segreto Vaticano, *S. Congregatio Concilii, Visite ad limina*, b. 251A, fols. 36r–37v. On Dall'Occhio, see AAUd, *S. Officio*, b. 86, reg. "Inventario dell'Archivio," fols. 1r–7v.

trial formulary are substituted. On one occasion the ritual opening remarks of a session are changed, while on another a question is asked in direct vernacular discourse, correcting an earlier version posed indirectly in Latin. Other modifications of this type introduce simple textual refinements. The records for the sessions of 22 February, 8 March and 7 May only contain corrections for errors of transcription and are probably copies. The proceedings for 17 and 19 May and for the final undated session, since they are all without date, are also not originals. For the first two this can be reconstructed from fols. 1r–v of the sentence.

Sentence and abjuration of 1584, trial for the commutation of the punishment. These documents are preserved in b. 58, fasc. "Sententiarum contra reos S. Officii liber II." They consist of fols. I + 35, numbered 1–37 in the hands of Fra Antonio Dall'Occhio, and written in the hands of Giovanni Ghibillino, hand *d* (from Concordia), and Terenzio Placentino.

Paleographically, the sentence and abjuration are preliminary versions, drafts of these documents set down by the notary, with corrections made orally by the inquisitor Fra Felice, as we can clearly deduce from the textual variants printed in the notes of the Italian edition of the present work.

Fascicle 285. The fascicle consists of folios I + 69, with fols. 1–52 recently numbered in pencil, including several blank leaves. The writings are in the hands of Leonardo Simon, Fra Girolamo Asteo, Fra Antonio Francesco Sinigardi d'Arezzo, chief notary of the Holy Office, and the priest Tiberio Asteo, notary of the Holy Office. The following signatures are autographs: the priest Ottavio di Montereale, the priest Curzio Cellina, Antonio Facineto, Matteo Sanudo, Pasqualin de Zanuto, Zuane de li Fabri de Pilon, and Andrea Patesio. Other documents are in the hands of the priest Giovanni Daniele Melchiori, Orazio Crasso, notary of the Holy Office, Gregorio Ferro, Fra Tommaso Rizzo, hand *e* (from Aviano), Fra Giulio Viano, Agostino Pisenti, Domenico Scandella, Ghibillino de Ghibillinis, Fra Zan Antonio Pisano, Fra Giovanni Battista Angelucci, and the priest Michele Carboni.

The title of the fascicle is written on the cover sheet: "1596. Trial against Domenico Scandella called Menocchio of Montereale." It is in the hand of Fra T. Rizzo and completed in the hand of Fra G. Asteo: "and Giovanni Mellina from Pedemonte of Aviano, officer of Polcenigo, both cases concluded in 1599." In a corner above it on the left Fra Antonio Dall'Occhio has placed the number 285, inserting between the two sections the words "7 March 1596." Under the fascicle number someone has written: "D. & J.," letters that resemble the "D" of fasc. 126.

It is difficult to establish paleographically if the various trial records are original or copies, because there are few variants and corrections. The depositions of 6 July 1599 written by Fra Tommaso Rizzo certainly were set down during the actual session. For the proceedings on 12 July, the first part of the records were written down during the session, but the second demonstrates obvious copying errors, for which the notary Orazio Crasso was responsible.

The present edition does not include fols. 13r–17v that contain the trial against Giovanni Mellina, who has no connection with Domenico Scandella. The proceedings against him are recorded in fasc. 285, probably for practical reasons, since he was denounced at the same time as Scandella by Michele del Turco on 28 May 1599, and both are interrogated between 5 and 21 July.

2. Earlier editions.

Many separate phrases and small portions of the text are published by Carlo Ginzburg in *The Cheese and the Worms*. He includes in extenso the first portions of the session for 12 May 1584, Scandella's autograph defense made on 17 May, his supplications of 18 January 1586 and 12 July 1599 (also autograph).[3] A small portion of the 17 May 1584 defense has been reprinted in facsimile by Raffaele Simone.[4]

---

[3] See Ginzburg, 54–56, 87–89, 93–94, 108–9.
[4] R. Simone, "Scrivere, leggere, capire," *Quaderni storici* 38 (1978): 692.

Denunciation Against Certain People of Fanna, Priest Andrea Ionima and Domenico Scandella

[June/July 1580–August/September 1583][1]

Iacomo del Re of Fanna, Dor de Re, Daniel del Re (brothers), *barba* Dor de Batistin, called Il Zotto: all these deny purgatory, and also say that the dead have no need for any prayers, to give alms to religious is to throw them away, and preaching is not needed. Zorzi Susit and Domenego "caligaro" (cobbler)[2] deny the most holy sacrament; when the body dies, the soul dies.

The witnesses are: the reverend Don Paulo Paulino[3] from Castel Iuliano in the Abruzzi, vice abbot of the abbey at Fanna, presently

---

[1] AAUd, *S. Officio,* b. 8, fasc. 135, unnumbered leaves, unbound leaf.

[2] The brothers Iacomo, Salvador and Daniele de Re, *alias* della Pupa, Salvador de Re de Batistin, Zorzi de Madalena called Zositto, Domenico "caligaro," Iacomo Colauzo, Piero "caligaro," son of the deceased Lorenzo were accused in two long anonymous denunciations lodged with the Holy Office at Venice between the end of 1579 and early 1580. On 16 June of the latter year the tribunal began its inquiry, and on 30 August ordered the arrest of Salvador de Re de Batistin, who was arraigned on 31 August. He was granted confinement in Venice upon personal security of 500 ducats and then released on 13 September after having the bond raised to 1000 ducats, with the obligation to present himself whenever summoned. Iacomo de Re was arraigned on 3 January 1581, but was eventually released after offering security of 200 ducats and accepting the obligation to respond when summoned: ASVe, *Santo Uffizio,* b. 46, fasc. "Da Re Salvatore, Dalla Puppa Giacomo, Dalla Puppa Isidoro, Dalla Puppa Daniele, De Madalena Giorgio. Fanna."

[3] The priest Paolo Paulino or Pauleni was vice abbot of Fanna from c. June 1578 to June 1580, definitely curate of Barcis from July 1580 to February 1584, when he moved to a chaplaincy at Fiume Veneto; in 1589 he was curate at Corbolone: Ibid, depositions of 21 July and 25 August, interrogation of 31 August 1580; AVPd, *Biblioteca capitolare, Visite,* b. 7, questioning of Paulino at Fiume, 28 September 1584; AAUd, *S. Officio,* b. 8, fasc. 135, interrogation of same by the inquisitor Fra Giovanni Battista Angelucci, 28 January 1589 apropos the accused persons of Fanna.

priest in the village of Barcis; the reverend Fedrigo Cresendolo,[4] previously assistant priest in Fanna; the reverend messer Piero Tuluso[5]), vicar of Porcia, previously vice abbot of Fanna; count Fantuz,[6] count Francesco; count Elia; the counts of Polcenigo and Fanna; messer Rinaldo of Fanna, presently notary at Fanna; messer Iosef of the white house in Fanna; master Francesco de Ione, blacksmith of Fanna; messer Daniel of Montereal, steward of count Fantuzo, all witnesses to the aforesaid things.

Montereale: the priest Andrea.[7]

Menego Scandella denies that he did not observe Lent and also [having] a vernacular Bible, and in his discussions he is continually quoting from the Bible.

---

[4] Federico Crescendolo was priest at Sant' Odorico di Sacile; in 1579–1580 he was priest at Fanna for a year, and then vicar at Maniago from June–July 1580 to 1591, accumulating additional benefices: ASVe, *Santo Uffizio*, b. 46, fasc. "Da Re Salvatore . . . ," first denunciation, deposition of 21 July 1580; Degani, *La diocesi di Concordia*, 449–50.

[5] The priest Piero Tuluso or Tulusio was vicar at Porcia until August–September 1583, when he was replaced by Giovanni Ricca: AVPd, *Biblioteca capitolare, Visite*, b. 7, interrogation of the priest Antonio Locatello on 30 September 1584.

[6] Count Fantussio (son of Giacomo Antonio) and his own son Antonio were received as witnesses by the inquisitor on 17 January 1589 at Polcenigo: AAUd, *S. Officio*, b. 8, fasc. 135.

[7] Priest Andrea Ionima: see xxi of the introduction.

First Trial Against Domenico Scandella

[Concordia] 28 September 1583[*]

The 28th day of September 1583

Since it came to the attention of the reverend and excellent Giovanni Battista Maro,[1] doctor in canon and civil law, canon of Concordia and vicar general, that reports were being widely circulated, originating not from malevolent persons, but from upright, honest people zealous in the Catholic faith, almost as a matter of common knowledge, that a certain Domenico Scandella, known as Menocchio from Montereale in the diocese of Concordia spoke heretical and most impious words about Jesus Christ our Savior, and that he impiously believed them, preached them and held them as dogma, therefore he [the vicar general] determined to launch an inquiry into these matters, examine witnesses and institute a trial, as follows, etc.

A summons was issued to the following witnesses so that they could give testimony truthfully, and their summoning was confirmed by Francesco Tirindel, officer of the episcopal court of Concordia.

29 October 1583

Before the most excellent and reverend Giovanni Battista Maro, doctor in canon and civil law, canon of Concordia and vicar general for

---

[*] AAUd, *S. Officio*, b. 7, fasc. 126.

[1] Giovanni Battista Maro, originally from Camerino, probably came to the diocese of Concordia in the train of his relative, Giovanni Maria Maro, who in 1553 resigned from his own canonry in his favor: BSPn, *Capitolo, Atti capitolari*, 1526–1558, fol. 134v. Giovanni Battista was vicar general of Bishop Pietro Querini in 1570, acting vicar from July to October 1579 and vicar general from after September 1581 to August 1585; he died between 21 March and 16 April 1587: ASVe, *Santo Uffizio*, b. 29, fasc. "Marcolino Antonio"; b. 45, fasc. "Colussi don Ottaviano"; b. 46, fasc. "De Melchiori don Daniele"; AVPn, *Visite*, b. 1, reg. "1573. Visite Querini," 17 August–28 September 1581 (S. Bonaverio), 14–16 August 1583; AAUd, *S. Officio*, b. 7, fasc. 119; BSPn, *Capitolo, Atti capitolari*, 1580–1602, fol. 31r (S. Bonaverio); 1586–1589, fols. 10v–11v.

spiritual and temporal matters, as well as before the reverend brother Fra Andrea da Sant'Erasmo,[2] minor Franciscan, commissioner of the Holy Office of the Inquisition, seated in the hall of the palace of the most illustrious Francesco Maria Minio,[3] worthy *podestà* of the city of Portogruaro, with the participation of the aforesaid *podestà*, there appeared as witness Ser Francesco, son of the deceased Daniele Fasset of the village of Grizzo, in the parish of Montereale, duly sworn, cautioned and diligently examined as follows, specifically interrogated whether he knew a certain Domenego Scandella, known as Menocchio, of Montereale, he replied: "Yes sir, I know him because he is my relative."

Questioned on the reputation of the aforesaid Domenico, especially in matters of the faith, he replied: "He is always disputing with someone over the faith for the sake of argument, and also with the priest."

Questioned if he ever heard him say these formal words, specifically about his opinion that the air is God, he replied: "Yes sir, I heard him say 'What do you think God is? Everything that we see is God, and we are gods,' and similar words. I also believe that he mentioned the air, but I do not remember for sure."

Similarly asked if he had heard Domenico himself say that he considers it impossible that the Blessed Virgin could have given birth to Our Savior and remained a virgin, he replied: "I have heard the aforesaid Domenego say that he does not believe that the Blessed Virgin could have given birth through the Holy Spirit and remain a virgin, and he does not believe that the Holy Spirit governs the Holy Mother Church. And he says that priests want us under their thumbs just to keep us quiet, but have a good time for themselves and he has no faith in them and that he knows God better than they."

Questioned, he replied: "Already two months ago or more he said these words to me coming from Venice, and he also told me that he only believed in good works and he said this to me along the road as

---

[2] Fra Andrea da Sant'Erasmo, regent of the convent of San Francesco di Portogruaro, was substituting for the absent inquisitor: AAUd, *S. Officio,* b. 5, fasc. 85; b. 7, fasc. 119; b. 8, fasc. 136.

[3] It is impossibile to specify the dates of his service because the apposite register is missing from ASVe, *Segretario alle voci, Elezioni del Maggior Consiglio.* His presence is dated erroneously 1585 by E. A. Cicogna, *Documenti storici inediti pertinenti alla città di Portogruaro* ... (Portogruaro: Società di Storia, 1982), 116.

we were walking. And it was during this journey that he spoke about the air and the other words I mentioned above; there was no one else with us."

Asked if he had heard the aforesaid Domenico say that it would have shown little wisdom by Our Savior, since he is omnipotent, as it is preached, to have allowed himself to be killed, [he replied]: "Yes sir, he did say that if he had been God he would not have allowed himself to be crucified, and he did not believe that Our Savior Jesus Christ was crucified. And he spoke these words to me alone in the precincts of Montereale, I do not remember when, but in the more than twenty years that I have known him, he said them more than once."

Questioned if he had heard Domenico say that to blaspheme God and the saints is not a sin, he replied: "I have heard him say that it is not a sin to curse the saints, but not God too."

Asked if he had heard Domenico say that without so much preaching and doing, it is enough for salvation not to harm one's neighbor, he replied: "I have heard Domenego say, 'I do not want anything else except to do good.'"

To another question, he answered: "Yes sir he knows how to read and write, but I do not know if he has other books besides the Bible. I do not know about any other books pertaining to Holy Scripture."

Asked whether all the things to which he testified above he [Menocchio] had said seriously or jestingly or repeating what he had heard from others, he replied: "He said them himself and as the truth."

Questioned whether he had testified out of hate and whether he had omitted anything, he said: "I have said these things out of zeal to do good and in my conscience," adding: "Domenego once told me that if he should ever fall into the hands of the law over this, he would like good treatment, but if he should be dealt with harshly he would like to speak out loudly against our superiors for their bad deeds."

About generalities, he said: "I am a relative, as I told you earlier, but I have spoken the truth." And he took the oath to maintain silence.

There appeared as a witness Daniele Fasseta of Grizzo, in the parish of Montereale, in the diocese of Concordia, and having been sworn, cautioned and diligently examined as follows, he testified under oath, and when questioned if he knew Scandella called Menocchio, he replied: "Yes sir, I knew him from when we were little, because we are both from the same parish."

Asked about what reputation he [Menocchio] had concerning our faith, he replied: "It has been said that he has a wrong opinion about things pertaining to our Catholic faith."

Questioned whether he had heard Domenico himself say that he believed that the air was God, he replied: "Yes sir I have heard him say that the air is God and the earth is our mother. And he told me this in Montereale, walking along the road and there were others present, but I do not remember their names precisely."

Asked if he had heard the aforesaid Domenico say he considered it impossible that the Blessed Virgin could have given birth to Our Savior Jesus Christ, remaining a virgin, he replied: "Returning from Davian[4] with him and another person from Montereale called Menego de Marchiò, Menocchio said that he believed Jesus Christ was born from the Virgin Mary. It is not possible that she gave birth to him and remained a virgin; it may very well be this, that it was some respectable man or the son of some respectable man. And he told me this more than three years ago."

Asked if he had heard the aforesaid Domenico say that it would have shown little wisdom by Our Savior, since he is omnipotent as it is preached, to have allowed himself to be killed on the cross, he replied: "I have heard tell by others that Menocchio said that if Jesus Christ had really been omnipotent, he would not have let himself be crucified, and this was reported to me by Domenego de Marchiori, walking on the road to Montereale."

Questioned whether he had heard Domenico Menocchio say that cursing was not a sin, he replied: "No sir."

Asked if he had heard Domenico say that without so much preaching and doing, it is enough for salvation not to harm one's neighbor, he replied, "No sir."

Questioned if he knew that the aforesaid Domenico possessed prohibited books, he replied: "I know how to read and write and I know that he has a Bible, but I do not know if it is in the vernacular or Latin."

Questioned if the above things to which he had testified had been said [by Menocchio] seriously and not in jest, or repeating them as the sayings of others, he replied: "I believe that he said them seriously from the heart."

On generalities he replied properly on all matters, saying also:

---

[4] Aviano.

"The aforesaid Domenego said that if he did not fear for his life, he would say so many things that would astonish, and I think he meant about the faith."

There appeared Bernardo, son of the deceased Domenico del Ceta of Grizzo, in the parish of Montereale, in the diocese of Concordia, summoned, sworn, cautioned and diligently examined as below, when specifically questioned if he knew a Domenego Scandella called Menocchio of Montereale, he replied: "Yes sir, I have known him for five or six years and spoke with him a few times."

Asked if he knows what reputation this Domenego Scandella has concerning the things of the faith, he replied: "I have heard said by others that he has the name of a bad man in matters of the faith."

Asked if he has heard Domenico say that he considers the air to be God, he replied: "I have not heard it said by him but by others who claim that he said it, and especially by Daniele Fasseto."

Asked if he has heard Domenico say that he considers it impossible that the Blessed Virgin could have given birth to Our Savior Jesus Christ, remaining virgin, he replied: "No sir."

Also asked if he had heard Domenico say that it would have shown little wisdom by Our Savior Jesus Christ to let himself be killed on the cross, he replied: "No sir."

Asked if he had heard Domenico say that our good deeds have no merit before God, he said he did not know.

Asked if he knows that he [Menocchio] possesses prohibited books, he replied: "I have heard it said by others and especially by Blas de Caligo of Montereale that he has prohibited books."

And to further questions, he added: "I have heard it said publicly that he never observes Lent or fasting," and about other things he did not know.

About generalities he replied properly and he took the oath to maintain silence.

The 30th of October 1583, Concordia

Before the most reverend and excellent Giovanni Battista Maro, aforesaid vicar, seated under the arcade of his habitation, present the reverend Ottavio Collucci,[5] canon of Concordia, and the reverend

[5] Ottavio Collucci was definitely the chief notary of the episcopal Curia of Concordia between 1567 and 1569 and presumably became a canon in 1581: B. Pighin, *La diocesi di Concordia nella dinamica della riforma tridentina* (San Vito al Tagliamento: Ellerani, 1975), 2. He

priest Gaspare, chaplain of the benefice called Frattuccia, in the diocese of Concordia, appointed to this duty that morning, there appeared Ser Giovanni Povoledo of Montereale, diocese of Concordia, son of the deceased Leonardo Povoledo, as witness. Cited, sworn, cautioned, examined and interrogated, he gave his oath and testified as below, and asked specifically if he knows Domenico Scandella, called Menocchio of Montereale, he replied: "I have known him for thirty or forty years, because we are from the same place and are neighbors and I often speak with him."

Asked about the reputation of the above mentioned Domenico and especially about matters that pertain to the faith, he replied: "As for the things that pertain to our faith, he has a poor reputation, namely that he holds evil opinions following the sect of Luther and frequently I have heard him speak and dispute about matters of the faith."

Asked if he had ever heard Domenico stating and affirming that he believed the air is God, he replied: "I have heard him say that the sky, earth, sea, air, abyss and hell, all is God. And I heard him say this many times, in the presence of many, whom I do not remember."

Asked if he had ever heard Domenico say and affirm that he thought it impossible that the Blessed Virgin could have given birth to Our Savior Jesus Christ without sinning, nor remain a virgin after the birth, he replied: "I have heard him say that the Blessed Virgin could not have given birth to Our Lord Jesus Christ without sinning, nor remain virgin after the birth and I do not remember who was present. It is true that it may be about two or three months since I have heard such words uttered by Domenego Scandella."

Asked if he had ever heard Domenico Scandella say and affirm that it would have shown little wisdom by Our Savior Jesus Christ, being omnipotent as it is preached, to let himself be killed on the cross, he replied: "I have heard Domenego say that if Jesus Christ Our Savior had been omnipotent and the savior of the whole world, he would not have allowed himself to be killed on the cross. I have heard him say this in our village of Montereale, but I do not remember who

---

engaged in controversy with the vicar general Scipione Bonaverio over a canonry in 1577, a fact which may explain Collucci's denunciation of Bonaverio to the Venetian Holy Office on 19 May 1579: BSPn, *Capitolo, Atti capitolari*, 1580–1602, fol. 18v; ASVe, *Santo Uffizio*, b. 45, fasc. "Colussi don Ottaviano"; AAUd, *S. Officio*, b. 5, fasc. 81.

was present, but that he should have saved himself if he was omnipotent."

Asked if he had heard Domenico ever say and affirm that to blaspheme is not a sin, he replied: "Yes sir, I have heard it said by Domenico many times and it is of public and notorious knowledge in the town."

Similarly asked if he knew that the aforesaid Domenico Scandella ate meat and other prohibited foods during Lent, he replied: "Yes sir, I do know that he does not observe Lent and eats cheese and eggs, but not meat, that I know of."

Questioned, he answered: "I know because he told me and said that he had a weak constitution and could not do without them."

Similarly asked if he had heard the above mentioned Domenico say that our good works are of no merit with God, he replied: "I have heard said by Domenico himself that when we are dead, we are no longer anything, but are like worms and like the beasts. And in the twenty-five or thirty years that I have known him, I have always heard him say this."

Asked if he knows whether Domenego had prohibited books in his house, he replied: "I do not know if he has anything besides a vernacular Bible and I know this because I have seen him read it at home."

Similarly asked whether, taking all the aforesaid things into consideration, he knew if the things to which he has testified were said by Domenico Scandella in jest, or repeated as said by others, or spoken as true and truly believed by him, he replied: "I believe that Domenico was speaking seriously and from the heart."

Similarly asked if he was testifying out of hate and rancor, or if he had omitted saying anything out of love or to do a favor, he replied: "I have heard him say that in the beginning this world was nothing and that the water of the sea was whipped into a foam and coagulated like a cheese, from which then were born a great number of worms and these worms became angels, of which the most powerful and wise was God, to whom the others rendered obedience. And there was an evil one with his legions, Satan, who tried to fight against this God but he was beaten, and this God, like a great captain, sent his son as an emissary to men in this world, who let himself be hung up like a beast. And I heard this narrated by Pelegrin de Zanin eight days ago, as we were walking along the road on our way to the market in Pordenone. He said that Ser Domenego de Marchiori had heard this from Domenico Scandella, namely that Domenico Scandella thus spoke and believed."

About generalities, he said: "I am neither his relative nor his enemy, nor do I bear him ill will, but I have told the truth because of the sacrament I received." And then the oath not to reveal the things to which he had testified was imposed on him.

The 9th of December 1583

Done in the convent of San Francesco, in a room of the residence of the inquisitor,[6] in whose presence appeared as witness Giovanni Antonio Melchiori of Montereale in response to a summons he had received from an emissary of this Holy Office some days earlier. After taking an oath and having been cautioned to speak the truth, to a question he answered: "In Montereale, although several people are talked about, there is a certain Domenego Scandella, called Menocchio. It is said that he has books in the vernacular and, as far as we can conjecture, against the faith."

Questioned, he replied: "About three months ago, approximately, speaking with a brother of mine named Domenego Melchior, Domenego Scandella told him: 'It is not true that Christ was crucified, as many say, but he was a certain man who was then hanged.' And he told me that he had spoken those words in the presence of Bartolomeo, son of the deceased Andrea."[7]

Questioned, he replied: "He said these words to me only once when we were cutting wood."

Questioned about the reputation of the aforesaid Domenico Menocchio, he replied: "Everybody says that this man talks loosely about matters that pertain to the faith, that he says things which are not right; but he's not out of his head nor crazy, as you ask."

---

[6] Fra Felice da Montefalco, regent and lector of the convent of San Francesco in Udine, inquisitor in the dioceses of Aquileia and Concordia from 10 December 1579 to 14 June 1584. In 1593 he was appointed Visitor to the Franciscan province: AAUd, *S. Officio*, b. 73. reg. "Liber denunciarum . . ."; b. 71, reg. "Liber actuum . . ."; L. Wadding, *Annales minorum* . . ., t. 23, Ad Claras Aquas, 1934, 107.

[7] This personage, who is interrogated under different names on 2 February 1584 and on another occasion is indicated as being present at this conversation of Menocchio, is called Bartolomeo di Andrea, since a person of Montereale with such a name is recorded in the apostolic visitation of 1584 and we have no information about a Bernardo: see above, cxiv.

Questioned, he replied: "It was about twenty-five years ago in the house of messer Francesco Lazaro of Venice in the square of Montereale, and the priest, who is now at the parish of Valvasone,[8] was outside with the aforesaid Menocchio, and I recognized their voices because they were talking loudly about matters of the faith, and I heard the priest say to Menocchio: 'Don't you recite the Credo?' And Menocchio answered yes, to which the priest added: 'Don't you say: credo in unum Deum, patrem omnipotentem...?' and coming to that article: 'et in Iesum Christum,' Menocchio interrupted: 'I do not believe in it,' or these other words: 'That's not for me.' And it is not so long ago that I recalled these words to the priest."

Questioned, he replied: "One day when I was at Polcenigo the priest[9] told me that while he was making wafers this Menocchio came up to him and seeing the wafers exclaimed: 'By the Virgin Mary, these are big beasts.'"

Questioned, he replied: "He told me this apropos the fact that, when I told him he had been summoned to Concordia by the Holy Office, he answered that yes, it must be about Menocchio: 'And I want to tell you a good one that he told me here.' And he reported the above words, while he and I were in his house."

And in response to other questions, he said that he did not know. And then he was sworn to silence. About generalities he answered properly, etc.

Summoning of the witnesses
Montereale, 2 February 1584

Fra Felice da Montefalco, inquisitor general especially appointed by the Holy Apostolic See for the entire patriarchate of Aquileia and the diocese of Concordia, to all individuals to whom this present summons shall have been presented, in virtue of holy obedience under penalty of a sentence of excommunication and a fine of ten ducats to be applied by each one of you to the Arsenal of the most illustrious

---

[8] Priest Leonardo of Grizzo was presented by the Counts of Valvasone to the Chapter of Concordia on 2 December 1561, which appointed him parish priest: AVPn, *Visite*, b. 2, reg. "Sacrarum visitationum Nores ...," fol. 40v. In 1555–56 he had taught school in Portogruaro, disseminating, among other matters, a religious idea that "postulated a natural intuition of divinity, independently of revelation": cf. Seidel Menchi, *Erasmo in Italia*, 138, 395.

[9] Priest Giovanni Daniele Melchiori.

and renowned Venetian government, in the event that any of you do not heed our order, we request, summon and caution you to appear personally before us and our office in the church of Santa Maria in Montereale to testify and answer in regard to that about which you will be questioned, otherwise, etc. In token of which, etc.

Montereale, 2 February 1584.

(Seal) To be returned to the person who submits it so that it can be presented to the others.

Valerio Canipa, notary, commissioned.

2 February 1584

Done in the sacristy of the church of Santa Maria of Montereale, where the reverend father inquisitor has gone with the intention of examining witnesses to better learn the truth of what has happened, with the consent of the reverend and most excellent Giovanni Battista Maro, vicar of Concordia, etc.

Before him, etc. appeared as witness Ser Giulio, son of the deceased Stefanut, summoned, sworn, cautioned to speak the truth, he testified under oath as follows: "I do not know for certain why I was summoned, but I believe that it is on account of Domenego Menocchio, because I was summoned to Concordia on another occasion by our curate, but due to my poverty I could not go, and also I believe because of certain discussions that have taken place in recent days over the many things that this Domenego Menochio used to say."

Asked whether there is anyone in this village who does not live as a Catholic and is suspect in matters of the faith, he replied: "I only know two, one is Domenego Scandella and the other Melchiore of Grizzo."

Asked about Domenico Scandella, he said: "I have doubts about him because he utters many things against the faith of Christ, and among other things says that to blaspheme is not a sin. And I have had a falling out with him over this, particularly in the tavern in the house of Piccin, the innkeeper of Montereale, and I told him that if the monsignor who has left now had still been here, I would have gone to accuse him and this took place just a short time after the most reverend monsignor left."[10]

---

[10] The reference is to the bishop or to the vicar general, but there is no information about a visit to Montereale in the register which covers the years 1573 to 1583: AVPn, *Visite*, b. 1, reg. "1573. Visite Querini."

Questioned, he replied: "Many were there whom I do not remember, except for Nico of Grizzo and the innkeeper Piccin."

Questioned, he replied: "Several times he told me, talking about blaspheming, that everybody has his calling, some to plow, some to harrow, and I do mine, which is to blaspheme."

Questioned, he replied: "I remember another time, when he was standing on the street near the door of his house, that he said to me that he did not believe Christ was born from the Holy Spirit, but that he was the son of St. Joseph or was a bastard."

Questioned, he replied: "It may have been three years ago that he told me this and there were others besides the two of us, and he is always looking for the chance to talk about these things."

Questioned, he replied: "He tells everyone that it is possible to blaspheme without sinning. 'What do you imagine God to be? God is nothing else than a bit of air and whatever man imagines him to be.' And even when the body dies all that remains is that little bit of earth. He usually says these things when we are discussing going to the graveyard, or when we are returning from the Mass: 'Why are you giving these alms for those few ashes?'"

Questioned, he replied: "I told him many times, especially on our way to Grizzo that I love him, but that I cannot stand the way he talks about the things of the faith and that I would always fight him over this and even if he should kill me a hundred times and I returned to life, I would always let myself be killed for the faith."

Questioned, he replied: "This Domenego has a reputation for being a heretic in the town, and one of his relatives, named Fasseta,[11] told me that he said he could not see the face of God."

Questioned, he replied: "He is accustomed to introduce with everyone the subject of God and always interjects some sort of heresy and then he argues and shouts in support of his opinion."

Questioned, he replied: "I was not present, but I heard it from the priest who spoke with him and reproached him many times about these things."

Questioned, he replied: "From what I have heard him say many times, he does not believe in the pope nor in these rules of the Church."

Questioned, he replied: "I am certain that he does not observe

---

[11] Francesco Fasseta.

Lent because I have seen him eat meat, cheese, milk, eggs and other forbidden foods. And I reproached him that he should not eat these things so openly, at least eat them secretly so as not to set a bad example for others."

Questioned about Melchiore, he replied: "Going along one day together from Montereale to Grizzo, accompanying him home and speaking about Christ, and wishing for his help, he exclaimed, 'Oh Christ, if only you had escaped!' And he still discusses matters of the faith, and I have reproached him many times, but now I do not remember the words."

Questioned, he replied: "His father told me that he is a person who does not pay attention to Lent and eats eggs even in holy week."

Asked who might be able to provide information, he replied: "The priest here of Montereale, and Francesco and Antonio Fasseta, brothers."

And to other questions, he replied that he did not know. About generalities, he said: "I am a blood brother to both and I love them, but I do not like their way of acting." And he was administered the oath of secrecy.

There appeared as witness Bartolomeo, son of the deceased Andrea, summoned, sworn, cautioned to speak the truth and interrogated, he said under oath: "I do not know why I have been summoned, if you do not tell me."

Questioned, he replied: "I only know about a certain Merchiori de Sgiarbasso of Grizzo and about Domenico Scandella of Montereale who maligned and spoke badly about the things of the Church."

Questioned about Melchiore, he replied: "I have heard it said many times in the taverns that he does not believe in God and blasphemes very strongly."

Asked who could provide more information about this Merchiò, he replied: "Daniel Turchetto, who associates with him and Antonio the innkeeper at Grizzo."

Questioned about the reputation of Domenico Scandella, he replied: "Except for the opinions that he has, he is a respectable person and says: 'Do you want me to teach you not to do evil? Do not take the property of others and this is the good that one can do.'"

Questioned, he replied: "He talks cleverly about the things of the faith with this person and that because of a certain book he has, but I do not know what it is."

Questioned, he replied: "It could be he said that Christ was not born from the Virgin Mary, but I do not remember."

Then words were read back to him from the session in which Giovanni Antonio Melchiori had testified, and he stated: "I do not remember these precise words, but I indeed heard him say that Christ was a man like us."

To many other questions, he replied: "I do not know anything because I have few dealings with him and also when I heard him say crazy things, I reproached him and left because I did not want to hear them."

About generalities he said: "His wife is my cousin." And after having been sworn to silence, he was dismissed.

There appeared as witness Domenico Melchiori of Montereale, summoned, sworn, cautioned to speak the truth, interrogated under oath, he said: "I do not know why I have been summoned."

Questioned, he replied: "I do not know anyone in this village who is suspected of heresy and does not live like a Catholic, except Domenego Menocchio."

Questioned, he replied: "I have heard with my own ears from this Menocchio: 'What! Do you really believe that God was born from the Holy Spirit and that St. Joseph is as old as in the paintings? Christ was born from St. Joseph, not from the Holy Spirit.'"

Asked about the place and time and whether there were witnesses, he replied: "Once it was on the road, coming from Grizzo he and I alone, many years ago and I do not remember precisely."

Questioned on what occasions he began these discussions, he replied: "He usually talks about these things when he is in company and on a journey, and he introduces these subjects himself."

Questioned, he replied: "I have spoken about him with many persons, but I do not remember who they are, and it is possible that Domenego Menocchio still holds to these words of his."

Questioned about his reputation, he replied: "Everybody talks about it and it is public voice and fame that he is a heretic, and if you will question any one you will discover that it is the truth."

Questioned, he replied: "He likes to discuss with this one and that one, and when he wanted to argue with me, I told him: 'I am a cobbler and you a miller, and you have no education. What use is there talking about it?'"

Questioned, he replied: "I have heard this very Menocchio say, 'What do you think God is? It is this world, this air is God!'"

Asked about witnesses and the place, he replied that he did not remember. Questioned, he replied: "He believes in neither prelates nor the Church. 'What popes, what prelates, what priests!' He uttered these words disdainfully because he did not believe in them."

Questioned, he replied: "Once, when he and I and Bartolomeo, son of the deceased Andrea of Montereale, were on the road from Aviano, speaking about Christ, he said, since the world had become a bad place, God had to send either John the Baptist or Elias to preach, but instead he sent his Son, who let himself be hung up like a beast."

Questioned, he replied: "He holds and I have heard him say that he does not believe in God and that he is not God, but that he was born from St. Joseph and that he is merely a man like us. And when I used to hear him say these words, I told him: 'Good grief, Menocchio, for the love of God, do not let these words come out of you.'"

Questioned, he replied: "I myself heard him say and he says it in front of everyone that to blaspheme is not a sin and he blasphemes no end."

Questioned, he replied: "He says that when a man dies, he is like a beast, like a fly, and that when man dies the soul dies and every thing."

Questioned, he replied: "I have only seen him with a vernacular Bible, I do not know if he has other books."

Questioned, he replied: "I did not see him, but I have heard him say himself that he eats cheese during Lent."

Questioned, he replied: "This Domenego has said these words: 'If I could speak out without being afraid of men in this world, I would have a lot to say.'" Questioned, he replied that he did not know what this was.

Asked about Melchiori, he replied: "It is also said about him that he is suspect of heresy, but he is not like Domenego, but I cannot say anything in particular because he is from this other village."

About generalities, he answered properly, confirmed the testimony read back to him and took the oath of secrecy.

There appeared as witness Paolo Sgiarbassio of Grizzo; summoned, sworn, cautioned and diligently questioned, he replied: "I do not know why I have been summoned."

Questioned, he replied: "I have heard only that a certain Domenego Menocchio is being discussed and a son of mine called Merchiò."

Questioned about this son, he replied: "My son ate eggs during holy week, he tried to kill me and his mother and his sister and his brother."

Questioned, he replied: "This son of mine swears beyond measure."

Questioned, he replied: "In years past the priest had his hands full dragging him to confession and to communion."

Questioned, he replied: "He goes to Mass, but only God knows why."

Questioned about Domenico Scandella, he replied: "I never heard him say that Christ was not God, but once going to Aviano, he said these words, that if Christ had been God, when the Jews wanted to kill him, he should have killed them."

And about other questions, he replied that he did not know. On generalities he answered properly, confirmed what was read back to him and took the oath of secrecy.

There appeared as witness the reverend priest Andrea Hionima;[12] summoned, sworn, cautioned to speak the truth and questioned, he replied: "I do not know why I have been summoned."

Questioned, he replied: "He is one called Domenego Menocchio, who is suspect of heresy, and I do not know if there are others."

Questioned, he replied: "With my own ears I have heard him deny the authority of the pope and say that the pope has no more power than he, and that it will never be true that Christ gave him authority. And when I cited to him that saying from Scripture: 'Quodcumque negaveris, etc,'[13] he rejected it, saying that it was not true, and then I added: 'Be still, Domenego, do not say these things, because one day you may regret it.'"

Asked about the time, place and witnesses, he replied: "It may have been about a year ago, at the crossroad, in front of master Pecin, but I do not remember who they were."

Asked about rumors and his reputation, he replied: "He has become notorious, speaking thus with everyone, and all say he is a heretic."

Questioned, he replied: "He said: 'To go and confess to priests and monks, one might as well go to a tree. And what is this God? It is a fraud on the part of Scripture to deceive people and if there were a God he would let himself be seen.' And he spoke these words when we were talking about the sacrament of the altar and he said: 'I can

---

[12] Priest at Mareno di Piave until 1566, acting chaplain at the altar of saints Rocco, Sebastiano and Francesco: see p. xxi.

[13] "Quodcumque ligaveris super terram . . .": Mt 16: 19.

only see a piece of dough there, how can that be God? And what is this God, other than earth, water and air?' And he is always going around arguing carrying his vernacular Bible and he imagines that he bases himself on it and is obstinate in these views of his."

Questioned, he replied: "He pays no heed either to indulgences or to Lent, saying 'Who ordered this Lent?' He told me, in fact, that he had never observed Lent."

Questioned, he said: "He denies that the Holy Spirit governs the Church, in fact he says: 'What is this Holy Spirit?' And he insists specifically that this Holy Spirit is not there [in the Church]."

Questioned, he replied: "He said that if Christ really had power, he would not have been crucified."

Questioned, he replied: "Once when someone said that he would end up falling into the hands of the Holy Office, he answered, 'So what?' In fact, once when I reproached him, saying, 'Don't you remember that you have already been once in the hands of monsignor in Concordia and you promised him that you would say nothing more,' he retorted, 'When monsignor commits me, I shall never say anything again.'"

Questioned, he replied: "He told me: 'When man dies, he goes to the house of the Devil,' and he rejects purgatory."

On generalities, he answered properly, confirmed the testimony read back to him, and after taking the oath of silence, he was dismissed.

There appeared as witness Pelegrino, son of the deceased Francesco of Montereale, summoned, sworn, cautioned to speak the truth and questioned, he replied: "In the past it was public knowledge that a certain Domenico Scandella did not live as a Catholic, but after he went to Concordia, it seemed that he mended his ways."

Questioned about his opinions, he replied: "He believed that when man dies, he becomes nothing."

Questioned where these opinions of his came from, he replied: "I believe, to the best of my knowledge, that a certain Marchiò had a book and occasionally let Domenego have it and from it he got those fantastic ideas."

Questioned, he replied: "He used to say that God was the sun, the air and that which you see."

Asked about blasphemy, he replied: "He says that to blaspheme is not a sin."

Questioned, he replied: "Marchiò says such things, as if they come from a mad man and also because he gets drunk."

About generalities, he responded properly, confirmed what was read back to him and he took the oath of secrecy.

There appeared as witness Ser Francesco Fasseta of Grizzo, summoned, sworn, cautioned to speak the truth and questioned, he replied: "I have been questioned another time about Scandella at Concordia and I stand on what I said then."

About generalities, etc. and he was sworn to secrecy.

Antonio Fasseta appeared as witness, summoned, sworn, cautioned to speak the truth, questioned, he replied: "I know Marchiò de Sgiarbas of our village, who does not have a very good name in matters of the faith and he is a companion of this Scandella."

Questioned, he replied: "Once when we were on the holy ground before the church, he said: 'I wouldn't give a red cent either for priests or Masses.'"

Questioned, he replied: "Coming down the mountain once with Menocchio at a time when the empress[14] was passing through, he said about her: 'This empress is greater than the Virgin Mary.' And another time conversing about Christ, he said: 'It is not true that Christ was crucified; it was Simon the Cyrenian.'"

Questioned, he replied: "I did not hear it from him, but from others, that he said when the body dies, the soul dies."

Questioned, he replied: "He said many things, but so long ago that I do not remember."

About generalities, he said: "I am somewhat related to him." He confirmed the records read back to him and he took the oath to secrecy.

There appeared as witness the reverend Odorico, priest in the church of Santa Maria in Montereale, summoned by Tirindel, as he reported, sworn, cautioned to tell the truth, and questioned, he testified under oath: "In my parish I know that there is no one, except Domenego Menocchio, who has been denounced to this Holy Office,

---

[14] The empress Mary of Austria came to the Friuli in 1581: see Ginzburg, 138.

and I myself brought him once to Monsignor Mauro, vicar in Concordia, and I told him [Menocchio]:'These fancies of yours are heresies, and to get you straightened out, we are going to monsignor the vicar, who will explain that this is all heresy.' And so he promised me that, if monsignor the vicar could show him, he would never do it again, but he did not stick to it."

Questioned about Melchiore, he replied: "It seems that I heard from the aforesaid Marchiò that he had a book, with which he let it be understood that he could do wonderful things."

Questioned about Domenico Scandella, he replied: "In my opinion and from what I have heard, everyone considers him to have evil ideas about the faith."

Questioned, he replied: "It is true that he has argued with many people and especially with me, but I do not remember details."

Questioned, he replied: "He said many times, and I heard this from several people, that if he were not afraid of certain persons in this world, he would say things that would astonish."

Questioned, he replied: "I seem to have heard from many that he said how it is impossible that the Virgin Mary could have given birth to Christ and remained a virgin."

And on other matters, he said: "I do not remember in particular what he said because I have a bad memory and have been occupied with other things."

For the exoneration of his conscience he said: "To clear my conscience, so that there be no blemish on it, there is a house in Montereale belonging to the Notti. The old man is called Noto and his son, Bartolomio,[15] who, from what I gather, never observe Lent and even if they come to Mass, they do so for the sake of appearance."

Asked who could corroborate this fact, he replied: "Lunardo Fagnon, Zulian del Negro, Simon Corneto and Picin Feminussa."

He added that once Domenego said: "I would like to have no other privilege than to go before the pope, bishops and cardinals to unburden my soul, and if I have erred, even if they should kill me, I could not feel a more welcome thing."

About generalities, he spoke properly, confirmed what was read back to him, and took the oath of silence.

---

[15] On Noto and Bartolomeo Margnani, see lxxxiv.

Summoning of Domenico Scandella
Montereale, 2 February 1584

Fra Felice da Montefalco, especially appointed inquisitor by the Holy Apostolic See for the entire patriarchate of Aquileia and diocese of Concordia, to Domenico Scandella beloved of Christ, residing in the village of Montereale, at the request of the Holy Office of the Inquisition, with this summons that can be delivered by any sworn messenger, by virtue of holy obedience under pain of excommunication as well as under pain of having to pay a hundred ducats to the Arsenal of the illustrious Venetian government, as well as other penalties, we order and command that as soon as you are presented with this summons, you must appear personally before us at our seat in the church of Santa Maria in this village to obey and answer the questions that you will be asked, etc., etc.

Valerio Canipa, assistant notary.

2 February 1584

The emissary Ser Francesco Tirindel reported that today he went to the house of Domenico Scandella and ordered him, subject to the penalties noted in our summons, to appear personally before the Holy Office of the Inquisition in the church of Montereale to obey and reply to the questions he will be asked, as per the aforementioned summons.

The aforesaid Domenico appeared before the father inquisitor in the aforementioned church and there to his face the inquisitor informed him that he must appear within three days and present himself before the office of the most holy Inquisition, and not to leave the place without first obtaining written permission from the Holy Office under pain of passing a sentence of excommunication, and a fine of a hundred ducats to be applied to the Arsenal of the illustrious Venetian government, and other penalties and punishments at the discretion of the office of the most holy Inquisition.

The same day

The reverend father inquisitor ordered me, as notary, accompanied by a legally deputed assistant of the village of Montereale, to go to the house of Domenico Scandella and make a diligent search of it, and bring away to his reverend paternity any books that I found. And so I went there and making a careful search found some books that were neither suspected nor prohibited so that the reverend father inquisitor ordered that they be returned to him, as was in fact done.

3 February 1584

The reverend father inquisitor, having examined the trial proceedings, decreed that the aforesaid Domenico Scandella should be arrested. Consequently, he commanded Ser Francesco Tirindello, emissary of our court, who requested the assistance of members of the nobility of Maniago, who volunteered three men from that town, to make the arrest with our officer and conduct him to the city of Concordia.

The aforesaid messenger reported that he had arrested Domenico Scandella for the purpose of taking him, etc.

Saturday, 4 February 1584, in Concordia

Francesco Tirindel, officer of our episcopal court in Concordia, reported that tonight he had escorted in fetters to the prisons of this episcopal see the aforesaid Domenico Scandella, called Menocchio of Montereale, arraigned as above, in execution of the decree issued by the reverend father Fra Felice da Montefalco, inquisitor general for all the patriarchate of Aquileia and the whole bishopric and diocese of Concordia, especially delegated by the Holy Apostolic See, on the 3rd day of the present month of February. For greater safety in conducting the aforesaid accused to prison, he had as companions and assistants, by order of the reverend inquisitor himself, as far as the town of Vivaro, five men loaned by the counts and commune of Maniago, and from there to Concordia he had four men, replacing the first group, volunteered by the commune of Vivaro. And thus the accused was confined in the prison and placed under close surveillance by the aforesaid Francesco Tirindel, etc.

Tuesday, 7 February 1584, at Concordia

Held in the episcopal palace, in the inner room, where the most reverend and excellent Giovanni Battista Maro, doctor in canon and civil law, canon and vicar general, having seen of the most reverend father Fra Felice da Montefalco, inquisitor general for all the patriarchate of Aquileia and the diocese of Concordia, especially delegated by the Holy Apostolic See, his decree dated the 3rd of the present month of February, contained in the trial dossier and concerning the arrest of a certain Domenico Scandella, called Menocchio of Montereale, of the diocese of Concordia, and having also seen the report made by Francesco Tirindel, emissary of the episcopal court, in execution of the aforementioned decree, that he had performed the above mentioned arrest and had consigned Domenico Scandella to prison, in continuation of the trial, decided to interrogate the prisoner, in the presence of the reverend Ottavio Collucci, canon of Concordia and the reverend Flaminio Palmira, mansionary of Concordia, who took the oath of secrecy in the present case. Then he ordered Giovanni Battista Parvis, a jailer, to bring the aforesaid Domenico Scandella from his cell.

The guard then led out the prisoner, who was wearing a certain vestment, and over it a cloak and cap and other pieces of clothing all of white wool. He was asked to take an oath to tell the truth about himself and his companions, and then asked by the reverend vicar: "Who are you?" He replied: "I have the name of Domenego Scandella, called Menocchio."

And asked if he knew why he was standing there in the presence of monsignor the vicar, he replied: "The father inquisitor had me summoned in Montereale and asked me who I am, and I replied that I was Domenego Scandella. His lordship informed me that I had been denounced to the Holy Office. Then under penalty of a hundred ducats I had to show up at Maniago, where that father had me arrested and led handcuffed to Concordia."

Asked where he was born, he replied: "I am from Montereale, in the diocese of Concordia. My father was called Zuane and my mother Menega and I have lived in Montereale most of my life, except for two years when I was banished, of which I spent one in Arba and one in Cargna,[16] and I was banished for being in a brawl."

Questioned, he replied: "My trades are that of miller, carpenter, sawyer, builder of walls and other things."

Questioned, he replied: "Yes sir, I do know how to read, write and do figures."

Asked if he knows how to say the Credo, as every faithful Christian is obliged to do, which is called the symbol of the apostles, and that other Credo which the holy Roman Church still uses and is recited on Sunday at Mass and on certain holy days, he replied: "I know how to recite the Credo and also the one said in the Mass; I have heard it spoken and have helped to sing it in the church of Montereale."

Asked: "Since you know the Credo, what do you say about that article 'et in Iesum Christum, filium eius, unicum Dominum nostrum,

---

[16] Carnia.

qui conceptus est de Spiritu Sancto, natus ex Maria virgine?' What did you say and believe about it in the past, and what do you believe now?" And when asked, do you understand the words: 'qui conceptus est de Spiritu Santo, natus ex Maria virgine?' he replied: 'Yes sir, I understand.' And he added: Since I made confession many times with a priest of Barcis,[17] I told him: 'Can it be that Jesus Christ was conceived by the Holy Spirit and born from the Virgin Mary?' But I would add that I believed it, but that sometimes the Devil tempted me about this, and he replied yes, that I should believe it firmly, and this happened two or three years ago. This idea of mine was based on the fact that so many men are born in the world and none are born from a virgin woman, and since I had read that the glorious Virgin was married to St. Joseph, I believed that our Lord Jesus Christ was the son of St. Joseph, because I read in some stories that St. Joseph called our Lord Jesus Christ son. I read this in a book called *Il fioreto della Bibia*."[18]

Asked whether he had said these words in the form of preaching or exhortation in front of people, he replied: "It is true that I spoke these words to different people, but not to make them believe them. On the contrary, I exhorted many people, saying: 'Do you want me to teach you the true way? Do good and walk in the path of our predecessors and do as holy mother Church commands.' But those words above I spoke because I had been tempted and not because I believed them or wanted to teach them to others. It was the evil spirit who made me believe those things, and he also instigated me to say them to others."

Questioned, he replied: "I recall saying those words to a Francesco Fasseta, but I do not remember saying them to others, and I told him this coming from Venice to Montereale last March."

Asked to repeat what he had said about the Holy Spirit on several occasions, he replied: "I said that I believe he is in all men and that it is God."

Asked about what he believes and said concerning that article of the faith which states: 'passus sub Pontio Pilato, crucifixus, mortuus et

---

[17] Priest Paolo Pauleni or Paulini. See note 3 of the denunciation (1).

[18] For the numerous editions of the *Fioretto della Bibbia*, see A. J. Schutte, *Printed Italian Vernacular Religious Books 1465–1550: a Finding List* (Geneva: Droz, 1983), 94–96. See the quotation in the 1517 Venice edition by Giorgio Rusconi, fol. O5v; Ginzburg, 28–31, 150 and passim.

sepultus,' and if he ever said these or similar words: that it showed little wisdom on the part of Our Savior Jesus Christ, since he is omnipotent, as it is preached, to let himself be killed on the cross, he replied: "I said that if Jesus Christ was eternal God, he should not have let himself be caught and crucified. And I was not certain on this point, but had my doubts, as I said, because it seemed an important thing that a Lord should let himself be taken like this. And so I wondered whether, since he had been crucified, he was not God, but some prophet, some great man sent by God to preach in this world. I discussed this too with that Francesco Fasseta."

Asked what he had said about God and what he had believed and believes that God is, because he has been heard to say that God is only air, earth, etc, he replied: "I believe that the whole world, that is air, earth and all the beautiful things of this world are God, and that the sun is a creature of God, because we say that man is made in the image and likeness of God[19] and in man there is air, fire, earth and water and from this it follows that air, earth, fire and water are God."

Asked if he had ever said that in the beginning this world was nothing and that the water of the sea was beaten into a foam, which coagulated like a cheese, from which a great multitude of worms was born, and these worms became men, of which the most powerful was God, to whom the others rendered obedience; and that there was one evil one with his legions, Satan, who tried to oppose God and was conquered, and this God, similar to a great captain, sent his son as an ambassador to men in this world, who let himself be hung up like a beast, he replied: "I have said that, in my opinion, all was chaos, that is, earth, air, water, and fire were mixed together; and out of that bulk a mass formed—just as cheese is made out of milk—and worms appeared in it, and these were the angels. The most holy majesty decreed that these should be God and the angels, and among that number of angels, there was also God, he too having been created out of that mass at the same time, and he was made lord, with four captains, Lucifer, Michael, Gabriel, and Raphael. That Lucifer sought to make himself lord equal to the king, who was the majesty of God, and for this arrogance God ordered him driven out of heaven with all his host and his company; and this God later created Adam and Eve and people in great number to take the place of the angels who had been

---

[19] Gn 1: 26.

expelled. And as this multitude did not follow God's commandments, he sent his son, whom the Jews seized, and he was crucified." He added: "I never said that he allowed himself to be hung up like a beast. Indeed, I really said that he let himself be crucified, and he who was crucified was one of the children of God, because we are all God's children, and of the same nature as the one who was crucified and he was a man like the rest of us, but with more dignity just as the pope is a man like us, but of greater rank, because he has power, and he who was crucified was born of St. Joseph and Mary, the Virgin."

Questioned, he replied: "I said this to Francesco Fasseta and I said Mary, the Virgin, because she was called virgin having been in the temple of the virgins. There was a temple where twelve virgins were kept, and as they grew up they were married off. And I read this in a book called *Il lucidario della Madonna*,[20] which was loaned to me when I was in Arba."

Asked if he had ever said, speaking of the most holy sacrament of the Eucharist: "This is a piece of dough and not God, and I do not believe in a God you cannot see," he replied: "I have said that the wafer is a piece of dough, but that the Holy Spirit comes down from heaven in it, and this I really believe."

Asked what he thinks the Holy Spirit is, he replied: "I believe he is God."

Asked if he knows how many are the persons in the Holy Trinity, he replied: "Yes sir, I do, the Father, Son and Holy Spirit."

Questioned: "In which of these three persons do you think the Eucharist is converted?" he replied: "Into the Holy Spirit."

Asked again which person precisely of the holy Trinity is in that host, he replied: "I believe that it is the Holy Spirit."

Questioned, he replied: "I did not say that I do not believe in a God I cannot see."

Questioned: "When your parish priest preached on the most holy sacrament, what did he say was in that most holy host?" he replied: "He said that it was the body of Christ, nonetheless I thought it was the Holy Spirit, and that is because I believe that the Holy Spirit is greater than Christ, who was a man, and the Holy Spirit came from the hand of God."

---

[20] Fra Alberto da Castello, *Rosario della gloriosa Vergine Maria* . . . , Venezia, Domenico de Franceschi, 1575, fol. 42r; Ginzburg, 34.

Asked what he had said and believed concerning the confession that Christians make to their priests, he replied: "I have said that when someone goes to confess, he needs to confess to the majesty of God in his heart and beseech him to pardon his sins, and then he can go to the priest and tell him his sins, so that he can receive penance."

Questioned, he replied: "Yes sir, I have been to confession and took communion this past year from the priest of Maniago.[21] Four years have passed since I confessed myself to our priest, but I have received communion from him, and as I have said I confessed myself at Maniago Libero to priest Macor[22] for two years and two in Barcis with priest Paulo Pauleni."

Asked whether he has said that priests and monks do not have the authority to absolve those who go and confess themselves to them, and that the confession made to priests is of no use, he replied: "I did not say this, in fact I believe that they can absolve and have the authority to do it."

Asked what he believes about the souls of the Christian faithful, he replied: "I have said that our souls return to the majesty of God, with which he does what he wishes depending on how they have lived: he assigns paradise to the good and hell to the bad, and purgatory to some."

Questioned, he replied: "I did not say that when the body dies the soul dies."

Asked by whom he believes this Holy Church is governed, he replied: "I believe that it is governed by Christ, who left St. Peter to govern it, and afterwards to the pope, cardinals and bishops."

Told: "It appears from the trial that you said that you did not believe in the pope nor in these rules of the Church, and that any person has as much authority as the pope," he replied: "I beg the omnipotent God to let me die on the spot, if I know that I said what your lordship asks me."

Questioned about rites for the dead, he replied: "I have said that one should be doing good as long as he is in this world, because afterwards it is the Lord God who disposes of souls, and the prayers and charities and Masses that we do for the dead, we do them, as I believe, for the love of God, who then does as he pleases, because

---

[21] Priest Federico Crescendolo. See note 4 of the denunciation (2).

[22] Priest Ermacora de Philipponis: cf. AVPd, *Biblioteca capitolare, Visite,* b. 6, fol. 48r.

those souls do not receive those prayers and alms, and it is left to God to receive these good works for the benefit of either the living or the dead."

Cautioned to consider the truth more carefully, the reverend and most excellent lord vicar had him led back under close guard to his cell. After the foregoing testimony was read back to Ser Domenico, he ratified and signed it.

And I Domenego Scandella of Montereale ratify what I have testified to above.

At this point the aforesaid Domenico added: "Sir, that which I have said either out of the inspiration of God or of the Devil, I do not confirm it is either the truth or a lie, but I ask for mercy and I will do whatever is taught me."

A short time later the jailer attested that he had conducted the aforesaid Domenico to his cell and had left him under close guard.

[Odorico Vorai] to Domenico Scandella
[Written in Montereale, delivered to Concordia, 7 February 1584].

My dear Ser Domenego, since this recent event of yours and any suffering by you are the cause of common unhappiness among all your relatives and friends, be assured that if they could set you free with their own blood, they would do so more than gladly, but since they cannot act in any other way, they are wholly ready to consult about the matter with the most excellent lawyers to discover every possible remedy and help possible. And in doing this they will not spare their own life, nor goods to help you, provided that you wish to be helped, holding firm and adhering to what the lawyers will advise you, and not deviate from it in anything. And to us it seems good and for your benefit, first and principally that you should confess and be firm in the opinion that about everything that you have said against the Holy Church and our faith, you are a thousand times penitent and beseech mercy for it of our Lord God and of their most reverend lordships, promising full obedience to the Holy Church, and say that you do not believe nor ever will believe except when it is commanded by our Lord God and the Holy Roman Catholic and apostolic Church, and, in fact, if need be you would give your life and a thousand lives, if you had them to give, for the love of our Lord God and of the holy Christian faith, as recognition that you have your life and all that is good from his majesty. And if you will thus stand firm, it is common opinion that

our Lord God and his ministers will have mercy on you, because his
majesty does not wish for the death, but rather the conversion of the
sinner.[23]

To this then and to patience you are now being exhorted for the
love of God by your relatives and friends, all of whom greet you from
the heart and with tears in their eyes, and they do not fail, nor will
they fail, to pray the Lord God for your salvation, because at present
they cannot help you in any better way.

Giovanni Scandella to [Valerio] Trapola[24]
Montereale, 14 February 1584

Praise God. 1584, 14 February, in Montereale.

Your excellency, doctor, sir, by this I wish to ask your lordship to
please give an accounting of everything that has happened up to now
to my father, Ser Domenego Scandella of Montereale. As you know,
we talked with you asking if you would be willing to convey information about the whole matter; we enclose in the present communication,
an affidavit prepared by the commune of Montereale, as you will read.
If you deem it proper, share it with the most excellent monsignor the
vicar, to use it as he wills, beseeching him for the love of God that he
keep us informed of everything, and begging him to go to the prisoner
and tell him that his son Zanuto has been to Serravalle to see the
father inquisitor and spoke with him and he promised to write from
here and has read the present affidavit, and he was beseeched to
conclude the case because of his infirmity. And I pray that you will be
willing to take on this case on behalf of this poor man, so that the
proceedings be expedited, and you will be rewarded graciously. And if
you need to have a sworn statement from the authorities in Montereale
that the prisoner has confessed and taken communion every year, the
priests will prepare it; and if you need an affidavit from the commune
that he has been mayor and rector of the five hamlets, and administrator of the parish of Montereale, and that he did his duty as an upright
person, and that he had been tithe collector of the parish church of
Montereale, all this will be done; in performing his duties for the

---

[23] Ez 33: 11.

[24] In those years he was governor and judge of the city of Concordia: AVPn, *Processi,*
fasc. "Nonnulli processus ab anno 1578 usque ad annum 1585," fasc. I, fol. 1r (7 August
1585); fasc. V, dated 25 September 1583. He was definitely vicar general beginning from
1591: AAUd, *S. Officio,* b. 58, fasc. "Sententiarum contra reos S. Officii liber II," fol. 65r.

church he has aroused the ill will of many people in the village of Montereale. I hope that you will be willing to tell him to be stout-hearted in the grace of God and not to worry, and that as soon as we shall have a reply from your lordship, we shall come there, and shall do whatever you command. And I commend myself to him and to your lordship. May the Lord God preserve you from harm.

Signed, Zanut, son of Ser Domenego Scandella.

Thursday, 16 February 1584

The reverend and most excellent, the aforesaid lord vicar, with the intention of moving forward with the proceedings, decreed that Domenico Scandella should again be interrogated, with the assistance of their most illustrious lordships Ottavio Collucci and Flaminio Palmira, and ordered the guard to conduct the aforesaid Domenico before him. In an inner room of the episcopal residence, he asked Domenico to swear to tell the truth more distinctly and clearly both about himself and about his companions or accomplices. He then asked him to tell truthfully how long it had been since his last confession, and to whom he had confessed; he replied: "I have always gone to confession and the last time was Lent of this past year at Barcis with priest Pauleni, as I said earlier."

Asked when it was that he raised that doubt with him about the conception of Our Lord Jesus Christ, he replied: "The year before the last time I confessed to him."

Asked his age and if he has children, he replied: "I am fifty-two years old and have had eleven children, of whom four died and the rest are living."

He was told: "You have said that you talked about these ideas of yours with various people, and then you reduced it to one, saying 'I told it to Francesco Fasseta.' Therefore tell us now who the others are with whom you discussed and believed these things." He replied: "My lord, upon my faith as a Christian, I know only about that Francesco Fassetta. I do indeed believe I talked about it with others, but I do not remember for sure."

Asked what book it was that Marchiò of Grizzo showed him, which is said to contain marvelous things, he replied: "Sir, he never showed me a single book."[25]

---

[25] This was the vernacular Bible kept at home by Sebastiano Scandella and possessed by Domenico Gerbas. Melchiorre knew it well: cf. 33–34 and note 27.

Asked if he had been to Barcis and to whom had he talked, he replied: "Yes sir, I had dealings with different people, especially with Tita dell' Anna, Florit de Salvador, and Zanmaria de Salvador."

Asked, "What book is it that you gave to Tita?" he replied: "I gave him *Il fioreto de la Bibia,* which I bought in Venice for two *soldi.*"

Asked: "This *Lucidario della Madonna,* where you said that you read all the things that you testified about, do you have it at home?" he replied: "I had it when I was at Arba, a woman loaned it to me, and it was in 1564, a woman named Anna, and I returned it to her."

He was then asked: "Is this Anna still alive and what family does she belong to?" He replied: "She is dead and she was called Anna de Cecho, and I kept this book for about a month. Anna had a son called Zorzi,[26] and in this book it was written about the life of the Madonna and about the temple of the twelve virgins, which I mentioned in the first session, and in it was also said that the Madonna was called queen of the virgins."

Questioned, he replied: "I don't remember clearly if that book was called *Rosario* or *Lucidario,* but it was printed."

Questioned: "You said in the first session that everything had been chaos and that the most holy majesty decreed that from that mass the angels and even God should be born. What was this most holy majesty?" He replied: "By that most holy majesty I mean the spirit of God, which always existed."

Questioned: "You say that our souls return to the majesty of God and you also stated that God is nothing else but air, earth, fire and water. How then do these souls return to the majesty of God?" He replied: "It is true I said that air, earth, fire and water are God, and I cannot deny what I have said. And as for souls, they came from the spirit of God and thus they must return to the spirit of God."

Asked if the spirit of God and God are one thing and if this spirit of God is incorporated in these four elements, he replied: "I do not know," and then added: "I believe that all men have a spirit from God, which is happy if we do good works, and if we do bad works that spirit is angry."

Asked if he meant that the spirit of God is the same as the one born from that chaos, he replied: "I do not know."

And told to tell the truth, and resolve this question, namely if he

---

[26] Giorgio Capel.

really believes that souls return to the majesty of God, and God is air, water, earth and fire, how then do they return to the majesty of God, he replied: "I believe that our spirit, which is the soul, returns to God since it was he who gave it."

At this point, the reverend and most excellent lord vicar cautioned him to better consider telling the truth, to which he replied: "I have said that all the things of the world are God, and as for me I believe that our souls return to all the things of the world to enjoy as God deems fit." And then added: "Those souls are like the painted angels near Our Lord God, who keeps them close by him in accordance with their merits, and some who have done evil he disperses around the world."

Questioned whether he has ever said that when the body dies, the souls are dissolved into nothing, he replied: "I do not remember ever having said this, or even believing it."

At this point, the reverend lord vicar again cautioned him to better consider telling the truth and ordered him to be conducted back to his cell under close guard. And after the proceedings were read back to him, he confirmed and signed them.

And I Menego Scandella affirm the above.

A short time later the aforesaid guard reported that he had conducted Domenico back to his cell and had left him there under close guard.

22 February 1584, in the morning

Held in Concordia, in an internal room of the episcopal palace, where the most reverend and excellent Giovanni Battista Maro, doctor of canon and civil law, vicar of Concordia, considering that the aforesaid Domenico Scandella, accused, arraigned and imprisoned, had not confessed in the previous interrogation the truth of the facts in a clear and distinct manner, therefore decided to question him again, with the assistance of the reverend Ottavio Collucci, canon of Concordia, and the reverend Giovanni Battista Crescendolo, also a canon of Concordia, and both were asked to swear an oath to observe secrecy.

Following this the reverend vicar ordered the guard to lead Domenico Scandella from his cell to his presence, where he was asked to swear to tell the truth both about himself and about others. And then he was questioned: "You have said, according to the trial records, that when we die we become nothing, and are like worms and beasts; that when the body dies, the soul dies. Therefore, tell the truth and speak more clearly than you have done in the last session." He replied: "About what you have just asked me, I talked with Zulian de Stefenut and with Marchioro de Gerbas and with Francesco Fassetta, and I did state formally those words that when the body dies the soul dies, but the spirit remains."

Asked if he believes that in man there are body, soul and spirit and that these things are distinguished one from another, and that soul is one thing, spirit another, he replied: "Yes sir, I do believe that soul is one thing, spirit another; the spirit comes from God, and is that thing that when we have to act on some matter, inspires us to do it or not to do it."

Asked if he believes that what he is talking about are one or two spirits, he replied: "I believe that they are two spirits, one opposed to the other, which, when the body dies, return to God."

Questioned: "When the body dies, does the soul die?" he replied: "As I said earlier, when the body dies, the soul also dies. And this is my opinion, but I don't know if it is good or bad, but I think that it must be more bad than otherwise."

Questioned: "Why did you tell it to so many people, if it is bad, and pass it off as good?" He replied: "I did not talk about it as if it was good, but the Devil or something tempted me."

Questioned: "About blasphemy, we have noted in the trial records that you said blaspheming is not a sin; therefore, tell us the place, the time and the situation that made you say it." He replied: "Yes sir, I did say that to blaspheme is not a sin."

Asked to explain why he does not think it is a sin to blaspheme, he replied: "Because it only hurts oneself and not one's neighbor, just as if I have a coat and want to tear it up, I only hurt myself and not others. And I believe that he who does not harm one's neighbor is not sinning, because we are all God's children if we do not do wrong to one another, just as if, for example, a father has many children and one of them says, 'Curses on my father,' and the father forgives him; but if he breaks the head of someone else's son, he cannot be forgiven without paying. And thus I have said that to blaspheme is not a sin, because no one is hurt."

Asked to tell what book it was that many years ago he had received from Fior, the wife of Domenego Gerbas, which was half a foot tall and heavy like a Missal, and most of it in red letters, he replied: "This large book that I received from my uncle Domenego de Gerbas was a printed vernacular Bible, and I do not know where it was printed.[27] And this Domenego loaned me another book called *Il luchien-dario de' santi*, printed in the vernacular."[28]

Asked what he had done with these books and where they were now, he replied: "*Il lucendario de' santi* got wet and we tore it up, and the Bible, a cousin of mine, Bastià Scandella, had it at home and loaned it to me many times, but six or seven months ago told me that his wife burned it in the oven, but it was a shame to have burned that book."

Questioned: "Tell me, who were your companions who held these ideas with you?" He replied: "Sir, I have never known anyone who had these ideas, and whatever ideas I had came out of my own head. It is true that I once read a book that was loaned to me by our chaplain the priest Andrea da Mareno,[29] who now lives in Montereale, and this book was called *Il cavallier Zuanne de Mandavilla*, I believe it was French, printed, in the vernacular Italian language,[30] and it may be five or six years ago that he loaned it to me, but I returned it at least two years ago. And this book was about a journey to Jerusalem and about certain errors held by the Greeks about the pope, and it also told about the great Khan, the city of Babylon, of the priest John, about Jerusalem, and about many islands where people lived in this way and that; and this knight went to the sultan who asked him about priests, cardinals, the pope and the Church, and he said that Jerusalem belonged to the Christians and due to the poor government of the Christians and of the pope, God took it away. In one place it also said

---

[27] The description of the Bible given by the vicar had been provided by Melchiorre Gerbas in the session of 18 February 1584: AAUd, *S. Officio*, b. 8, fasc. 132. Editions of the Bible with a red letter title page are few, namely the Venetian imprints of 1492, 1494, 1517, 1525. The editions by Bernardino Bindoni in 1546 and by Lucantonio Giunti in 1538 have lettering in red and black. They all print the version by Nicolò Malermi, except for Bindoni's which has Sante Marmocchino's: Schutte, *Italian Religious Books*, 83–85; M. Sander, *Le livre à figures italien ...* (Milan: Hoepli, 1942), 989–1005; *Catalogo e suo supplemento ... della collezione ... Guicciardini ...* (Florence: Giuseppe Pellas, 1877), 28. Cf. A. Del Col, "Appunti per una indagine sulle traduzioni in volgare della Bibbia nel Cinquecento italiano," in *Libri, idee e sentimenti religiosi nel Cinquecento italiano*, ed. A. Biondi and A. Prosperi (Ferrara & Modena: Panini, 1987), 165–88.

[28] See the many editions of Jacopo da Varazze, *Leggenda aurea*, translated by Nicolò Malermi, cited in Schutte, *Italian Religious Books*, 321–23.

[29] Andrea Ionima, ex-parish priest of Mareno di Piave (see note 12).

[30] There are many Italian editions of Mandeville's *Voyages*, for example the Venetian of 1534 entitled: Ioanne de Mandavilla, *Qual tratta delle più maravigliose cose....* Cf. Ginzburg, 29–30, 41–49, 147, 151.

that when a person died ..." [the text breaks off here].

Asked if the book said anything about the chaos, he replied: "No, sir, but I read this in the *Fioretto della Bibbia,* but the other things that I have said about this chaos, I made them up in my head." Then, he added: "This same book by the knight Mandeville also related how when men were sick and near death they would go to their priest, and that priest beseeched an idol, and that idol told them whether someone had to die or not, and if he had to die the priest suffocated him, and they ate him in company: and if he tasted good he was sinless, and if he tasted bad he had many sins, and they had done wrong to let him live so long. And from there I got my opinion that when the body dies, the soul dies too, since out of many different kinds of nations, some believe in one way and some in another."

Having received this testimony, since the hour was late, he had Domenico conducted back to his cell. And when the proceedings were read back to him, he confirmed and signed them.

And I Domenego Scandela confirm the above.

Then the guard returned and reported that he had personally escorted Domenico Scandella back to his cell where he was locked up under close watch.

Saturday, 25 February 1584

It was reported by Ser Battista Parvis, jailer in the episcopal court of Concordia, that on the 7th of the present month after dinner he was shown the present letter[31] by Giovannino, son of the prisoner Domenico Scandella, so that it could then be given to the said Domenico, and the guard accepted the letter and read it word for word to the said Domenico Scandella, and then turned it over to the reverend and most excellent vicar, who ordered him not to show the letter in any way to Scandella, except with the permission of the most excellent vicar himself and to observe this provision in the future, etc.

A little later the same jailer reported that Domenico Scandella had told him that the aforesaid letter addressed to him had come from Ser Domenego Femenussa, a lumber and linen merchant in Montereale.

Thursday, 8 March 1584, in the morning

Held in Concordia in the episcopal palace, in an interior room,

---

[31] The letter of the priest Odorico Vorai to Domenico Scandella, 28–29.

where the reverend and most excellent vicar, intending to continue the case against Domenico Scandella, presently a prisoner of the Holy Office of the Inquisition, decreed that he be further questioned, with the assistance of the reverend Antonio Fagagna, who was obliged to swear to maintain silence, and the reverend Ottavio Collucci, both canons of Concordia. Subsequently the guard was ordered to conduct before the aforesaid reverend and most excellent vicar the said Domenico, and when he appeared, and after he swore on the Holy Gospels of God, physically touched, to tell the truth both about himself and his other companions, questioned by the reverend and most excellent vicar, he replied: "As I already said, I believe that when man is born he is like an ox and a beast and that God then gives him an angel and I believe that when we are in the mother's womb, we are just a pulp and dead flesh, but as soon as we are born, God sends us this angel, but before that, as I said, we are dead flesh, like a worm still without spirit or breath. And when man grows up, whether it comes from God or from the Devil, another spirit comes into us which fights with that angel. And when man dies, both spirits go where it pleases God."

Questioned, he replied: "I say that it is a greater teaching to love one's neighbor than to love God, because I read in a *Historia del giudicio* that on Judgment Day, he will say to that angel: 'You are wicked, you have never done anything good for me.' And that angel replies: 'Lord, I have never seen you so that I could do a good deed for you.' 'I was hungry and you did not feed me, I was thirsty and you did not give me drink, I was naked and you did not clothe me, when I was in prison you did not visit me.' And because of this I believed that God was that neighbor, because he said: 'I was that poor one.' "[32]

Asked who is that God who will judge, he replied: "It will be that most holy majesty which I mentioned before, who existed before the chaos, and Christ will be there, as the one who will remind the most holy majesty that he taught the way to them to do good together with the most holy fathers."

Questioned, he replied: "When speaking with Francesco Fasseto and arguing with him and saying that when the Madonna was to be married, there were many who wanted her, and they gave her to St.

---

[32] See Ginzburg, 37–38, where he quotes the *Iudizio universal overo finale*, in Firenze, appresso alle scale di Badia, [n.d. but 1570–1580]. The passage that he reproduces is a paraphrase in verse of Mt 25: 31–46.

Joseph who was old and because I had read that he found her pregnant and so wanted to leave her,[33] so I said that Christ was the son of St. Joseph, or rather the bastard of some other man. And I said this last May in the year 1583, returning from Venice with Francesco Fassetta."

Questioned, he replied: "I said that if Christ was born from the Holy Spirit and was the Son of God, he would not have let himself be crucified."

Questioned, he replied: "It may be I said that this Christ let himself be hung up like a beast, but I do not remember."

Questioned, he replied: "A certain Nicolò, painter of Porcia. I know him, but it may be a year that I have not seen him. He lives in Porcia, and he said to me once when he was in my house: 'Are you observing Lent?' because it was Lent, and I said: 'I eat a little milk, cheese and an egg now and then. And do you observe it?' He replied: 'I do it out of fear.' I know that he had a book called *Zanpollo,* a buffoon, according to him, who died and went to hell and joked with the demons there; and if I remember he said that he was with a companion, and that a demon had taken a liking to the buffoon, and when his companion learned that the demon was fond of the buffoon he said to him that he should pretend to be unhappy; and as he was doing this, the demon said to him: 'Why do you look unhappy? Speak honestly, regardless, because one should be honorable even in hell.'"[34]

Questioned, he replied: "I never said that all men go to hell, and I do not know that I ever spoke about this, but I did say that when man dies, I believe he is no longer anything."

Questioned, he replied: "That night when the father inquisitor said to me: 'Tomorrow come to Maniago,' I was like a wild man and I wanted to go out in the world and do something crazy."

Asked what crazy things, he replied: "I wanted to kill priests, burn churches, and be reckless, but because of my two little children, I checked myself and went to Menego della Feminussa where I found a messer Alessandro Policreto, a lawyer in Aviano but a native of Pordenone, who had represented one of my sons in a case, and I told him: 'I want to go to Concordia.' And he replied: 'You are right to want to

---

[33] Menocchio is referring to a scene from frescoes in the parish church which portray the wedding of the Madonna according to the traditional iconography. What he read is in Mt 1: 18–19.

[34] A. Caravia, *Il sogno dil Caravia,* In Vinegia, nelle case di Giovanni Antonio di Nicolini da Sabbio, 1541, fols. Gv–G2r; Ginzburg, 22–27.

go and get rid of this bother, but say, even if you said it, that you did not put faith in it or believe it.' And he had with him another young man of Pordenone called Hetor,[35] the brother of the priest Decio of Fiume and Menego Femenuzza, and the three were eating supper together and there was nobody else that I remember."

Questioned, he replied: "It will never be shown that I said there is no Holy Spirit; on the contrary, the greatest faith that I have in the world is my belief that there is a Holy Spirit and that he is the word of the most high God that lights up the whole world."

And warned to think about telling the truth more fully, the proceedings were read back to him and he signed them.

And I Menego Scandella ratify as above.

And subsequently the guard was sent to escort diligently the aforesaid Domenico to his cell. He returned and reported that he had conducted, as ordered, Domenico Scandella to prison and left him under careful watch.

16 March 1584

Before the reverend and most excellent vicar, sitting in Concordia, there appeared the reverend Giovanni Daniele Melchiori, priest of Polcenigo, cited as witness in the trial and taken *ex officio,* summoned, having taken an oath from the hand of the reverend vicar, cautioned and diligently questioned, he replied: "I do not remember the time precisely, but I believe that it is over ten years ago that Domenego Scandella of Montereale was in my house at Polcenigo, where I was making wafers, and he said to me: 'By the Virgin Mary, these are big beasts.' And I warned him to watch what he was saying, and he replied: 'They are not consecrated yet, I am just talking about the dough.'"

Asked if he remembered anything else about this matter concerning Scandella, he replied: "I heard it said by many people, whose names I do not remember, that he had wrong ideas about the faith. For example, one day on the road from Grizzo to Dalmanins[36] someone remarked to him, I do not remember who because fifteen years have passed: 'Great is the goodness of the Lord God in having created

---

[35] Ettore da Napoli of Pordenone: cf. AAUd, *S. Officio,* b. 8, fasc. 137, interrogation of A. Policreto, 14 May 1584.

[36] Probably Malnisio, from the forms Malnis, Manins; less likely Domanins.

these mountains, these fields and this so beautiful machine of the world.' To which he, Menocchio that is, replied: 'Who do you think created this world?' and when the reply came 'God,' Menocchio retorted: 'You are fooling yourself, because this world was made by chance. And if I could just speak out I would, but I cannot speak.' And I do not know anything else."

Asked, "Sir, were you present when Domenego Menocchio was asking whether he should come to Concordia at the order of the father inquisitor," he replied: "No sir, I was not there when he was asking advice on this matter, but I can tell you that many days ago, perhaps about four months ago, Menocchio told me in his own house that the Holy Office of the Inquisition was preparing a trial against him and asked my advice about what he should do. I advised him that if he wanted to do the right thing and to his benefit, he should go spontaneously to the Holy Office and tell, confess the errors into which he had fallen, because in this way, going voluntarily, he would be shown greater mercy."

Asked whether "You gave him the form in which he should answer," he replied: "No, sir but I told him these precise words: 'I have read that if an offender presents himself voluntarily to the Holy Office, he has to be received charitably, and if summoned shall appear and be punished according to his crime and if he does not appear when summoned, he shall be totally expelled from the company of the good.'"

Asked if he knew anything else, he replied: "No, sir." On generalities, he answered properly and he took the oath of secrecy.

21 March 1584, in the morning

There appeared before the reverend and most excellent vicar the priest Andrea Ionima, chaplain of Montereale, and pursuant to the order he had received, he presented to his lordship a book in quarto with wooden boards, written in the vernacular, entitled *Il libro de Zuan de Mandavila,* lacking a title page, which began: "Here beginneth a short treatise." Then after an oath to tell the truth about this book as well as about other things, he stated: "I found this book by chance when I was going through certain notarial writings in the town of Mareno, perhaps four years ago. I brought it back to Montereale and read it now and then."

Asked how it ended up in the hands of Domenico Menocchio, he replied: "I think that a certain Vincenzo Lombardo, who knows how to read a little, took it from my house and, since he had it, he may have shown it to Menochio, and it was returned to me by this Vicenzo Lombardo."

To generalities, he replied properly, etc.

27 April 1584

The reverend and most excellent lord vicar and the reverend father inquisitor, wishing to proceed in the present trial in conformity with the instructions contained in certain letters from the most serene Dominion of Venice which laid down certain provisions affecting the Holy Office of the Inquisition,[37] and wishing to bring the previous interrogations of the aforesaid Domenico into line with the requirements set forth in these letters, ordered that he be brought with a sufficient escort to the city of Portogruaro so that in the presence of the most distinguished *podestà* he might ratify and confirm the proceedings that had transpired, and to effect this they requested the assistance of the illustrious *podestà* himself.

The same day

The most distinguished Pietro Zorzi,[38] *podestà* of the city of Portogruaro, so requested by me, Giovanni Ghibillino, chief notary, in the name of the Holy Office, ordered one of his guards and officers to escort the aforesaid Domenico with every care and diligence to the city of Portogruaro, as had been asked by the Office of the Holy Inquisition.

The 28th day of the same month

Held in the city of Portogruaro in the palace that is the residence of the most celebrated *podestà,* specifically in the lower chamber of audiences, in the presence of the reverend Giovanni Battista Maro, canon and vicar of Concordia and the reverend father Felice Montefalco, inquisitor general for the entire patriarchate of Aquileia and diocese of Concordia, and of Pietro Zorzi, *podestà* of the aforesaid city. Led before them was Domenico Scandella, called Menocchio, conducted by Battista Parvis, a guard attached to the episcopal court, and by the guards of the most distinguished *podestà* of Portogruaro. The

---

[37] See xxxiv–xxxvi.

[38] It is impossible to indicate the dates of service, since the register for those years is missing in ASVe, *Segretario alle voci, Elezioni del Maggior Consiglio.* His presence in 1585 is attested by Cicogna, *Documenti storici,* 116.

judges ordered that the aforesaid Domenico be released from his bonds and set at liberty, which was immediately done, and they ordered that all the previous trial records be read to him, so that, after hearing them, he could ratify, confirm and approve them under oath, and he took that oath and was cautioned to tell the truth.

There, in the presence of the persons named above, after the preceding trial records were read to Domenico by me, chief notary, in a loud and audible voice, namely the records of the first, second, third and fourth sessions, he ratified, confirmed and approved them, saying that everything had been written down and had been said by him, and he signed in confirmation of the aforesaid ratification.

And I Domenico Scandela confirm and ratify as above.

After this was done, the aforesaid reverend lord vicar and father inquisitor decided to interrogate Domenico anew in the presence of the above-mentioned *podestà*. When he was asked how long he had persisted in his opinions, he replied: "For five or six years, since I was given that book entitled *Il cavallier Mandavilla*."

And when he was told that it was more like thirty years that he had held these opinions, he replied: "In this book, *Mandavilla*, it seems that I read there was a Simon Magus who turned into an angel[39] and the first time I ever spoke of it was when I was going to Pordenone for a lawsuit with some people of Maniago. When they said that God had made them lose it, I told them: 'God! God does not care about lawsuits.' And I do not remember who they were, but I think one was Iacomo di Cella."

Questioned, he replied: "When my father and my mother died, I was small and I never had any business with anyone who was a heretic, but I have a subtle mind and I sought after lofty things which I did not know about. And of the things I said, I do not know if they are true, but I want to be obedient to the Holy Church, and I did have some ideas that were bad, but the Holy Spirit enlightened me and I beseech the mercy of Almighty God, of the Lord Jesus Christ and of the Holy Spirit, and may he kill me if I am not telling the truth."

Questioned, he replied: "I beseech God to let me die if I ever told anyone: 'Believe this about Christ and the Virgin Mary and do not believe that,' and if I ever said it, I would certainly know it. It may be

---

[39] Simon Magus is never named in the book: cf. Ginzburg, 157 and the introduction, lvii.

some bad people who maliciously accused me of it. And it is true that I had dealings with that painter of Porcia, but I do not know that he is a Lutheran, although it is true that he said he observed Lent out of fear. I do not know if not observing Lent makes a person a Lutheran, but I do believe that one who goes around teaching bad things and eats meat on Friday and Saturday is a Lutheran."

When he was told to name all his companions, otherwise more rigorous measures would have to be taken against him, because it seems impossible to this Holy Office that he should have learned so many things and not have companions, he replied: "Sir, I do not remember ever teaching anyone, nor have I ever had any companions in these opinions. And the things I said I got from that book of Mandeville that I read."

Questioned, he replied: "For the last twenty years I have not observed Lent because I ate cheese and milk."

When he was told: "It emerges from the trial that you never observed Lent," he replied: "As for eating meat, I never ate meat, but during Lent I always ate milk, cheese and also some eggs, and I also told others that to eat cheese and milk at Lent is not a sin."

Asked if he has grown-up children and if they too share these opinions, he replied: "Yes sir, I do have them and God forbid that they should have these opinions."

Asked to whom he spoke the aforesaid words, he replied: "I may have said them to Francesco Fassetta and I do not remember any others, and also with Marchiò Gerbas, to him too I told all these opinions of mine."

Asked if his wife is alive, he replied: "Yes sir, and I never talked to her about these things."

Questioned, he replied: "Yes sir, I believed that to eat eggs, milk and cheese at Lent was not a sin, being in a place where you could not get anything else."

Questioned, he replied: "It is true I said that if I were not afraid of the law, I would say a lot of things to shock people, and I also said that if I had the grace to go before the pope, or a king or a prince who would listen to me, I would say many things, and then if I was killed for it, I would not care."

When he was asked to tell everything that was on his mind and that he wanted to say, he replied: "I have this idea that to speak Latin is a betrayal of the poor, because in a lawsuit poor people do not know what is being said and are harmed by it, and if they want to say four words they need a lawyer. It seems to me that under this law of ours the pope, cardinals and bishops are so great and rich that everything is the Church's and the poor are hurt by it, who if they have two rented fields, they belong to the Church, to some bishop or cardinal. It also appears to me that these Venetian rulers have a lot of thieves in that city, so that if one goes there to buy something and asks: 'What do you want for that stuff?' they say one ducat, even if it is only worth three *marcelli*, and I wish that they would show some justice.

I wish that everyone believed in the majesty of God and were honorable people and did as Jesus Christ asked, who answered to those Judeans who asked him what law there should be 'Love God and your neighbor.'[40]

The majesty of God has given the Holy Spirit to everyone: to Christians, to heretics, to Turks and Jews, and they are all dear to him and are all saved equally. And you others, priests and monks, you want to know even more than God and are like the Devil and want to become gods on this earth and have the same knowledge as God, in the guise of the Devil, and the more one thinks he knows, the less he knows.

I believe that the law and the commandments of the Church are just a business and they live on it.

I like this about the sacrament, that after one has confessed, he goes to take communion and receives the Holy Spirit and one's spirit is joyful.

As for the sacrament of marriage, it was not God who made it, but men: once man and woman exchanged vows and this sufficed, and then later came these human inventions.

Of the sacrament of confirmation, I believe it is just a business, the invention of men, since everyone has the Holy Spirit, and they seek to know and know nothing.

Of the consecration and ordination of priests, I wish they were done at age sixty and I believe that the spirit of God is in all people, and when man does good works, the spirit rejoices. I believe that anyone who has studied can be a priest without being consecrated, because it is all a business.

As for extreme unction, I do not believe it is anything and is worth anything, because it is the body that is anointed and the spirit cannot be anointed.

---

[40] Mt 22: 34–40.

About the sacrament of baptism I believe that as soon as we are born we are baptized, because God who has blessed all things baptizes us. And this baptism is an invention and priests begin to devour souls even before they are born and devour them continually even after their death.

As for the sacrament of the Eucharist it is a way of governing men, devised by men through the Holy Spirit; and the Mass was thought up by the Holy Spirit, just as the adoration of the host, so that men will not be like beasts.

I like the preaching about men living in peace, but as for preaching about hell, Paul says one thing, Peter another. I think it is just a business, the invention of men who know more than others.

I read in the Bible that David made the Psalms when he was being persecuted by Saul.[41] I believe that the Holy Scripture was given by God, but then was added to by men. Four words only would suffice in this Holy Scripture, but it is like the books of battle that grew and grew. As for the things in the Gospels, I believe that some are true and some the evangelists made up out of their own heads, as we see in the Passion narratives where one says it one way and one in another way."

When he was asked: "Did you say that Holy Scripture was devised to deceive men?" he replied: "Yes sir, I said that."

Questioned, he replied: "I believe that the saints were honest men who did good works, and because of it Our Lord God made them saints, and I believe that they pray for us. As for their relics, such as an arm, a body, a head, a hand or a leg, I believe that they are just like ours when they are dead and we should not adore or revere them."

Questioned, he replied: "We should not adore their images, but only the one God, who created the heavens and the earth. Don't you see that Abraham cast down all idols and all images and adored only one God?"[42]

Questioned, he replied: "As for indulgences, I believe that they are good, because if God has put a man in his place, who is the pope, and he sends a pardon, that is good because it is as if we receive it from

---

[41] 2 Sm 22: 1; Ps 18: 1–2.

[42] Gn 12: 1–9; 17: 1–27, which speak of the one God of Abraham, but not of idols and images, while it is Moses who smashes the golden calf after his descent from Sinai and receives the divine order to destroy the altars, pillars, and sacred totems of the Canaanite gods: cf. Ex 23: 23–33; 32: 1–35; 34: 11–17.

God, since these indulgences are given by someone who is acting as his steward."

Asked if he believes that indulgences come from the merits of the saints and from Our Lord Jesus Christ, he replied: "Indulgences come only from the Holy Spirit, and this Holy Spirit is the will of God."

Questioned, he replied: "I believe that Our Lord God gave free will and the Holy Spirit to the body and said: 'Do good, and you will be treated well in the things of the world; but if you offend the world, you will be offended by the world, and if you offend God, you will be offended by God.'"

Questioned, he replied: "No sir, I do not believe that on the day of judgment we will be resurrected in the body, which to me seems impossible, because if bodies were resurrected they would fill the heavens and the earth. And the majesty of God will see our bodies with his intellect. It is not different than if we wanted to build something, shut our eyes and visualized it in our mind and intellect, and thus saw it with that intellect."

Questioned, he replied: "I believe that the empress in this world is greater than the Madonna, but in the hereafter the Madonna is greater, because there we are invisible."

Questioned, he replied: "Yes sir, it is true that when the empress passed through I said she was greater than the Madonna, but I meant in this world. And in that book about the Madonna, she was never sent or paid so many honors. In fact, when she was brought to be buried, she was dishonored when someone tried to lower her from the shoulders of the apostles and his hand would not come unstuck. And this was in the life of the Madonna."[43]

At the conclusion, since the hour was late, the aforesaid Domenico was ordered to be conducted back to the episcopal prison in the city of Concordia. At which point he exclaimed: "My lords, I beg you, by the passion of our Lord Jesus Christ, to settle my case; and if I deserve death, send me to it; and if I deserve mercy, exercise it, because I want to live as a good Christian." The proceedings were read back to him, and he ratified and signed them.

And I Domenego confirm as above.

---

[43] See Iacopo da Varazze, *Legendario de le vite de tutti li santi* . . . , (Venice: Girolamo Scotto, 1566), 262; Ginzburg, 34–36.

28 April 1584, Concordia

Ser Giorgio Capel of Arba, son of the lady Anna of Arba, now
deceased, sworn in as witness and questioned, testified: "I am, as I
have said, the son of the lady Anna of Arba. I am about 36 years of
age and know how to read and write a little."

Asked if he knows Domenego Scandella, he replied: "I have
known him for about 20 years, because he had a mill in Arba."

Asked if he knew what book it was that Domenego had borrowed
from his mother the lady Anna, he replied: "I do not know; my mother never told me."

Questioned, he replied: "Yes sir, I have a book called *La vita de'
santi*,[44] and two or three other books, which were returned to me by
messer Zanbattista, our parish priest,[45] and a few others he kept himself, saying 'They will want to burn these.'"

Questioned, he replied: "I do not remember having seen at home
any book called a *Lucidario* or *Rosario della Madonna*. I do not have
any other books than those three returned by the priest."

At the conclusion, he was ordered, under pain of excommunication, to bring to Concordia within six days all the books he had
received from the priest.

Tita, son of Domenico Coradina, of Barcis, now deceased, sworn
in and questioned, replied: "I am called Tita, son of Domenico Coradina. I am 25 years old and know how to read and write."

Questioned, he replied: "It may be about four months ago that
Domenego Scandella loaned me a book called *Il fioreto della Bibbia* in
the vernacular and I read only one page, I read about when Adam and
Eve ate the apple."[46]

Questioned, he replied: "I burned this book when the parish priest
told me it was prohibited."

Gasparino son of Daniele Gasparini of Barcis, now deceased,
sworn in, was questioned and replied: "I am called Gasparino, son of

---

[44] Probably the book just cited in note 43.

[45] Priest Giovanni Battista, son of the deceased Giulio of the Counts of Maniago:
AVPd, *Biblioteca capitolare, Visite*, b. 6, "Visitatio apostolica ... Concordiensis ... ," Arba.

[46] See *El fiore de tutta la Bibbia hystoriato* ... , (Venice: Francesco Bindoni, 1523), fols.
[B5]r–v, the chapter entitled "Come il demonio s'ingegnò d'ingannare Adam et Eva per
invidia" ("How the Devil out of envy plotted to deceive Adam and Eve").

Daniele Gasparini, and I am 25 years old."

Questioned, he replied: "Yes sir, I do know that Menego Scandella loaned *Il fioreto della Bibia* to my friend Tita."

Questioned, he replied: "On the oath I have sworn, I tell you that I saw it burned by this Tita. I do not know if Menocchio loaned books to anyone else."

Questioned, he replied: "I do not know if Menocchio ever preached, except that sometimes he argued with the priest and took pleasure in it. I do not know if he has any companions who share his opinions, but I have heard people arguing with him."

Monday, 7 May 1584

Held in Concordia in the episcopal palace, in the interior room, where the reverend judges assembled, since the most celebrated *podestà* of Portogruaro would have to be absent for several days, and since the aforesaid judges did not want to further prolong the affairs of the Holy Office, they decided to again interrogate the aforesaid Scandella, so that he might more clearly speak the truth, and they ordered him to be summoned before them.

And then the aforesaid Domenico was sworn in, cautioned to tell the truth, and questioned: "In the previous session we told you that it appeared that your mind was full of these humors and evil doctrines, and this holy tribunal asked you to bare your soul to it." He replied: "My mind was lofty and wished for a new world and way of life, that the Church should act well and that there should not be so much pomp."

Questioned: "In the previous sessions you showed yourself very perplexed and in doubt over the article of the most Holy Trinity, so state your opinion." He replied: "I believe that the eternal God, out of that chaos that I mentioned before, removed the most perfect light in the way that is done with cheese, where the most perfect is taken, and from that light he made those spirits that we call angels, then he chose the noblest among them and bestowed on him all his knowledge, all his will, and all his power, and this is the one whom we call the Holy Spirit, and God placed him over the creation of the whole world, since God had already seen everything that had to be done and drawn up, so that this Holy Spirit is like a steward of God. This Holy Spirit then selected four captains, or should we say stewards, from those angels that had been made, namely Lucifer, Michael, Raphael and Gabriel, and placed them over the building of the whole world. Then Lucifer rose up and wanted to be equal with God, but since every creature knows that it cannot be equal to God, he wanted to be equal to the Holy Spirit and be as great as he for the works he did. And so he was removed from these works by the Holy Spirit, which no longer wanted him involved in the things of this world, but arranged it so that the other three made the whole world and chased Lucifer and all his company away from the thrones."

Questioned, he replied: "After the Holy Spirit received knowledge, will and power, he knew everything that God wanted to do and what God had seen, and this Holy Spirit commanded those captains that with their followers they should make the seven heavens corresponding to the seven days of the week, which we call the seven planets, and thus they were made. And God stopped closer to the sun, and I believe that it is not the sun that gives light, but it is God that shines and that the sun is like a mirror, which reflects God who is the true light.[47] The sun sends forth the light which is the light of God."

Questioned: "You have spoken of the Father and of the Holy Spirit, you must now declare yourself about the Son." He replied: "I believe that the person of the Son is [...] as that of the Holy Spirit, because he did all things: the will of God elected Abel as the son of God, but not pleased with him he elected Noah, and not being pleased with Noah, he elected Abraham, whom he blessed; and not being pleased with Abraham, he elected Isaac, son of Abraham, whom he blessed and permitted him to multiply in the world like the stars in the sky, and not being pleased he elected Jacob and when he came to his house, he battled with the Holy Spirit until morning, and when the Holy Spirit asked to be let go, Jacob replied that he would not stop until he received a blessing and thus the Spirit blessed him and said: 'In the future you shall not be called Jacob, but Israel'; and still not pleased, he elected Moses, and not pleased with Moses he finally elected Our Savior Jesus Christ, in whom he was pleased, and this is the Trinity."[48]

Questioned: "What do you think God is?" he replied: "Light,

---

[47] Cf. Jn 1: 9.

[48] For Abel, see Gn 4: 1–16; for Noah, 6: 5–22; 7: 1–9, 17; for Abraham 12: 1–3; for Isaac 17: 1–22; 22: 17; for Jacob 27: 1–45; 32: 23–33; the quote is 23: 29; for Moses Ex 3: 1–22; for Jesus Christ, Mt 1: 1–16; 3: 17 and parallels. The Trinity is present in the account of the baptism of Jesus: in fact God's Spirit descended on Christ and the Father said that he was well pleased with his Son.

happiness, consolation, this signifies the Trinity. The Trinity resembles a candle: the wax is the Father, the wick is the Son, and the light is the Holy Spirit. I believe that there is the Trinity in the sacrament of the Eucharist because there is happiness, consolation and light, and what makes me believe this is that when I go to this sacrament of communion repenting for my sins and having done my penance, I feel happiness, consolation and light."

He was told: "For the person of the Father, it appears that you mean God, for that of the Holy Spirit that angel created by the Supreme God who has been given knowledge, will, and power by God, and the Son you understand to be that person made by the Holy Spirit through the will of God, who is Our Lord Jesus Christ." He replied: "The Father is God who existed before the chaos, the Holy Spirit after the chaos, as also Christ the Son."

Asked where God was, he replied: "He was a certain light, a certain intellect, a certain will."

Questioned, he replied: "This God was in the chaos, just as a person in the water wants to spread out, or a person in a forest wants to stretch. Similarly, this intellect, having received knowledge, wants to enlarge and create this world."

Questioned: "Was God eternal and did he always exist with the chaos?" he replied: "I believe that they always existed together and were never separated, that is chaos without God, nor God without the chaos."

Questioned: "Did this God make, create or produce any creature?" he replied: "He made the design and gave the will through which all things were made."

Questioned: "Is the Holy Spirit God?" he replied: "It is that angel to which God gave his will and God entered into that angel with his will, knowledge and power."

Questioned: "Did God exist before there was a Holy Spirit?" he replied: "I believe yes."

Questioned: "What was the Son: man, angel or true God?" he replied: "A man, but in whom there was the spirit."

Asked what was this spirit that was in Christ, he replied: "The soul of Christ was one of those angels made in the beginning, or it may have been made anew by the Holy Spirit from the four elements or from nature itself. Things cannot be done well if they are not three, and thus God, since he had given knowledge, will and power to the Holy Spirit, thus gave it to Christ so that they could then console each other." He added: "When there are two who cannot agree in a judgment, when there is a third, if two agree then the third joins in, and thus the Father has given will and knowledge and power to Christ, because it has to be a judgment."

Questioned: "This Christ, is he really man like us, or is he something else?" he replied: "I believe that he is a man like us, born from man and woman like us, and that he had only what he received from the man and the woman, but it is true that God sent the Holy Spirit to elect him as his son."

Questioned: "Do you believe that Christ performed miracles and that he performed all those miracles written in the Gospels?" he replied: "Yes Father, because since God elected him a prophet and gave him great knowledge and sent him through the Holy Spirit, I believe he did do miracles."

Questioned: "Do you believe that Christ had a soul?" he replied: "I believe he has a spirit just like ours, because soul and spirit are the same thing." And then he added: "That man Christ, before he died, could bless and curse."

Questioned: "This soul of Christ, from whom does it come?" he replied: "Either one of those angels created in the beginning or a Holy Spirit created it from the elements, as we are created."

When asked: "Earlier you said that when the body dies, the soul dies, thus we should like to know if the soul of Christ dies when he dies," he replied: "I shall tell you: in man there is intellect, memory, will, thought, belief, faith and hope, which seven things God gave to man and are like souls, and because of which we must do works. And this is why I said that when the body dies, the soul dies." And he added of his own accord: "I will tell you how it is: these seven things are given by God to man in the same way as to a carpenter who wants to build things. So just as a carpenter with a hatchet and saw, wood and other instruments does his work, so God has given something to man so that he can also do his work; and not doing this work, there is no value at all."

And since the hour was late, it was decided to resume the questioning after dinner, and meanwhile the guard was ordered to return the prisoner to his cell, and he confirmed the trial records when they were read back to him.

And I Menego Scandela confirm the above.

The guard Battista Parvis returned with the information that he had led back Scandella and left him closely guarded.

The same day after dinner

Held as above, in the presence of the above, with the participation of the reverend Svetonio Canevalis, canon of Concordia, etc., the aforesaid Domenico appeared and after taking an oath to speak the truth, was interrogated: "In Christ die the intellect, memory, will, remembrance, and what else is given to our souls, do they die in the body of Christ when Christ dies?" he replied: "Yes sir, because up above there is no longer any need for working."

Asked if by that spirit given to Christ, he means the angel or the soul, he replied: "Spirit, angel and soul are one thing."

Asked "From whom was Christ born?" he replied: "It was announced by the Holy Spirit, I believed he was born of St. Joseph and Mary Virgin."

Questioned: "Did this Christ suffer death and the passion?" he replied: "Yes Father, and this is because he wanted to speak about the Father and about true things and those people, the Jews that is, took offense, and because of the miracles he was doing they gave him death and the passion."

Questioned: "Was this death and passion of benefit to anyone?" he replied: "It was of benefit for us Christians in this sense; as a mirror, that since he was patient and suffered for love of us, that we should die and suffer for love of him, and that we should not be amazed if we have to die, because God willed that his Son should die."

Questioned: "Did not Christ die for our sins?" he replied: "If a person has sins, he himself must do penance."

Questioned: "Did Christ sin?" he replied: "No Father."

Questioned again: "Why did he die?" he replied: "As an example for us." Then he added of his own accord: "He died without sin because he was always doing the works of the Father."

Questioned: "When Christ died, where did his soul go?" he replied: "It went to the throne of God."

Asked about Christ's body, he replied: "I do not know and cannot judge anything, whether it was carried to heaven or left on earth."

Asked if Christ's body was buried, he replied: "Yes Father, but I do not know if the eternal Father brought it away, because there was an angel who said it had been resurrected."[49]

Asked if the soul of Christ descended into limbo, he replied:

---

[49] See Mt 28: 5–6.

"Some say yes, but I do not know, because he told the thief: 'Today you will be with me in heaven.' "[50]

Questioned: "Was this Christ resurrected?" he replied: "As for me, I do not believe that he was resurrected, but that since he had risen to the heavens, the Father and the Holy Spirit sent down his spirit, saying to him: 'You are one like the others, dead, but go, raise up those who are in darkness and show yourself, that they will believe you.' "[51]

Questioned: "Will this Christ come back to judge in the Last Judgment?" he replied: "The Father chose him so that they three would judge." And he added spontaneously: "The thrones were filled with celestial spirits, but they shall be filled with the most chosen and carefully selected terrestrial spirits, since we have in our heart an evil spirit who is always tempting us. And those who die without having extinguished their light and who have performed works, will go up to heaven because the spirit of his Son Christ is terrestrial."

Questioned: "What do you mean by this word 'selected?'" he replied: "It does neither good works nor bad works, but God is the author of good but does no evil, and the Devil is the author of what is evil and does no good; and if man takes the part of the Devil he does not go to heaven and his light is extinguished, but if he does good works he goes to heaven and his light is not extinguished."

Questioned: "What are these works of God?" he replied: "To love him, adore him, sanctify him, revere and thank him, and one must also be charitable, merciful, peaceful, loving, honorable, totally obedient to one's superiors, pardon injuries, keep one's promises, and doing these things, we go to heaven and they suffice to go there."

Questioned: "What are the bad works?" he replied: "To rob, assassinate, commit usury, be cruel, do shameful things, vituperate and kill, and these things are seven works which displease God and are pleasing to the world and the Devil."

Questioned: "What are God's commandments?" he replied: "I believe that they are those I mentioned before."

Questioned: "To mention the name of God, to sanctify holy days, are these not God's precepts?" he replied: "This I do not know."

---

[50] Lk 23: 43.

[51] There is no mention in the four Gospels of a similar statement after Christ's resurrection. It is, instead, an indirect quotation from something said to Abraham by the rich glutton: "But if some one goes to them from the dead, they will repent": Lk 16: 30.

Questioned: "After the establishment and creation of the planets, what else was made at the beginning of the world?" he replied: "The earth, trees, animals and man, the sea was separated from water, fishes and all the creatures were made."

Asked by whom were all these things done, he replied: "By the Holy Spirit by means of his angels working through the will of God."

Questioned: "Well then, when all this was done, was there the Son of God?" he replied: "No sir, but he had the will to make him."

Questioned: "Were men all made at one time, all together?" he replied: "I believe so, because I read there were so many generations of men, I believe that they were made in different parts of the world."

Questioned: "By whom were these men made?" he replied: "By the Holy Spirit through the will of God and by his ministers, just as a steward joins the work of his own ministers, so too the Holy Spirit lent a hand."

Questioned: "Of what were these men made?" he replied: "I believe that they were made of earth, but of the most beautiful metal that could be found and this is because man desires these metals, and gold above all others. Men are composed also of the four elements and participate in the seven planets, and because of this some participate more of one planet than another, and a person may be more mercurial or more jovial, depending under what planet he was born."

Questioned: "Is this man composed of soul and body?" he replied: "First comes the body, then the soul."

Questioned: "Is man made in the likeness of God?" he replied: "Yes sir, just as the Holy Spirit is made of the four elements of the world, so man is made of the four elements just like the Holy Spirit."

Questioned: "Is this spirit that is given to man man himself, or something separate from man?" he replied: "It is separate from man, has the same will as man and sustains and governs this man."

Asked about original sin, if man in the mother's womb has any sin at all, he replied: "No sir, but he begins to sin when he begins to feed on the mother's milk after he leaves her womb."

Questioned: "When does man receive his spirit?" he replied: "When he has left his mother's womb, because before he does not yet have a voice. If he already had the spirit, it could be heard, but when he leaves the womb he receives the spirit and can be heard."

Questioned: "Did the Virgin Mary have sins?" he replied: "I believe that all men in the world are tempted, because our hearts are in two parts: one light, the other dark. In the dark is the evil spirit, in the light the good spirit. And so Mary Virgin was not a sinner like us, but she too sinned in some part."

Asked about Christ, if he had the two spirits like ours and was tempted like us, he replied: "Yes sir, but he was humble and patient."

Questioned: "Did Christ ever sin?" he replied: "I do not know, but I think he never sinned because he was inspired by the Holy Spirit and did not fear the Devil."

Asked what he believed about the universal church, he replied: "I wish that it would be governed more charitably, as it was established by Our Lord Jesus Christ."

Asked what he meant by "governed," he replied: "There is too much pomp, Our Lord Jesus Christ does not want pomp."

Asked about burial, he replied: "I think it would be better outside the church."

Questioned: "Should we pray to God for the dead?" he replied: "Yes sir, because God will put the dead person a little ahead, and will illuminate it a little more."

Asked about fasting, he replied: "If one fasts lovingly that is good, but if a person is a laborer and wants to fast, he sins more than receives grace." And he added on his own: "Fasting was devised for the intellect, to keep those humors from setting in, and as for myself I wish that we ate three or four times a day and did not drink wine, because then those humors would not come over us, and it would not happen as it does to those who eat more at one meal than they should in three, and I wish that during the time of fasting we ate only bread and water."

Asked about the glory of heaven, he replied: "I believe that it is a place that surrounds the entire world, and that from there all the things of the world can be seen, even the fish in the sea. And for those who are in that place it is like when we celebrate a feast day in this world, seeing thunder, . . . and serpents and every thing and those who remain here, who do not ascend up there and remain behind, remain without light and do not see." And he added on his own: "With these eyes of the body we cannot see all things, but with the eyes of the mind we can penetrate all things, the mountains, walls and every thing. We must do like those who go to Piazza San Marco to prepare a place for themselves."

Questioned: "Shall we see God in that beatitude?" he replied: "God is invisible but we shall see him then because he is spirit and spirit can see other spirits."

Questioned: "All the things that we shall see, shall we see them in God or outside God?" he replied: "That one seated above those thrones will want to see all things and it will be like a gentleman who drags out all his belongings to see them."

Questioned: "After the Judgment will we be in heaven with both our body and our soul?" he replied: "The body will not be there, because God sees that body where it is and will show that resemblance to those spirits."

Questioned: "Before you presented yourself to the Holy Office, with whom did you consult?" he replied: "I did not speak with anyone except with messer Alesandro Policreto and messer Hetor, brother of the priest Decio of Fiume, and I told him that I wanted to go before this Holy Office and he told me to come and confess everything and say that I did not believe them or hold them as true." Questioned: "Were these the precise words that he spoke to you?" he replied: "Yes Father." Questioned: "Would you say this to his face?" he replied: "Yes Father." Questioned, he replied: "That Hetor heard them, but I do not know if that other one did."

Questioned: "Did you not speak with the parish priest of Polcenigo before presenting yourself?" he replied: "Yes Father, but before I was summoned, at the time that the witnesses were being summoned."

Asked what that priest had said, he replied: "He told me that I should come down here even before being cited, that it would be good; and that if I was summoned I should appear because it would shorten things, and if I should delay and not appear, the affair would be dragged out. And tell them what they ask you and try not to talk too much and do not start recounting all these things, and answer only to those things they will ask you."

Questioned: "Who was present when you spoke to that priest and where was it?" he replied: "It was in my house in Montereale, but I do not know if anybody else was there; it is true that my wife was going back and forth but I do not think she heard anything."

Questioned: "Did you have business with him?" he replied: "I did not have business with him, but he came because he was my friend and because we had grown up together."

At the conclusion, the foregoing proceedings were read back to him and the aforesaid Scandella confirmed them and signed, and he was ordered to be led back to his cell.

And I Menego Scandella ratify the above.

And then the aforesaid guard reappeared and reported that, as ordered, he had returned Domenico to his prison and left him under close guard.

Saturday, 12 May 1584, in the morning

Held in the place as above, before the reverend lord judges as above, in the presence of the reverend lord Gaspare, there appeared the fore-named Domenico, and after he took the oath to speak the truth, he was told: "It appears that you contradicted yourself in the previous examinations speaking about God, because in one instance you said God was eternal with the chaos, and in another you said that he was made from the chaos: therefore clarify this circumstance and your belief." He replied: "My opinion is that God was eternal with chaos, but he did not know himself nor was he alive, but later he became aware of himself, and this is what I mean that he was made from chaos."

Questioned: "You said previously that God had intelligence; how can it be then that originally he did not know himself, and what was the cause that afterwards he knew himself? Explain also what occurred in God that made it possible for God who was not alive to become alive." He replied: "I believe that it was with God as with the things of this world that proceed from imperfect to perfect, as an infant who while he is in his mother's womb neither understands nor lives, but outside the womb begins to live, and in growing begins to understand. Thus, God was imperfect while he was with the chaos, he neither comprehended nor lived, but later expanding in this chaos he began to live and understand."

Questioned: "Did this divine intellect know everything distinctly and in particular in the beginning?" He replied: "He knew all the things that there were to be made, he knew about men, and also that from them others were to be born; but he did not know all those who were to be born, just as those who tend herds know that from them, others will be born, but they do not know specifically all those that will be born. Thus God saw everything, but he did not see all the particular things that were to come."

Questioned: "This divine intellect in the beginning had knowledge of all things: where did he acquire this information, was it from his own essence or by another way?" he replied: "The intellect received knowledge from the chaos, in which all things were confused together: and then it [chaos] gave order and comprehension to the intellect, just as we know earth, water, air, and fire and then distinguish among them."

Questioned: "Did this God not have will and power before he

made all things?" he replied: "Yes, just as knowledge increased in him, so will and power also increased."

Questioned: "Are will and power the same thing in God?" he replied: "They are distinct just as they are in us. Where there is will there must also be the power to do a thing: for example, the carpenter wants to make a bench and needs tools to do it, and if he does not have the wood, his will is useless. Thus we say about God, that in addition to will, power also is needed."

Questioned: "What is this power of God?" he replied: "To operate by means of skilled workers."

Questioned: "These angels that you think are God's ministers in the creation of the world, were they made directly by God, or by whom?" he replied: "They were produced by nature from the most perfect substance of the world, just as worms are produced from a cheese, and when they emerged received will, intellect, and memory from God as he blessed them."

Questioned: "Could God have done everything by himself without the assistance of the angels?" he replied: "Yes, just as someone who is building a house uses workers and helpers, but we say that he built it. Similarly, in making the world God used the angels, but we say that God made it. And just as that master carpenter in building the house could also do it by himself, but it would take longer, so God in making the world could have done it by himself, but over a longer period of time."

Questioned: "If there had not been that substance from which all those angels were produced, if that chaos had not been there, could God have created the entire apparatus of the world by himself?" he replied: "I believe that it is impossible to make anything without matter, and even God could not have made anything without matter."

Questioned: "That spirit or supreme angel that you call Holy Spirit, is he of the same nature and essence as God?" he replied: "God and the angels are of the same essence as chaos, but there is a difference in perfection, because the substance of God is more perfect than that of the Holy Spirit, since God is the more perfect light: and I say the same about Christ, who is of a lesser substance than that of God and that of the Holy Spirit."

Questioned: "This Holy Spirit is he as powerful as God? And Christ also is he as powerful as God and the Holy Spirit?" he replied: "The Holy Spirit is not as powerful as God, and Christ is not as powerful as God and the Holy Spirit."

Questioned: "Is what you call God made and produced by someone else?" he replied: "He is not produced by others but receives his movement within the shifting of the chaos, and proceeds from imperfect to perfect."

Questioned: "Who moves the chaos?" he replied: "It moves by itself."

Asked about predestination, after it was explained to him what it signified, he replied: "I do not believe that anyone has been preordained by God to eternal life."

Questioned: "When God contemplates making men, does he not contemplate placing them in the thrones from which the angels fell?" he replied: "It is true that he contemplates having them come to these thrones, but he does not have in mind this or that person in particular, but rather whoever was more worthy, whoever had better performed the works of God and whoever had been born under the better planet and had a better fate."

Questioned: "Those who are to come to this glory, are they called by this God?" he replied: "Yes Father, he summons them all: Turks, Jews, Christians, heretics, and all equally, just like the father who has many children but calls them equally, even if there are some who do not want to do the will of the Father."

Questioned, he replied: "We could not do good works without the grace of God."

Questioned: "What is this grace of God?" he replied: "I believe that it is God who sends the Holy Spirit to enlighten us."

Questioned: "Do you believe that Christ acquired this grace for us?" he replied: "I believe he was sent to teach how we could acquire that grace."

Questioned: "What do you understand about justification?" and after it was explained to him what was meant by justification, that it frees from blame, from eternal punishment and restores us to the grace of God, he replied: "I believe that justification is repenting for past sins, confessing to God and receiving penances from the confessor, and that we are thus freed from blame, eternal punishments and are restored to God's grace."

Questioned: "Who is it that justifies us?" he replied: "The Holy Spirit, the will of God and the words of Jesus Christ."

Questioned: "Do we receive justification through the passion of Christ?" he replied: "Through the death of Christ we learn that we must patiently bear the death of Christ ourselves."

Questioned: "Did you not say that it is the same to go to confess to a tree as to a priest?" he replied: "If that tree knew how to teach us about penance, it would suffice. Some men go to priests because they do not know about the penance that we must perform for our sins, so that they will teach it to them, but if they already knew it, there would be no need to go to them, and those who already know it have no need to go."

Asked what he believed about holy water, he replied: "I believe that all water is blessed by God and when priests bless it in the name of God they add nothing to it, but demonstrate that it is blessed by God, because if they blessed it, they would make it increase, it would never diminish, because what God blesses, he increases."[52]

Questioned: "Are the benedictions that priests make over all things useful?" he replied: "The Devil enters things and injects his poison into them, but when they are blessed by the priest he removes that poison, and the priest's holy water chases away the Devil."

Questioned: "If somebody other than a priest did the blessing, do you think it would be of equal use?" he replied: "Yes Father, if the layman knew the words, it would be of the same use as when the priest did it, because God gave his power equally to all, and not more to one than to another."

Asked about processions, he replied: "They are good."

Questioned: "Do you believe that there is an earthly paradise?" he replied: "I believe that the earthly paradise is where there are gentlemen with a lot of property and live without tiring themselves out."

Questioned: "Did you receive a letter in prison?" he replied: "The guard read it to me while I was in prison." And when he was shown a letter that began: "'My dear Ser Domenego,'" and which ended: "'help you in any better way,'"[53] a letter that had been presented by Ser Battista, guard in this Holy Office, on 25 February 1584, he replied: "This is not the letter."

Then the aforementioned guard was summoned, he was shown the letter and asked if this was the letter which he had read in the prison, and he answered: "This is the one." And in the presence of Domenico he stated and affirmed that it was the one.

Questioned: "From whom did you receive this letter and who

---

[52] It is a free rendering of Gn 1: 22: "And God blessed them, saying, 'Be fruitful and multiply and fill the waters in the seas, and let birds multiply on the earth.'" Cf. also Gn 9: 1.

[53] It is the letter published at 28–29.

brought it?" he replied: "It was brought by Zanut, my son, who told me: 'Take this letter that Domenego Femenuzza sends to you.'"

Questioned: "Is this Femenuzza a relative of yours?" he replied: "No Father." Asked: "Do you have close relations with him?" he replied: "I have no other dealings, except that he comes to my mill and occasionally lends me money."

Questioned: "Have you ever been reproached by anyone for these opinions of yours?" he replied: "I was reproached by the parish priest, by now many times, but I felt hostility towards him and did not take into account his own situation."

Questioned: "Were you ever conducted before monsignor the vicar by the priest?" he replied: "Yes Father, it was when we had discussed these opinions of mine together, and I told him: 'If it were one of these great people who said it to me, I would believe him,' and he replied: 'Shall we go to monsignor the vicar?' and I said: 'Let us go.' And so we went and found that he was away, and then the priest asked me: 'What should we do?' and I replied: 'I will do whatever you wish.' And when we got there, we exchanged some words, and I went to confess myself to the priest of Maniago Libero."[54]

Questioned, he replied: "I was also reproached by those priests who confessed me."

And at the conclusion, the records were read back to him, he confirmed and signed them.

And I Menego affirm the above.

At the conclusion, the aforementioned reverend lord judges ordered the guard to conduct him back to the prison, and then the guard returned to report that he had brought him back to his cell and left him under a close guard.

[12 May 1584]

The reverend lord judges gave the order to inform Domenico Scandella that he should make his defense in whatever form he intended, otherwise, etc.

[17 May 1584]

The guard, Ser Battista Parvis, reported that he had personally intimated to the aforesaid Domenico that he should make his defense,

---

[54] Priest Ermacora de Philipponis: cf. note 22.

and that Domenico had replied that he did not wish to make any other defense, except to present a statement in his own hand and throw himself upon the mercy of the court.

Autograph defense of Domenico Scandella
Portogruaro, 17 May 1584

In the name of the Father and of the Son and of the Holy Spirit.

I Domenego Scandella, called Menocchio of Montereal, am a baptized Christian and have always lived in a Christian way and have always performed Christian works, and I have always been obedient to my superiors and to my spiritual fathers to the best of my power, and always, morning and night, I crossed myself with the sign of the holy cross, saying, 'in the name of the Father and of the Son and of the Holy Spirit.' And I recited the Pater Noster and the Ave Maria and the Credo with a prayer to our Lord and one to the Madonna. It is indeed true that I thought and believed and said, as appears in the trial records, things against the commandments of God and of the Holy Church. I said them through the will of the false spirit who blinded my intellect and memory and will, making me think, believe, and say what was false and not true, and so I confess that I thought and believed and said what was false and not true and so I gave my opinion but I did not say that it was the truth.

I want to say four words briefly as an example from Joseph, son of Jacob, when he was speaking with his father and with his brothers about certain dreams that revealed that they should adore him. For this his brothers became angry with him and wanted to kill him, but it did not please God that they should kill him, but, rather, that they should sell him. And so they sold him to certain Egyptian merchants who took him to Egypt where he was thrown in prison because of some transgressions. And the king Pharaoh had a dream where he thought he saw seven fat cows and seven lean ones, and no one could interpret this dream for him. He was told that there was a youth in prison who would know how to explain it, and so he was taken from prison and led before the king. Joseph told him that the fat ones meant seven years of plenty, and the lean ones seven years of famine in which it would not be possible to find grain even to buy. And it came to pass that in Canaan it was not possible to find grain, even to buy, and so the king believed him and made him chief and governor over the entire kingdom of Egypt. Then came the abundance and Joseph set aside enough grain to last for more than twenty years; then came the famine when it was not possible to find grain, even to buy. And Jacob knew that grain was being sold in Egypt and sent ten of his sons with their animals to Egypt. They were recognized by their brother, and with the king's permission he had his father summoned with all his family and goods. And so they lived together in Egypt and the brothers stayed unwillingly, fearful because they had sold him. When Joseph saw that they were staying unwillingly he said to them: 'Do not be unhappy because you sold me, it was not your doing but the will of God so that he could provide for our needs; so be of good cheer because I forgive you with all my heart.'[55] Similarly, I had been speaking with my brothers and spiritual fathers and they accused me, sold me as it were to the most reverend father inquisitor, and he had me brought to this Holy Office and put in prison. But I do not blame them, because it was the will of God. Although I do not know if they are spiritual brothers or fathers, however, I pardon them all who were the cause of it, so that God may forgive me just as I forgive them.

There are four reasons why God wanted me to be taken to this Holy Office: first, to confess my errors; second, to do penance for my sins; third, to free me from the false spirit; fourth, to give an example to my children and to all my spiritual brothers, so that they would not fall into these errors. Therefore, if I thought and believed and said and worked against the commandments of God and of the Holy Church, I am sad and sorrowful, repentant and unhappy. So I say '*mea colpa, mea massima colpa*,' and for the remission of all my sins I ask forgiveness and mercy of the most Holy Trinity, Father and Son and Holy Spirit, and next of the glorious Virgin Mary and of all the saints in paradise,[56] and also of your most holy and most reverend and most illustrious justice, so that you will want to pardon me and have mercy on me. And so I beg you in the name of the passion of Our Lord Jesus Christ that you should not want to sentence me either in anger or in justice, but rather with love and with charity and with mercy. You know that Our Lord Jesus Christ was merciful and forgiving, and

---

[55] The account of Joseph in Egypt is in Gn chaps. 37; 39–45. The saying attributed to Joseph recalls Gn 45: 5–8.

[56] It is an echo of the *Confiteor*, which was recited at the commencement of the Mass both by the priest and those assisting him: "Confiteor Deo omnipotenti, beatae Mariae semper Virgini, beato Michaeli archangelo, beato Ioanni Baptistae, sanctis apostolis Petro et Paulo, omnibus sanctis (. . .), quia peccavi nimis cogitatione, verbo et opere: mea culpa, mea culpa, mea maxima culpa": see any *Ordo missae* in a Latin missal.

is and always will be; he forgave Mary Magdalen who was a sinner, Saint Peter who denied him, the thief who stole, the Jews who crucified him, and Saint Thomas who would not believe until he had seen and touched.[57] And so I firmly believe that he will forgive and have mercy on me.

I have done penance in a dark prison one hundred and four days, in shame and disgrace and with the ruin and desperation of my house and my children. Therefore, I beg you for love of Our Lord Jesus Christ and of his glorious mother the Virgin Mary that you change it in charity and in mercy and not be the cause of separating me from the company of my children whom God gave to me for my happiness and my comfort. And so I promise never again to fall into these errors, but instead to be obedient to all my superiors and to my spiritual fathers in everything they will command me to do, and nothing else. I await your most holy, revered, and illustrious sentence with its lesson to live as a Christian, so that I may teach my children to be true Christians.

These have been the causes of my errors: first, I believed in the two commandments, love God and love your neighbor, and that this was enough;[58] second, because I read that book of Mandeville about many kinds of races and different laws, which sorely troubled me; third, my mind and thought were making me know things that were improper; fourth, the false spirit was always tormenting me teaching me what was false and was not the truth; fifth, the disagreement that existed between me and the parish priest; sixth, that I worked and exhausted myself and became weak and because of this I could not obey the commandments of God and of the Holy Church in all things.

And so I make my defense with a plea for pardon and mercy, and not anger or justice, and I ask of Our Lord Jesus Christ and of you mercy and forgiveness and not anger or justice. And do not pay attention to my falseness and ignorance.

---

[57] See respectively Lk 7: 36–50; Mt 26: 69–75 and parallels; Lk 23: 39–43; 23: 34; Jn 20: 24–29.

[58] Mt 22: 36–40.

[17 May 1584]

Since the reverend and most excellent the aforesaid lord vicar, as well as the father inquisitor, desired to come to a resolution of the present trial, sitting in the audience chamber of the palace of the most illustrious *podestà*, in the presence and with the participation of the lord Pietro Zorzi, most worthy *podestà* of the land of Portogruaro, having summoned before them the excellent signor Girolamo Pigozzino and the excellent signor Valerio Trappola dai Colli to have their opinion, they ordered that the present trial records be read loudly, and they were read by me the notary word for word.

[19 May 1584]

The excellent aforesaid doctors, after having consulted between themselves with deliberation and diligence, and after having carefully examined, discussed, and considered all the legal acts in the present trial, declared that the forenamed Domenico was not only a formal heretic, but also a heresiarch.

28 May 1584

Held in the church of San Francesco in Portogruaro, before the forenamed reverend father inquisitor, present Ser Sebastiano Scandella of Montereale, who, after he took an oath and physically laid his hand on Scripture, was questioned by the reverend father inquisitor, and replied: "I no longer have the book[59] that your lordship asks me about, because when I got it back from my uncle Menego it was burned, as was ordered by the priest, and my wife burned it in the oven."

Signora Flor, wife of Sebastiano Scandella, questioned after taking an oath to tell the truth administered by the reverend father inquisitor, replied: "I threw the book that your lordship asks me about into the oven and I burned it as was ordered by the reverend priest."

Day [lacking date]

The reverend lord judges ordered the aforesaid Domenico to be summoned to hear his sentence in the church of Sant' Andrea on the next day and this morning the guard Battista Parvis reported that the summons had been delivered.

See the sentence in the book of sentences.

---

[59] It is the vernacular Bible: cf. note 27.

Abjuration of Domenico Scandella
Portogruaro, 20–31 May 1584

I, Domenego Scandella, called Menocchio of Montereale, of the diocese of Concordia, standing personally before you the venerable and reverend lord Giovanni Battista Maro, canon of Concordia and vicar general, and the reverend father Fra Felice Montefalco, doctor of sacred theology and for the entire patriarchate of Aquileia and the diocese of Concordia inquisitor general especially delegated by the Holy Apostolic See, with the sacrosanct Gospels before me and touching them with my own hands, I swear that I believe in my heart and confess with my mouth this holy Catholic and apostolic faith, which the Holy Roman Church believes, confesses, preaches and observes. Consequently, I abjure, revoke, detest and renounce every heresy of whatever condition and sect raised against the Holy Catholic and Apostolic Roman Church. Moreover, I swear to believe in my heart and confess with my mouth:

that the authority of the supreme pontiff and priests of the holy Church is true; that they are supported and governed by the Holy Spirit and what they do in guiding the Church is in accord with the regulations, orders and will of God; that they have a better knowledge of God than I; that the supreme pontiff and the priests of the Church have a greater power than I; that such authority comes from Christ and was left by him to the Holy Church, and that authority: 'Whatever you bind on earth, etc.,'[60] I confess to be true;

similarly that the statutes, orders and laws of the Church are true, that they can be fulfilled, and that they are not a business; that the Church is supported and governed by the Holy Spirit, and that it is supported and governed according to the regulations and injunctions given by Christ;

similarly that the saints are to be adored and revered, that their relics are to be revered and honored, that they are of greater reverence than ours, when we die; that we must adore and revere the image of Christ and of the saints as is commanded and desired by the holy Roman Church;

similarly that indulgences are founded on the merits of Christ and in the merits of the glorious Virgin and saints of God;

that the prayers we offer in Church assist souls to be freed from

---

[60] Mt 16: 19.

purgatory; that the prayers and ceremonies that are performed by the Church and by the faithful over the burial places of the dead are of value; that the Masses, prayers, charities and other deeds done for the dead are of value; that the good works done after this life are of value for souls in purgatory;

similarly that Lent should be observed at the time and in the way commanded by the Holy Roman Church; that fasting calls for a single meal in a day; that fasting not only purges the intellect, but is a meritorious act; that on fast days man must abstain from foods prohibited by the Holy Church;

similarly that in sermons it is permissible to bring in the authority of the saints in Sacred Scripture; that the preacher may preach about hell and heaven; that the preaching practiced in the Church of God is not a business;

similarly that the New and Old Testaments are revealed by God, that they are not human inventions nor commerce invented by men; that what is written in the books of the Gospels is all true and there is no real contradiction, and that the evangelists have written through revelation and what was dictated by the Holy Spirit, that Scripture does not deceive, but assures men's spiritual life, that it does not perpetrate fraud of any kind and that it especially speaks the highest truth when it testifies about the existence of God and where it is written by David in the Psalms not through the human spirit, but under the dictation of the Holy Spirit;

similarly that the precepts of God are those found in the sacred writings of either Testament and not those devised by men out of their own invention; that the injunction to love God is greater than the one to love one's neighbor; that at the Last Judgment God's love will not be lacking;

similarly that even though all creatures have been created by God, just the same they can be blessed by priests; that priestly blessing brings sanctification to the object blessed; that the blessing performed by a lay person is not of the same value as that of the priest, even though the lay person should say the same words in the benediction as the priest; that God has not bestowed equally on everyone the faculty of imparting benediction, but more on priests than on others, and more on popes than on priests;

similarly that the earthly paradise at the beginning of the world

was created by God as holy Genesis tells us;[61] that the homes of the
rich are not the earthly paradise;

similarly that God created the universe out of nothing, that chaos
was not eternal with God, that the world was not created nor formed
from chaos; neither is it true that the elements collided in the chaos
and that from this collision was generated a foam, nor that from this
foam worms were generated, nor men from worms, nor is it true that
the supreme man is God. It is true that the world was made and
created by God instantly; that God not only foresaw what was to be
done, but made everything; that the world was not made or constructed by angels; that the sphere of the sun is not the chamber of God
where he bestows his bliss; and the splendor that we see radiating from
the sun comes from the sun; that there are not two principles in the
universal world, good and evil, namely God and the Devil, but one
only, who is God;

similarly that the angels were not made from worms; that the
opinion is false that states a substance resembling rotten cheese formed
out of the chaos and is the substance from which were formed worms
and from worms angels; that angels are not of the same nature as God,
angels are made by God, angels were not produced by nature, angels
were not made at the same moment in eternity as God; that it is false
to say angels were made out of the same mass and substance as God
because angels were created; that it is false to claim that the Holy
Spirit is of the same nature as angels, and that angels made the whole
world, or that God selected a supreme angel and made the Holy Spirit
bestowing upon him his knowledge, will and power, so that this
supreme angel governed the world in the guise of God's steward, and
that this angel taught the other angels how to create the world; that
angelic nature is not divided into four orders, but in nine;

similarly that Lucifer was created the supreme angel by God, and
desired to be equal to God; that the vacant celestial thrones shall not
be filled by spirits made from air, water, earth, and fire, but created
from nothing;

similarly that at the beginning not many men, nor in diverse parts
of the world, but one single man only was created by God; that man
was made by God and not by the angels, whose soul was created by
God and the body formed from the earth and not out of metal; that

---

[61] Gn 2: 8–17.

man is made in the image and likeness of God, as told in the sacred book of Genesis;[62] it is false to say that man was made in the image of an angel and not in the image of God; it is false to say that the image and resemblance that man shares with the Holy Spirit means that since the Holy Spirit is made from the whole world and from the four elements, man is made in the same way. It is true that the infant in the mother's womb after a determinate period receives a rational soul, as all sacred theologians teach, and not as soon as it is born; that the angel given to it by God is not the soul;

similarly it is true that the soul is immortal and when the body dies the soul does not die, and even if the soul is separated from the body, it does not die when the body dies; that in man there are not two rational souls, one good and the other bad; that when the body dies, intellect, memory and will do not die, and after the present life our soul possesses intellect, memory and will; that after the present life the soul comprehends, remembers and wills; that soul and angel are not one and the same thing; that the soul is created out of nothing and not made from the elements; that the soul is not an angel, nor made from the four elements, nor issues from human seed;

similarly it is true that original sin is contracted in the maternal womb since man has a soul in the mother's womb and can receive original sin; that man does not sin before he can reason; that when he leaves the mother's womb and begins to nurse, he does not sin; that the types of mortal sins are those identified by the Holy Church and not those thought up by man on his own; that to blaspheme God and the saints is a sin; that to blaspheme is not an art; it is false to say that it is the only sin to harm one's neighbor and nothing else;

similarly that of human kind some have been eternally predestined by God to enjoy the benefits of eternal life, that those who have been predestined to enjoy eternal life are preordained by God, that some in particular were foreordained to enjoy the benefits of eternal life, that all those who were preordained were predestined; that God has special knowledge of all those who are to be saved; that those who predestined shall attain eternal bliss will do so through the grace of God, as St. Paul said: 'He saved us, not because of deeds done by us in righteousness, but in virtue of his own mercy';[63] that without grace our own

---

[62] Ibid. 1: 26.
[63] Ti 3: 5.

works would not have sufficed for our salvation; that we are not saved because we are born under a lucky star or have good fortune;

similarly that God summons a few to himself who have a particular vocation, whom he then justifies; but Turks, Jews, Marrani, heretics, Christians and all the people in the world are not called equally to a special vocation;

similarly that of those who are justified, all are by means of the passion and death of Christ, and that the grace we receive in the justification from God is through the merits of Christ;

similarly it is false to say that a person, as soon as it is born, is baptized by God; baptism is one of the sacraments of the Holy Church, to baptize is not a human invention, baptism was ordained by God; it is false to say that priests devour souls before they are born and continue to devour them even after their death;

similarly confirmation is one of the sacraments of the Church and instituted by Christ, is not an invention of men, nor is it a business for ecclesiastics; it is false to say that everyone has the Holy Spirit and does not need confirmation; it is false to say that ecclesiastics announcing this sacrament pretend to know the divine will and do not know it;

similarly marriage is one of the sacraments of the Church instituted by Christ, and not a mere human invention; it is not sufficient for a man and a woman to touch each other's hand, but the words of those present are necessary which give form to the marriage;[64] that the ceremonies used by the Holy Roman Church in this and in other sacraments are not damnable;

similarly that confession is necessary, is one of the sacraments of the Church, and was instituted by God; it is false to say that confessing to priests is of no more use than confessing to a tree; it does not suffice to confess to God when we can have a confessor for our salvation; we have to confess our sins to priests not only to receive penance, but also absolution; it is false to say that man needs to go to priests just to learn his penance; the layman, however well he may know the penances that are given for sinning, cannot hear confession, however much he may know of what is needed to atone for one's sins, and thus people must go to priests to confess themselves;

similarly that in the host consecrated by the priest there is the true

---

[64] See the decisions on the rites of marriage taken in 1563 by the Council of Trent in *Conciliorum oecumenicorum decreta*, 755–57.

body of Christ, that the bread was transubstantiated into the true body of Christ; that it is heresy to say it is only a piece of dough, since under those elements is the true body of Christ, and thus divinity needs to be there, even though one does not see one or the other; that it is one of the sacraments instituted by Christ; to say that only the Holy Spirit and not Christ descends there is false; to say that when man goes to communion and takes that sacrament he receives the Holy Spirit and not Christ is false; to say that it is a human invention is false;

similarly that holy orders is one of the sacraments of the Church, was instituted by Christ, and is not a business for the benefit of churchmen; to say that since the spirit of God is in everyone, therefore all are priests, is false; to say that everyone, as long as he has studied, can be a priest without being ordained is false;

similarly that extreme unction is one of the sacraments of the Church, was established by Christ and is necessary for those who are close to death; that anointing the body benefits the spirit;

similarly that the universal resurrection shall be as proclaimed in Scripture; it is not impossible for man to be resurrected;

similarly to say that in the Universal Judgment Christ will not proclaim the sentence, but will only reconcile men with God, is false;

similarly to say that the Holy Spirit is presently given to all—to Turks and Jews—so that they can be saved, is an error; to say that all will be saved—Jews, Turks, pagans, Christians, heretics and infidels— is an error; to say that all will be saved in the same way and that they will attain the same level of bliss is an error; to say that our bliss consists in being placed where we can see all the things of this world is an error; to say that our bliss does not lie in God is an error; that our bliss consists only in seeing the things of this world is an error; that the blessed in their bliss do not see everything in God, but in their own beings, is an error; that only the bliss of the soul and not that of the body is dispensed is an error;

similarly that the Blessed Virgin conceived by the Holy Spirit, who was a virgin during the birth and after the birth, brought forth Christ without sin; to say that any human creature is greater than the Blessed Virgin is an error; to say that the Blessed Virgin was an adulteress is an error; to say that Mary was a sinner is an error;

similarly to say that air and everything that we see is God is an error; to say that God was made from worms is an error; that God is a bit of air, and whatever is in man is an error; to deny that God exists is an error; to say that God does not look after things here is an error; that God was made from chaos is an error; to say that God received energy in the movement of the chaos is an error; to say that God grows from imperfection to perfection is an error; that God did not exist before the chaos is an error; to say that God in the instant of eternity does not know anything and is not alive is an error; to say that God at the beginning of time began to understand is an error; to say that God at the beginning of time began to live is an error; to say that comprehension and life came to God as they come to an infant in the mother's womb is an error; to say that the divine intellect, when it began to comprehend, received awareness of all things universally and not in particular is an error; to say that God does not know all the single things that have occurred, are presently occurring and shall occur is an error; to say that the divine intellect is not moved by its own essence in the comprehension of all things is an error; to say that the divine intellect grasps confusedly its awareness from the chaos in which are all things confusedly is an error; to say that the divine intellect, in the same way as ours, proceeds from confused to precise knowledge is an error; to say that in God grows awareness, will and power, as it does with us is an error; to say that will and power are actually separate in God is an error; that will is not sufficient to God, but he also needs power, as with us is an error; to say that the power of God is nothing else than accomplishing a task through skilled workmen is an error; to say that God made nothing himself is an error; to say that he created everything by means of angels is an error; to say that God could not have so quickly created the world as he did through the angels is an error; to say that God cannot create out of nothing is an error.

Similarly I say with my mouth and confess with my heart that in the most holy Trinity there are three distinct persons in a unity of essence, possessing the same nature, the same divinity, equality in glory, co-eternal majesty, equality of power; none of the three has been created or made; all are immense, infinite, eternal, and omnipotent; the Father is God, the Son is God, the Holy Spirit is God, but they are not three Gods, but one only God; to say that the Holy Trinity was made by chance is an error; to say that it was made only for the Universal Judgment is an error.

Similarly I say with my mouth and confess with my heart that the eternal Father does not have precedence over the Son and the Holy Spirit, that he together with the Son and the Holy Spirit, is God and is of one substance with the Son and the Holy Spirit, with the same divinity, the same glory, the same majesty, the same power, the same intellect, the same memory, the same will; to say that he was with chaos from eternity and was made from the chaos, is an error; to say that in the beginning he was imperfect and then became perfect is an error.

Similarly I say with my mouth and confess with my heart that God has a natural Son, that the eternal Word is the natural Son of God, that Christ is the Son of God by nature; that Abel, Noah, Abraham, Isaac, Jacob, Moses are not the sons of God as is Christ, who is of the substance of the Father, who is of the same perfect substance as the Father, and not less, who is of the same substance and perfection of substance as the Holy Spirit, and has the same divinity as the Father and the Holy Spirit, who is God, co-equal in glory to the Father and the Holy Spirit, is co-eternal in majesty with the Father and the Holy Spirit, has the same intellect, memory and will as the Father and the Holy Spirit, the same omnipotence as the Father and the Holy Spirit, is uncreated, immense and infinite, is not later in time or lesser in nature to the Father or to the Holy Spirit, he is not inferior to the Father or to the Holy Spirit, receives his essence from the Father, and not from the Father and the Holy Spirit; whatever he has, has all been received from the Father; Christ is not pure creature, but God and man, and he was in the beginning and in the instant of eternity, since God was with God and was God, as John teaches;[65] he is the author of the world: everything is done for him and without him nothing can be done;[66] his acts cannot be measured in time; he became flesh in the womb of Mary Virgin through the work and power of the Holy Spirit; his mother was a virgin before the birth, during the birth and after the birth; to say that Christ was a bastard or the natural son of St. Joseph is an error; to say that the soul of Christ either is one of the angels made at the beginning of the world, or made by the Holy Spirit from the four elements like ours is an error; to say that he had two spirits in his heart, one good and the other bad is an error; to say that Christ is not God, but a prophet or a great man sent by God is an error; to say that it showed little wisdom on Christ's part, if he is omnipotent, as he is said to be, to let himself be killed, and to say that Christ let himself be hung like a beast is an error; Christ cannot sin by

---

[65] Jn 1: 1.
[66] Ibid. 1: 3.

nature and was tempted outwardly not inwardly; he was crucified; when Christ died, his intellect, memory, and will did not die; when Christ died, his most holy soul did not die; Christ died for our sins; to say that the death of Christ is of no other benefit than that of serving as a mirror to us of his patience is an error; when Christ died, his most holy soul descended into limbo and did not immediately rise up to heaven; Christ was resurrected on the third day; the body of Christ is in heaven united to his soul and to his divinity; after his resurrection he reappeared to his disciples for forty days before ascending to heaven; he is the object of our bliss; to say that after the spirit of Christ ascended to heaven, he was sent by the Holy Spirit to free the souls in limbo, is an error.

Similarly I confess with my mouth and believe with my heart that the Holy Spirit exists, that he has the same being, essence and nature as the Father and the Son, that he is not less perfect in his essence than the Father and the Son, that he is not more perfect in his essence than the Son, that he shares his divinity with the Father and the Son, that he is God and not a creature, that he is not the noblest angel in the sky; he has equality of glory, co-eternity of majesty with the Father and the Son, has the same intellect, memory and will as the Father and the Son, and has the same power as the Father and the Son; he is uncreated, immense, eternal and infinite, not made from the substance of the chaos, proceeds from the Father and the Son, is neither made nor created, but proceeds, not helped by the nature of the chaos; what he has is from the Father and the Son; he does not precede or come after the Father and the Son, nor is he inferior to the Father and the Son; he was at the beginning and in the instant of eternity with the Father and the Son, and made everything with the Father and the Son without angelic ministry, and can create from nothing and is not a simple steward of God, and from eternity knew what had to be done to create the universe; that he governs the Holy Church, that he is not given equally to all, but in measure; to say that he is given to all people in the world, Jews, Turks, heretics and Christians, is an error.

And consequently I abjure, renounce, detest, and revoke that heresy damned by the holy Catholic, Roman and apostolic Church which falsely and untruthfully affirms:

that the authority of the supreme pontiff and priests of the Holy Church is not true; that the aforesaid prelates are not sustained and governed by the Holy Spirit; that what they do in maintaining the Church is not in accordance with the regulations, ordinances and will of God; that God is known more perfectly by me Domenico Scandella, who is simple and ignorant, than by the priests of the Church; that the supreme pontiff and prelates of the Church do not have greater power than a layman; that their authority does not come from Christ and that their authority was not left in the Holy Church by Christ; that the injunction 'Whatever you bind on earth, etc.'[67] is false;

similarly that the statutes, ordinances and laws of the Church are not true; that they cannot be done anew, that they are all a business run by ecclesiastics; that the Church is not sustained and governed by the Holy Spirit, that the Church is not governed in accordance with the regulations and injunctions laid down by Christ;

similarly that saints are not to be adored, that their relics are not to be revered and honored, and are not deserving greater veneration than ours when we die; that images of Christ and the saints are not to be adored and revered as commanded and desired by the Holy Roman Church;

similarly that indulgences are not based on the merits of Christ, indulgences are not based on the merits of the glorious Virgin nor of the saints;

similarly that the prayers we offer in Church to free the souls in Purgatory are of no value; that the prayers and ceremonies performed in Church and by the faithful at burial places of the dead are damnable and of no utility whatever; that the Masses, prayers, charity and other good works performed for the souls of the dead are of no utility; that the good works done after the present life for souls in purgatory are of no value.

Similarly I abjure, renounce, detest and revoke that heresy damned by the Holy Church which falsely and untruthfully affirms that we should not observe Lent at the time and in the way commanded by the Holy Roman Church; that while fasting we can eat three or four times a day; that fasting earns no merits of any kind; that on fast days we do not need to abstain from foods prohibited by Holy Mother Church;

similarly that in sermons it is not permissible to invoke the authority of saints or of Holy Scripture; that it is an error for the Catholic preacher to preach about hell and heaven; that preaching is just a business;

similarly that the New and Old Testaments were not revealed by

---

[67] Mt 16: 19.

God, that they are a human invention, and the commerce of men; that what is written in the books of the Gospels is all a lie, that in the Gospels there is a real and true contradiction, that the evangelists did not write through revelation and the dictation of the Holy Spirit; that Scripture betrays men, that Scripture is fraudulent and lying especially when it alleges that God exists; that what was written by David in the Psalms was not through the revelation of the Holy Spirit, but was made up out of his head;

similarly that the precepts of God are not those found in the Bible, but those that men make up themselves; that the precept to love one's neighbor is better than to love God; that in the Universal Judgment the precept to love God will receive no consideration.

Similarly I abjure, renounce, detest and revoke that heresy damned by the Holy Roman Church which falsely and untruthfully affirms that priests cannot bless since all creatures were made by God; that the priestly blessing does not sanctify the object blessed; that the benediction imparted by a layman is in itself of as much efficacy as that of the priest; that if the layman should use the same words in the benediction as employed by the priest, his benediction would be of as much value as the priest's; that God gave equal authority to everyone to bless, to priests and pontiffs and laymen in the same measure;

similarly that what the holy Genesis recounts about the earthly paradise being created at the beginning of the world is false,[68] that the real earthly paradise are the homes of gentlemen and the rich;

similarly that God did not create anything in the world, that the chaos was eternal with God, that the world was made from chaos, and that when the elements were jarred against each other in the chaos, from this agitation a foam resulted, which in turn generated worms, and from the worms came men; it is true that the supreme man is God; the world was not made and created by God immediately, and God foresaw what had to be done but did not make the entire world, because the world was made and established by angels; that the sphere of the sun is the chamber of God, where he dispenses bliss; that the splendor radiating from the sun is not from it, but is a splendor that comes from God; that there are two principles in the world, one good and the other evil: the Devil and God.

Similarly I abjure, renounce, detest and revoke that heresy damned

---

[68] Gn 2: 8–17.

by the Holy Roman Church which falsely and untruthfully affirms that angels were made from worms; that the opinion is true that teaches that from the chaos a substance formed in the same way as rotten cheese and from it came worms, and from the worms, angels; that angels are of the same nature as God, are not made by God, were produced by nature, and created in the same instant in eternity as God; that angels were made from the same mass and substance as God, and were not created by God; that the Holy Spirit is of the same nature as angels, and that angels made the whole world; that God elected a supreme angel and made it the Holy Spirit, giving to it his knowledge, will and power; that this supreme angel governs the world in the guise of a steward of God; that this supreme angel taught other angels how to make the world, and that angelic nature is divided into four orders and not as St. Dionysius divided them;

similarly that Lucifer was not the supreme angel created by God and that he did not desire equality with God; that the celestial thrones will be filled by spirits made of air, water, earth and fire;

similarly that in the beginning of the world not a single man, but many men were created in different parts of the world; that man was created by the angels and not by God, whose soul was not created by God and whose body was made of a pure metal which is gold; that man is not made in God's image and likeness, as is written in Scripture;[69] that man is made in the image of an angel and not in the image of God; it is true to say and affirm that the image and likeness that man bears to the Holy Spirit consists in this, that since the Holy Spirit was made from the whole world and from the four elements, so it made man; that the infant in the mother's womb never receives a rational soul, but does as soon as it is born; that the angel God gives to it is not the soul.

Similarly I abjure, renounce, detest and revoke that heresy damned by the Holy Roman Church which falsely and untruthfully affirms that the soul is mortal, that when the body dies, the soul dies, that since the soul is separate from the body, it dies with the body; that in man there are two rational souls, one good and one bad; that when the body dies, the intellect, memory and will die; after the present life the soul does not comprehend, remember or have desires; that soul and angel are one and the same thing; that the soul cannot be made from

---

[69] Ibid. 1: 26.

nothing, but is made from the elements; that the soul is either an angel or made by the Holy Spirit from the four elements, or extracted from the human seed;

similarly that original sin is not contracted in the mother's womb, since man does not have a soul in the mother's womb; that man sins before he has the use of reason; that when he leaves the mother's womb and when he begins to nurse, he sins; that the types of mortal sins are those that man makes up himself, and not those designated by the Church; that to blaspheme God and the saints is not a sin; that to blaspheme is an art; it is only a sin to harm one's neighbor, not something else;

similarly that no one who has human nature has been predestined by God to enjoy the fruits of eternal life; that all those who shall enjoy eternal bliss were not all foreseen in particular but universally; that God does not have particular knowledge of all those who will be saved; that those who attain eternal bliss will not do so through the grace of God, since our works will suffice without the grace of God; that to be born under a lucky star and good fortune are why we are saved.

Similarly I abjure, renounce, detest and revoke that heresy damned by the Holy Roman Church which falsely and untruthfully affirms that God does not call to himself and then save people with a special vocation; that all men in the world are called equally by God with a special vocation: Turks, Jews, Marrani, heretics and Christians;

similarly that the justified are not justified through the death and passion of Christ; that the grace which they receive in God's justification, is not through Christ's merits;

similarly it is true to say that as soon as one is born, he is baptized by God; that baptism is not one of the sacraments of the Holy Church, that baptism is a human invention and was not instituted by Christ; and it is equally true that priests devour souls before they are born and continually devour them even after their death;

similarly that confirmation is not one of the sacraments of the Church, that it was not established by Christ, that it is a human invention, and a business for the benefit of religious; it is true to say that everyone possesses the Holy Spirit and does not need confirmation, and that when religious proclaim this sacrament they pretend to know divine will, but do not know it.

Similarly I abjure, renounce, detest and revoke that heresy damned by the Holy Roman Church which falsely and untruthfully affirms that confession is not necessary, that it is not one of the sacraments of the

Church, and that it was not established by God; that to confess oneself to a priest is of as much use as confessing to a tree; that it is enough to confess to God; that we need to confess our sins to priests only so that we can receive penance; that lay persons who know the penance have no need to go and confess to priests;

similarly that in the host consecrated by the priest there is not the true body of Christ, that bread is not transubstantiated into the true body of Christ; that it is not a heresy to say the consecrated host is only a piece of dough, that the body of Christ is not under those components, that Christ is not in the host, or he would be seen; that it is not one of the sacraments of the Church, and not instituted by Christ; that only the Holy Spirit and not Christ descends into it; that when man receives this sacrament, he receives the Holy Spirit, not Christ; that this sacrament is a human invention;

similarly that holy orders is not one of the sacraments of the Church, was not established by Christ, and is a business for the benefit of religious; that all are priests, whether laymen or religious, because all receive God's spirit; that anyone who has studied can be a priest without being ordained.

Similarly I abjure, renounce, detest and revoke that heresy damned by the Holy Roman Church which falsely and untruthfully affirms that extreme unction is not one of the sacraments of the Church, was not established by Christ, is not needed by those about to die, and is of no value at all; that to anoint the body is of no avail to the spirit;

similarly that the universal resurrection will not take place, that it is not possible for man to be resurrected; equally to say that at the Universal Judgment Christ will not pronounce the sentence, but will be there only for the remembrance of God;

similarly that the Holy Spirit actually is given to all: to Turks, Jews, Christians, heretics, so that they will be saved; that all men of whatsoever generation not only will be saved, but will be saved in the same way, and all will attain a similar state of bliss; that our bliss consists in being placed where we can see all the things of this world; that our bliss does not consist in seeing God face to face; that our bliss consists only in seeing the things of this world; that the blessed in their bliss do not contemplate everything in God, but in their own beings; that only the bliss of the soul and not of the body exists;

similarly that the Blessed Virgin did not conceive through the Holy Spirit, that she was not a virgin during the birth and after the birth, and that she did not give birth to Christ without sin; that certain mere creatures are superior to the Blessed Virgin; that the Blessed Virgin was an adulteress and sinner.

Similarly I abjure, renounce, detest, and revoke that heresy damned by the Holy Roman Church which falsely and untruthfully affirms that air and whatever we see is God, that God is made from worms, that God is a little air and whatever is in man; that God does not exist, otherwise we would see him; that God does not look after the things of this world; that God came out of the chaos and received his power to act from the movement of the chaos; that God grows from imperfect to perfect and did not exist before the chaos; that God at the beginning of eternity did not know any thing, nor was he alive; that at the beginning of time God commenced to comprehend and to live; that as far as understanding and living is concerned, it was the same for God as for the infant in the mother's womb; that the divine intellect, when it began to comprehend, had awareness of all things universally but not particularly; that God does not know all the particular things that have been, are, and shall be; that the divine intellect is not moved by the divine essence in the cognition of all things; that the divine intellect received its cognition from the chaos in which all things exist confusedly; that the divine intellect, like ours, proceeds from a confused to a precise cognition; in God grew cognition, will, and power, as they do with us; that will and power in God are really distinct as they are with us; that will does not suffice to God, who also needs power, just as with us; that the power of God is nothing other than accomplishing his work through skilled workers; that God accomplished nothing himself and did everything through the angels, and that God could not have made the world as quickly as he did through the angels; that God from nothing cannot create or make anything.

Similarly I abjure, renounce, detest and revoke that heresy damned by the Holy Church which falsely and untruthfully affirms that there are not three divine persons in one unity of essence, that they do not have the same nature, the same divinity, the same quality of glory, the same co-eternity of majesty, or equality of power; that all three are not uncreated, that two have been made, that all three are not immense and infinite, but two are measurable and finite, that all three are not eternal and omnipotent, that the Father is God, and the Son and the Holy Spirit are creatures; that the Trinity was made by chance and made only for the Universal Judgment;

similarly that the eternal Father precedes the Son and the Holy Spirit, that he is God and not the Son and the Holy Spirit, that he does not have the same essence as the Son and the Holy Spirit, not the same divinity, not the same glory, not the same majesty, not the same power with the Son and the Holy Spirit; that he does not have the same intellect, the same memory, the same will as the Son and the Holy Spirit; that eternally he was with the chaos and made at the time of the chaos; that at the beginning he was imperfect and then became perfect.

Similarly I abjure, renounce, detest and revoke that heresy damned by the Sacrosanct Roman Church that falsely and untruthfully affirms that God does not have a natural Son, that the Word is not the natural Son of God, that Christ is not the Son of God by nature, that Abel, Noah, Abraham, Isaac, Jacob, and Moses are sons of God like Christ, that the Son of God is not consubstantial with the Father, that he is not of the same perfection of substance as the Father, but less, that he is not consubstantial nor of the same perfection of substance as the Holy Spirit, nor does he have the same divinity as the Father and the Holy Spirit; that he is not God but pure creature, that he is not co-equal in glory to the Father and the Holy Spirit, does not have the co-eternity of majesty with the Father and the Holy Spirit, does not have the same intellect, memory and will of the Father and the Holy Spirit, does not have the same power as the Holy Spirit; that he is not uncreated, nor immense, nor infinite; that he is later in time and inferior in nature to the Father and to the Holy Spirit; that he is less than the Father and the Holy Spirit; that he receives his essence from the Father and from the Holy Spirit; that what he has is all from the Father and from the Holy Spirit; that Christ is not God, but pure creature and pure man; that the Son was not at the beginning and from eternity; that he was not with God, was not God, that he is not the author of the world, nor was it made by him; that the world was made without him; that his actions are measured by time; that he did not become flesh in the womb of Mary Virgin through the act and power of the Holy Spirit; that his mother was not a virgin before, during and after the birth; that he was a bastard or the natural son of Saint Joseph; that the soul of Christ is either one of the angels made at the beginning of the world, or was made by the Holy Spirit from the four elements, like ours; that he had two spirits in his heart, one good and the other bad; that Christ is not God, but a prophet or some great man sent by God; that it would have shown little wisdom on Christ's part, being omnipotent, as it is said, to let himself be killed; that Christ let himself be hung like a beast; that Christ is not sinless by nature, that Christ was tempted externally and internally; that it was not Christ who was crucified but Simon the Cyrenian; that when Christ died, his intellect, memory and will died; that when Christ died, his most holy soul died; that Christ did not die for our sins; that the death of Christ is of no other benefit, than as a mirror of his patience for us; when Christ died, his most holy soul did not descend into limbo, but immediately ascended to heaven; that Christ did not rise again on the third day; that the body of Christ is not united with its soul in heaven; that he did not appear to his disciples after his resurrection for forty days before he ascended to heaven; that he is not the object of our bliss, and that after the spirit of Christ ascended to heaven, it was sent by the Holy Spirit to free the souls that were in limbo.

Similarly I abjure, renounce, detest and revoke that heresy damned by the sacred Roman Church which falsely and untruthfully affirms that the Holy Spirit does not exist because if it existed we would see it; that it does not have the same being, essence and nature as the Father and the Son, that it is of a less perfect essence than the Father and greater than the Son, that it does not have the same divinity as the Father and the Son, that it is not God and is a mere creature; that it is the most noble angel in the heavens; that it does not have the equality of glory and the co-eternity of majesty with the Father and the Son; that it does not have the same intellect, memory and will as the Father and the Son, nor the same power as the Father and the Son; that it is not uncreated, immense, eternal or infinite; that it is made from the substance of the chaos, proceeds from the Father and not from the Son, is neither created nor proceeding, but made, and formed from the nature of the chaos; that everything he has, he has from the Father and not from the Son; that he is subsequent in substance to the Father and prior to the Son, lesser than the Father and greater than the Son; that he was not at the beginning and from eternity with the Father and with the Son; that he did not make everything without the ministry of the angels; that he cannot create out of nothing, and is a simple steward of God; that in the instant of eternity he did not know what was to be done in the creation of the universe; that he does not govern the Holy Church, and that he is given equally to all: Jews, Turks, Marrani, Christians and heretics.

In addition, I swear and also promise that in the future I shall not hold, believe or consider any of the above heresies or any other; nor shall I dogmatize, teach or instruct anyone in any heresy whatever, nor will I knowingly keep prohibited and heretical books. In fact, I swear and promise that if I should know anyone infected with the stain of heresy, or who dogmatizes, teaches and instructs anyone in some heresy or error, or if I should learn that he has heretical books and writings, as soon as I shall be able and have the way to do it, I shall denounce and inform of it either you, monsignor vicar, or you, father inquisitor, or one of you or your successors or your vicars or their vicars.

In addition I swear and also promise that the penance which you will impose on me for the above sins, I shall not refuse nor oppose in any way, and shall fulfill to the best of my ability.

In addition I swear and also promise that I shall never try to run away, nor absent myself without your permission, license and approval; and, in fact, I swear and promise that each and every time I shall be sought out by both of you, or by one of you, or by your vicars and successors, or by any vicars under some other authority and summons, I shall present myself personally as promptly and conveniently as possible. May God help me and these sacred, saintly Gospels of God.

And if in the future I shall fail in any of the aforementioned things which I have sworn and abjured, or even some of them, God help me, that I may commit in the future, I want immediately to be considered a *relapsus,* and bind myself to the punishments reserved by law for the relapsed, after, however, they shall have been proven legitimately in judgment, or if I should confess that I have offended against the matters that I have here sworn against and abjured.

Sentence against Domenico Scandella
[Portogruaro, 20–31 May 1584]

Invoking the name of Christ, we Giovanni Battista Maro, doctor in canon and civil law, canon of Concordia and vicar general for spiritual and temporal affairs in the entire bishopric and diocese of Concordia of the most reverend and illustrious lord Pietro Querini, by grace of God and of the Apostolic See bishop of Concordia, and father Fra Felice da Montefalco, doctor of sacred theology, inquisitor general for the entire patriarchate of Aquileia and diocese of Concordia, especially delegated by the Holy Apostolic See, have considered that you Domenico Scandella, called Menocchio, of Montereale, in the diocese of Concordia, were denounced to us for heretical pravity both by public reputation and by persons worthy of faith, and that you have been infected with heresy for many years to the great ruin of your soul, an accusation which struck a harsh blow to our hearts. We, who through the office entrusted to us, have the responsibility of implanting the holy Catholic faith into all hearts and of extirpating heretical pravity from their minds, wishing, as we were and are obliged to do, to inform ourselves more certainly on these matters and to ascertain whether the rumor that had reached our ears was supported by some evidence, so that we could provide against it with appropriate measures if there was truth in the matter, we decided on 29 October 1583 to begin an inquest. On the 30th of the same month and on 2 February 1584 we examined witnesses, ordered your arrest on the 3rd of the same month and year, and interrogated you in the most appropriate way, based on the denunciations that we had received, on the following days: the 7th day of the above mentioned month and year, the 16th day, 22nd of the same, the 8th of March and 28th of April, and the 7th and 12th of May of the same year 1584. This was done under oath, and all the individual legal documents were compiled in accordance with the exigencies of justice and the obligations imposed by canonical sanctions.

In truth, desiring to conclude your case in an appropriate manner and see clearly what had emerged, whether you walked in the darkness or the light, and if you were infected with heresy or not, on the 12th of May we ordered that you be asked to prepare your defense, if you intended to make one. On the 17th of the current month you declined the offer, and instead presented only a statement written in your own hand. At the conclusion of the trial, we ordered that there assemble before us on the 17th day of this month a solemn college of experts in canon and civil law, since we knew that according to canonical norms, judicial proceedings are concluded when they are ratified by the opinions of a number of persons. We convoked it anew on the 19th day of the same month and received from it a sound, mature and carefully considered opinion from the forenamed experts, on the case as a whole and on its individual legal points. Having seen and diligently observed the merits of the trial and weighed on true scales everything it contained individually and as a whole, we found that you had fallen into multiple and almost unspeakable heretical pravity which you confessed yourself under oath. In fact, we determined that you had remained in this heretical pravity for about twenty years to the great peril of your soul and with scandal to the pious faithful, and that you were thus publicly judged by everyone, although you gave little thought to this poor reputation of yours until now.

You have possessed, kept and read books prohibited by the Holy Apostolic See and thus disregarded the sanctions of excommunication. We also learned that you often taught, argued and held doctrines against the Catholic faith not just with ecclesiastics, but also with simple uneducated people, with no little danger of corrupting their good intentions, which you could have accomplished very easily if God had not interposed his hand. We found that your soul was such, and so pertinacious in these heresies, that, even when warned, corrected and enlightened about the truth by many priests, including your own parish priest, nevertheless you remained with a hardened heart, despising everything.

We discovered the great evil that you uttered about the supreme pontiff and about the priests of the Church and their authority: you audaciously denied their sovereignty and power, affirmed that you did not believe in it, that the supreme pontiff and priests were not guided by the Holy Spirit and that all their works were directed only at deceiving the souls of the faithful and making them subservient to themselves; and you said that their acts and orders did not come from the divine will, and you so raised yourself against them that you dared say that you knew God more perfectly than they, and that the supreme Roman pontiff was not more important than you in dignity and power, but that you were equal to him in power; you asserted audaciously that his authority in the Church was not instituted by Christ, in fact if someone cited in support of the pope that phrase: "Whatever you bind on earth, etc.,"[70] you denied it pertinaciously, and finally you sullied their lives with blasphemous and unspeakable words.

Speaking publicly of the universal church you dared to say these blasphemous words: you stated that the statutes, norms and laws of the Church were not true and that men were not obliged to observe them, in fact that these laws and precepts were, as you vulgarly said, a business on which ecclesiastics lived. You affirmed with diabolical mind that the Church of God was not being governed on Christ's foundations, and that it was not sustained or governed by the Holy Spirit.

Of ecclesiastics you used to say that they were like the Devil, you despised them and said that they wanted to be adored on earth more than God; of their learning you asserted disparagingly that they wanted to know more than God; you wanted them to be so scorned that they

---

[70] Mt 16: 19.

would be esteemed inferior to every one, and you abominated them so that you dared to say you would sell them all for a *soldo;* and you were so malignant in their regard that like a raging mad man, without being one, you would have done everything you could to burn the churches of God and kill off these same ecclesiastics, if love for your children had not restrained you.

Speaking of saints, you asserted with assurance that they were not in the least way to be adored. About saints' relics, you said that they were not to be venerated and that there was no difference between them and our own remains. Not only did you not venerate the images held in such veneration by the Holy Mother Church, but you also affirmed that we should not honor or adore them, and you tried to prove your opinion by adducing the false example of the saintly patriarch Abraham.[71]

You firmly denied that indulgences had their origin in the merits of the saints, in fact, not even in the merits of Christ.

You said that we must not pray for the dead and you sharply reproved those whom you saw piously praying before the tombs of the departed faithful, with such words as: "Of what use are these prayers? For what purpose do you offer alms to ecclesiastics? At the end there is nothing but ashes." You thus affirmed that the alms, Masses and prayers and other pious works done for the dead were of no value and only what was done in life, not after death, was of utility to the dead person.

You did not leave intact holy fasting, in fact you disdained holy Lent with the words, "Who instituted it? Fasting was not invented so that we may earn merits, but so that the human intellect may not be weighed down by humors through overeating." And this, in fact, is how you said we should fast, namely that we can eat three or four times daily without breaking fast, and we discovered that you fulfilled by acts what you preached with your mouth, and that you never observed holy Lent, abstaining from prohibited foods and fasting, as taught by the Holy Roman Church, for the entire course of your life.

We learned that you also ranted against the sacred sermons. You wanted preachers to deliver their sermons to the people in such a way that they talked only about peace and not about hell or the precepts of the Church. In fact, even worse, if they quoted from the sacred letters

---

[71] See note 42.

of Paul, Peter, James and other passages taken from Holy Scripture, you affirmed confidently that this was a bad, human invention and, as you vulgarly said, a business. And finally you condemned with your blasphemous judgment the ritual and order observed by the Church in its preaching.

You did not leave intact the holy law of God, but, ripping it asunder, you stated that the Old and the New Testament were, as you vulgarly said, a human business, and that the Gospels written under dictation of the Holy Spirit were in part true, and in part the invention of the evangelists themselves. The malignant spirit led you so far as to affirm that not everything found in Sacred Scripture was revealed by God and not everything told about the passion of Our Lord Jesus Christ by the holy evangelists was true, because you said that they contradicted each other. You asserted that Holy Scripture could be reduced to a few words that came from God and that the other writings found in the Sacred Scripture had been added by men, no differently than in the books of battle, and, moreover, that the Psalms of David had not been dictated by the Holy Spirit, but were a pure invention of David's. Finally, with your filthy mouth you attempted to sully Sacred Scripture with these words: "Holy Scripture deceives us and was invented for this purpose, especially when it states that God exists."

You rejected the divine precepts contained in Holy Scripture and out of your own head decided that only some come from God and established a hierarchy among them. You asserted that the precept to love one's neighbor was greater than the one to love God, and that on Judgment Day men would have to give an account only of the love they bore their neighbor and not the love they bore God.

On the subject of holy water you spoke falsely and held the following things: since all water was blessed by God, it was not necessary that it also be blessed by priests, who added nothing saintly to it while they blessed it; in fact, if the benediction of the priest was true, the water would increase, as had happened when God blessed it; and if the benediction really confers anything, the benediction imparted by laymen would be of the same value as the priests' if the lay people pronounced the same words as priests over the things being blessed, and thus the blessing of lay people would be as valuable as the priests, since you stated that God gave the power to bless equally to all.

You rejected the earthly paradise and stated that it did not exist, and was in no place, if not in the homes of the rich.

Turning your corrupt head to the creation of the world, you

concocted out of your head the following heresies and errors: first, you dragged back to the light of day and firmly declared as true that opinion long ago condemned of an ancient philosopher who upheld the eternity of the chaos, from which derived all the things that are in this world. Moreover, you contrived the nefarious idea that the elements crashing against each other in the chaos produced a foam from which came worms, and from the worms men, of which the supreme one was God. Thus the world was not made by God and God only foresaw and determined what was to be done, and the world was subsequently made by the angels; and in the creation of the world the sun was not made resplendent with light, but you said that its splendor shone like a mirror that received its splendor from God and reflected it back. Similarly the splendor that we see is not the sun's, but God's. Finally, you brought back to the light of day the opinion of the Manichees on the double principle, namely of the good and of the bad, God, principle of the good, and the Devil, principle of what is evil.

Toward understanding the ranks of the holy angels' choir, you assented and affirmed your belief in the following errors: first of all you said that they were made in this way, that when that enormous mass of churning chaos became a single substance and became corrupted like cheese, from its putrefaction worms were born, and from the worms originated the angels. These angels were of the same nature as God, not made by God but from nature and the chaos, because they were produced in the same instant of time as was God and were made from the same mass and substance as God. Thus you denied the creation of the angels and audaciously affirmed that the Holy Spirit was of the same nature as the angels, that the universe was constructed by angels, that God selected out of the multitude of angels the most important and set it to the building of the world. This is the one that we call Holy Spirit, in whom God placed knowledge, will and power and entrusted the government of the world to it as to a steward. This supreme angel thus given precedence by God commanded the other choruses of angels and taught them how to proceed in the construction of the entire heaven and earth and of the entire world. Finally, you confused the supreme hierarchical order of the angels delineated by St. Dionysius and accepted by the Church, suggesting a different order among them, namely that the angels were divided into four parts in accordance with their four leaders, the first of which was Lucifer with his followers, followed by Michael and his angels, with Gabriel and his angels third, and Raphael and his last.

In speaking of the fallen angels, you declared that it had happened in this way: you stated, in fact, that Lucifer was not the greatest of the angels and did not want to be the equal of God; he erred only because he did not want to be subservient to the Holy Spirit, but only to God. The fall of the angels consisted in this, that they were deprived of their celestial places and were set to the universal construction of the world; in fact, you believed that the celestial places vacated by the celestial spirits would be filled by terrestrial spirits composed of air, earth, water and fire.

Considering the creation of man you distanced yourself from holy Genesis and from the doctrine of the Church, asserting that in the beginning not one man alone was created, but a multitude of men here and there in diverse parts of the world; that man was not created, but produced out of many things and that men in the beginning were not produced by God, but by the angels. You also said that the body of man was not formed out of earth, but from the purest metal, namely gold, and from this it followed that men always desired gold, and that man was of one with the seven planets, and thus one seemed jovial, and another mercurial. You did not hold that man was made in the image and likeness of God, and you said that it was in the image of the angels, and if man had some resemblance and similitude to the Holy Spirit, this lay in the fact that since the Holy Spirit was derived from the entire world and from the four elements, man also derived from that universe and from the same four elements. In regard to the infusion of the soul, not only did you set yourself against Holy Church, but also against all the philosophers. You stated, in fact, in one of your interrogations that the infant in the mother's womb receives neither soul nor spirit, but receives it as soon as it leaves the womb, and you attempted to demonstrate this with an utterly false and empty argument. Thus, for the entire time that the infant remains in the mother you say that there is no difference from brutish and irrational animals; but when the infant leaves the womb God sends an angel into it, which is its soul; this angel sent into man, which is, as you say, its soul, although it has the same will as man, nevertheless is distinct from him, and is not in the form of man, even though it is his soul, and only sustains and governs man. Finally, you affirm that in the heart of man there dwell two spirits, one good, the other evil in accord with the two parts of that very heart, of which one you call light, in which the good spirit reposes, and which sustains and governs man, and the other part you call dark, in which dwells the malignant spirit which continually agitates and subjugates man.

In discussing the soul, you stated that it vanishes at the death of the body, and that with the demise of the body nothing remains, except ashes. You were deceived by the argument that man's spirit is distinct from the soul, and thus for you only the spirit remains and you say that when the body dies, the soul dies. In man there are two opposed spirits, the first good, the other evil, and when the body dies, they both return to God. For you, when the life of the body ends, intellect, memory, will, and the recollection of man also end, because we do not need them after the present life, and they had been given by God to man as instruments in the present life. You considered these matters in a confused way and said that spirit, angel and soul were the same thing. You asserted that the soul was not created *ex novo*, but was made from the four elements, and you also asserted that the spirit sent by God to man after the birth, is either one of the angels created at the beginning, or newly made from the four elements, or taken from the nature of the material.

You wholly rejected original sin and, since the infant in the mother's womb does not have the spirit, neither is it possible that it can contract any original sin; but before the use of reason man can sin and, in fact, the infant begins to commit sins as soon as it leaves the mother's womb and begins to take nourishment.

You do not even have the correct idea about mortal sin and you decided in your head that certain sins are mortal, consequently rejecting those deemed such by God and by the Holy Church. The malignant spirit even led you to dare to say that blasphemy against God and the saints is not a sin, adducing for this purpose many frivolous and impious reasons, in fact you considered it your profession.

Raising your mind to the subject of ineffable and eternal predestination, you made grave and unspeakable statements: you actually denied that God had predestined and ordained anyone to eternal bliss, and even though you asserted that God might have foreseen at the beginning that some would be blessed, you asserted nevertheless that they were not predestined by God to the same bliss, and thus denied individual predestination; in fact, incredibly, you asserted that God knew universally that mankind would be predestined, but not specifically and particularly. You have also maintained as true the impious heresy that, even if some individuals should ascend to the bliss of heaven, this did not occur through the grace of God, but through human merits and good works; you even stated most impiously that this bliss came to them through the influence of the planets and fortune.

Considering vocation, even though you did not reject universal vocation, nevertheless you criticized the particular one espoused by Holy Mother Church: you asserted, in fact, that God calls everyone equally, Turks, Jews, Marrani, heretics, Christians, all men, and you tried to prove this with the example of the father that you poorly understood, and thus denied the particular grace of vocation.

Speaking of justification, you said most impiously that no one was saved through the passion and death of Christ, and that men received the grace of their own justification only from God and not through the merits of Christ. And so, according to this doctrine of yours, the passion of Christ became empty and useless in regard to justification.

And so that nothing would remain intact and uncontaminated by you in the Holy Church of God, you defiled all the sacraments of the Church. You rejected the sacrament of baptism and declared it unnecessary, because everything is blessed by God and every newly born baby is baptized by God. You denied that it was a sacrament, and that it was instituted by Christ. You held that the rite followed in the Church was a human invention, adding to this that priests devoured souls before birth, after birth and even unto death.

In regard to the sacrament of confirmation, not only did you deny its necessity, but even that it was a sacrament and that it had been instituted by Christ, because it was a simple human invention, and, as is vulgarly said, a business for the benefit of religious. To destroy this sacrament you said that every man had the Holy Spirit and that thus it was not necessary that he should receive the Holy Spirit through confirmation. And turning with your slanderous tongue to priests, you stated that when they spoke of this sacrament, they thought to know, but instead knew nothing.

Equally in regard to the sacrament of matrimony, you denied that it was a sacrament, that it was ordained by God, and said that it was a simple human invention, and that for the sacrament of marriage it sufficed if a man and woman gave their consent by joining hands, thereby rejecting the form and words used in this sacrament. Finally, you barked against the ceremonies used by the Church in this sacrament and said that they were human inventions.

Nor did you leave auricular confession intact, in fact you asserted against it that confession made to the priest was as beneficial as if made to a tree or to a plant, and thus you denied its necessity, that it was a sacrament and that it had been instituted by God and by Christ. You supported the notion of the heretics that it sufficed to confess one's sins to God, and that if someone confessed to the priest, this was only useful so as to receive salutary penances for the sins, and that if one could learn about penances for sins from a tree, confession to a priest would be unnecessary. You concluded that sins were confessed to priests only because they knew the penances, and that sins were told to them so that they would have that knowledge. You also asserted that if a layman knew this and that penance, he himself could hear confession. In fact, if the sinner could know the penances for his sins, there would be no need to confess sins to anyone but God.

And even though it emerges from the trial that you partook of the sacrament of the Eucharist almost yearly, nevertheless to the great detriment of your soul you did not believe about it anything that is believed by the Holy Roman Church. In fact, you spoke these impious words to wafers, which, although unconsecrated, had the image of our crucified lord: "That is a big beast." Nor did you hesitate to utter these impious words about the consecrated host: "It is a piece of dough," and that beneath these elements there was not the true body of Christ, thereby denying that the substance of the bread and the wine were transformed into the body of Christ. You said that God was not in the most sacred host, because if he was, he would be visible to men, and, persuaded by we know not what malignant spirit, you asserted that the Holy Spirit descended upon the host, and that Christ was not there, nor the Son of God, and, thus, whoever received the sacrament, did not receive the body of Christ. Moreover, you denied that it was a sacrament instituted by Christ and called it a simple human invention.

Rejecting the sacrament of holy orders, you dared say that, since the spirit of God reposes in all men, all men are priests, and anyone who endeavors to study can be a priest without being ordained. Finally, you denied that it was a sacrament and that it had been instituted by Christ, but you did affirm that it was, as is vulgarly said, a business for the benefit of religious.

And what did you say about extreme unction? You denied its necessity, said that it was not a sacrament, that it was not instituted by Christ, that it is of no value at all, and that it is an anointing only of the body and not of the spirit.

Thus you derided God, because you denied even the universal resurrection, insisting pertinaciously that it was impossible, and you tried to seduce others into this error with your false reasoning.

You acknowledged that there would be Universal Judgment, nevertheless you cast poison into this admission by saying that God would be the judge and Christ would recall events for him, as if God could not remember our actions.

You similarly believed falsely in regard to eternal bliss: first of all, you brought back to light Origen's heresy that all would be saved, Jews, Turks, pagans, Christians and infidels, because they all had received the Holy Spirit, and you asserted that they would all be saved in the same way. You sustained that the place of bliss circled the world, and that standing there all the things of the world could be seen, but that extraterrestrial things could not be seen and bliss could not be achieved; that this bliss did not consist in the vision of God, but in the vision of all the things of this world. You also affirmed that the things of the world could not be seen in God, but only in themselves, and thus you destroyed the idea of the bliss of the body.

Leaving nothing uncontaminated, with villainous mind and perverse mouth you directed these blasphemies against the immaculate and ever Blessed Virgin Mary: that she did not conceive through the Holy Spirit, that she was not a virgin during the birth and after the birth, that it is impossible she could have given birth to Christ without sin, that she is inferior to the empress Mary of Austria, and, horrible to hear as well as to say, you asserted that the Blessed Virgin was an adulteress and a sinner.

What is there to say? Your nefarious mind is so impiously, so inhumanly corrupted that it excogitated about God things that not even demons dared to suggest. First, something that all have asserted and no one can deny, you dared to affirm with the ignorant that God does not exist[72] and that he would be visible if he was really there high in the heavens; returning to yourself, you said that God exists, but so imperfectly that air and everything that we see is God, and, abominable to say, you were not ashamed to insist that he was made from worms, and you even denied that God looked after things below. You stated that he was made from the chaos, that he had his habitation near the sphere of the sun; that even though God was not made nor generated by others, nevertheless in the beginning he received his impetus from the motion of the chaos and thus came into being from imperfect to perfect, just as with all things human. Thus you believed that there was no God before the chaos, that in the instant of eternity he had no cognition either of himself or of others, nor did he have life.

---

[72] Ps 52: 1.

But at the beginning of time he commenced to understand and to live, and you tried to demonstrate this with the example of the infant in the mother's womb who at the beginning neither lives nor understands, and you compared God to this. Concerning the intelligence of the supreme and divine intellect, you affirmed that in the beginning, even if it could understand everything universally, it could not comprehend things in particular, and not only did it not understand individuals of all species, but not even of one, namely man. In this knowledge the intellect was not impelled by its own essence, but from things themselves; or you asserted that it had this knowledge from the chaos, in which everything remained confused. In this knowledge the divine intellect acted in this way, by passing from a confused to a distinct comprehension, as is the case with our own intellect; this knowledge increased daily and, as divine knowledge grew, you affirmed that in God will and power also increased. And just as with us will and power became so distinct to the point that one can be without the other, it occurs similarly in God, so that will can be without power and power without will. For you this divine power is nothing other than that possibility found in God, according to which he can perform everything by means of secondary causes. Thus you denied that God made some creatures directly himself, asserting, instead, that he made everything through angels. Finally, you spoke of this power so impiously, so inhumanely, so inanely, and stated that God cannot act in an instant, but only in a span of time, and that he is not able to create something from nothing.

Your malignant and perverse mind did not content itself sustaining all the things that have been recounted up to now, but you became even more daring, and you began to wage a battle of giants against the most holy and ineffable Trinity, launching missiles even more execrable than the Devil himself would have hurled. While acknowledging the three persons, you denied the unity of substance among them, the unity of nature, the unity of divinity, the equality of their glory, the co-eternity of their majesty, the equality of their power. You said that only one of the three persons is uncreated, the Father, and that the other two, namely the Son and the Holy Spirit, are made. You considered the first person immense, and the other two measurable and finite; you called the first person eternal and denied the eternity of the other two. You denied omnipotence to all three and made the Father God, but the Son and the Holy Spirit creatures. You asserted that the Trinity is light, joy and consolation. And what greater blasphemy can be uttered, if not that the sacred Trinity exists by chance and through fate, and that it was invented only for the purpose of the Universal Judgment, which you attempted to demonstrate with a comparison to a human, judicial judgment.

Just as you contemplated the entire Trinity in this execrable way, you also considered the single divine persons no less maliciously with an iniquitous and depraved mind. About the Father, you said that he was made from the chaos, that he had preceded in existence the Son and the Holy Spirit, that he was separate in his divinity from the other two persons, that he had a communicated essence with the Son and with the Holy Spirit, and that he did not share with them divinity, glory, majesty, omnipotence, nor the same intellect and will, that the Father was made from the chaos, and, most impiously, that he had proceeded in existence from imperfect to perfect, and, finally, about the eternal Father you made all the heretical statements that were said above about God.

The heavens are thunderstruck, all things become agitated, and any begin to tremble who listen to the inhuman and horrible statements you made with your sacrilegious mouth about Jesus Christ the Son of God. First of all, you denied that God the Father had a natural son, but rather a son by election. Thus, Jesus Christ is not the Son of God by nature, but by election, and God did not have a single son, but many: at the beginning, in fact, he chose Abel, but since he did not find him to his liking, he elected Noah, but the same ensued as with Abel; next he elected Abraham but it happened as with the others, so that he elected Isaac, and since he was not totally satisfied with him, he elected Jacob, then Moses, until finally he elected Christ, in whom God took great pleasure. In considering the nature of the Son of God, you dared to say that he is not consubstantial with the Father and not of such a perfect substance, but that he is less than the Father, that he is not consubstantial with the Holy Spirit and not of such a perfect substance, but that he is less; that the Son does not have the same divinity as the Father and the Holy Spirit. In fact, taking away all his divinity, you stated that he is only a man, that he is not co-equal in glory with the Father and the Holy Spirit, but that he is less than the Father and the Holy Spirit, that he does not have co-eternity of majesty with the Father and the Holy Spirit, nor does he have the same intellect and will. This Son of God is not omnipotent, infinite, uncreated, immense and eternal, but made from corruptible, finite, measurable and temporal substance. With a pertinacious mind you asserted that the Son is posterior to the Father and to the Holy Spirit, less than the Father and the Holy Spirit, proceeds from the Father and from the Holy Spirit, receiving his sonship from both. The Holy Spirit gave him intellect, will and power, and you sustained that this Son of God is pure creature and pure man, and that he is not different in nature from other men. And you thus affirmed that he was at the beginning and in the instant of eternity with the Father and with the Holy Spirit, but not with God, nor was he God, nor the author or artificer of this world. He did not create everything and everything did not derive from him, and everything that we say he did occurred in time. Regarding the doctrine of incarnation, you did not have a correct view of his incarnation, denying that he was conceived by the Holy Spirit, born from the Virgin Mary. And even if you thought correctly about his birth, that he was born from Mary, nevertheless you denied her virginity during the birth and after the birth, and, horrible to say, you asserted that he was conceived in sin and that it was common knowledge he was the son of St. Joseph. Concerning the soul of Christ, you iniquitously said these things: that it was either one of the angels made at the beginning of the world or that it was made *ex novo* by the Holy Spirit from the elements of this world, as is our own soul.

You dared to assert that this Christ was not sinless by nature and that he had two spirits in his heart, one good, the other bad, by which he was inwardly tempted; that this Christ was not God, but one of the prophets or a great man given by God to men. And you used to say that if this Christ had been omnipotent, as all Christians and the faithful believe, he behaved foolishly allowing himself to be killed.

You denied that he was crucified and asserted that in his place Simon the Cyrenian assumed death on the cross and that Christ himself like an irrational animal allowed himself to be hung. You acknowledged his death, but you asserted that in death his intellect, memory and will died, and that when the body of Christ died, his most saintly soul also died. And what is there more inhuman and more wicked than to state, as you did, that Christ did not suffer death for our transgressions and those of the whole world, but that his passion and death only were intended as an aid, to serve as a mirror of patience to us. You denied the doctrine of the descent into hell when you asserted that Christ's spirit immediately entered heaven when his body died and did not descend to hell, since you were deceived by the promise made to the thief: "Truly, I say to you, today you will be with me in Paradise."[73] Concerning the resurrection of Christ, not only did you doubt it, but you also rejected it, thereby making our faith meaningless; you doubt and are uncertain whether the most holy body of Christ exists in heaven; you have also questioned whether Our Lord Jesus Christ appeared to the apostles for forty days after his death before ascending to heaven. You also stated that after his ascension the spirit of Christ sent by the Holy Spirit descended into limbo to free the souls of the holy fathers which dwelt there. Finally, you denied that Christ was the cause of our bliss.

Even though you seem to have much faith in the person of the Holy Spirit, nevertheless your sacrilegious, iniquitous, malignant and perverse tongue and mind have uttered and believed the following heresies: for a time you denied the existence of the Holy Spirit, then, correcting yourself, you admitted his existence, but added these errors, namely that it is not of the same nature and substance as the Father and the Son, not of an equally perfect essence, but lesser; that the Spirit did not have the same essence and perfection of essence as the Son, but greater; that he did not share the divinity of the Father and the Son, that, in fact, the Spirit is not God, but a pure creature. That which is called by us the Holy Spirit you said was the most noble of the angelic spirits, which does not have equality of glory with the Father, but lesser, not equality of glory with the Son, but greater, not co-eternity of majesty with the Father and with the Son, not the same intellect and will of the Father and the Son, not a power equal to, but less than the Father and more than the Son; that the Spirit is not uncreated, immense, infinite and eternal, but made from the substance of the chaos with the angels, and is measurable, finite and temporal; that he proceeds only from the Father and not from the Son, that he is made and not produced; that this Spirit is not so much made by God, but from nature and from chaos; that he receives intellect, will and power from the Father himself and not from the Son, that he is posterior to the Father, superior to the Son, less than the Father, greater than the Son, was not at the beginning and in the instant of eternity with the Father and the Son. All things were not made immediately by the Spirit, but through the angels, he cannot create something from nothing, and is none other than a steward of God. You also iniquitously stated that the Holy Spirit was ignorant of what

---

[73] Lk 23: 43.

he had to do until the moment that he was made by the Father and received knowledge, will and power from him; and that he was made from the substance of the chaos and that the Church is not sustained and governed by the Spirit. Finally, you dared to assert that the Holy Spirit is found in all men, Jews, Turks, heretics and Christians, and that he was given by God to all equally without distinction.

Nevertheless, since our Lord mercifully permits some persons to fall into heresy and error, not only so that Catholic and literate men can exercise their knowledge of sacred doctrine, but also so that those who have thus fallen become more humble and exercise themselves in works of penance, after diligently discussing the merits of the present trial, we find that you, following frequent contact with us and with other upright men, and following a sounder course, wholesomely have returned to the bosom of Holy Mother Church and its unity, detesting your previous errors and heresies, recognizing the unshakable truth of the holy Catholic faith, and accepting it in your most intimate being.

Therefore, we have admitted you to the possibility of making an abjuration and of ratifying it under oath. We have obliged you to publicly abjure the aforesaid heresies and every other heresy; and, after the abjuration, we absolve you from the sentence of greater excommunication, to which you had been subjected through your fall into heresy. Reconciling you to the Holy Mother Church, we restore you to the ecclesiastical sacraments, provided that you have returned to the unity of the Church with a true heart and sincere faith, as we hope and believe that you have done. Nevertheless, because it would be unworthy to avenge injuries committed against temporal lords and serenely tolerate injuries toward the Lord of heaven and creator of all things, since it is much worse to violate eternal majesty than temporal majesty, and because God, merciful toward sinners, has mercy for you, and that you may be an example to others, your crimes not remain unpunished, and you become more cautious in the future, and less prone to commit and believe the above heresies, and all others, after repeating the name of Christ, we, vicar and inquisitor, the judges in this trial of the faith, presiding over this tribunal as judges, in accordance with the counsel furnished us by the legal experts, with the Sacred Gospels before our eyes so that our judgment comes from God and our eyes perceive what is just, with only God before us and the unshakable truth of the orthodox faith, we condemn and sentence you, Domenico Scandella, brought before our presence in the place, day and hour previously established to pronounce the definitive sentence and the imposition of the penance, mercifully sparing only your life. We condemn you:

First to wear a gray vestment in the form of a military tunic or a hoodless monk's scapular, emblazoned with crosses of yellow cloth front and back, two palms in length and half a palm in width; you must wear this vestment and its crosses over your other clothing for the rest of your life as a sign of your repentance, and if the vestment should be destroyed, you are obliged to have and wear another, because the crosses are the sign of a penitent man, and you must not reject them, but rather love them, just as Jesus Christ Our Lord himself humbly carried the cross on his own shoulders.[74]

Similarly we condemn you and assign to you as a penance to stand before the doors of the cathedral church of Santo Stefano in the city of Concordia, on the next five holy days and also on the feast day of St. Stephen himself, during the solemn Mass with your head bared, a lit candle in your hand and a leather thong about your neck.

Similarly we condemn you to be confined between two walls and to remain there forever and for your entire life, to endure with the bread of suffering and the water of misery, so that you may lament your sins and show your repentance;

similarly to fast every Friday on bread and water for the rest of your life;

similarly to confess all your sins twice a month and make your reconciliation with God;

similarly to read daily those articles of the faith that this holy tribunal will assign to you;

similarly to recite daily for the rest of your life the penitential psalms with the litany [of the saints] on your knees before an image of the crucifix, or the rosary of the Blessed Virgin Mary.

And since by law all your property, movable and immovable, that concerns you in any way is confiscated, we confiscate it and consider it confiscated by this sentence of ours. However, so that your sons and daughters may have food on their table, this holy tribunal, through its special grace, grants them the aforesaid property, with the condition that first they deduct from it your sustenance and what is required to support your existence, furnishing you with all your food and paying all the expenses connected with the present proceedings. We reserve to

---

[74] Cf. Jn 19: 17.

ourselves from certain knowledge and expressly the right to freely mitigate, increase, remove entirely or in part the above sentence and penances, if and when and how and as many times as we may choose.

Trial for the commutation of the punishment
Portogruaro, 18 January 1586

Before the most reverend and most illustrious lord, Matteo Sanudo,[75] bishop of Concordia, and the reverend father, Fra Evangelista Pelleo,[76] doctor in sacred theology and inquisitor general in the entire patriarchate and diocese of Aquileia, seated in a room of the habitation of the above named illustrious visitor in the convent of Sant'Agnese,[77] there appeared Giovannino, son of Domenico Scandella, who in the name of his father and also in the name of his brothers and of the wife of the aforesaid Ser Domenico, and his mother, presented, on his knees, a petition, beseeching that it be considered through merciful eyes because of the compassion used by the Holy Office, and, considering the just causes it describes, that it be received and acted upon as requested.

Supplication of Domenico Scandella
[Concordia, before 18 January 1586]

Presented on behalf of Scandella, 18 January 1586.

"Most illustrious and most reverend monsignor, and reverend father inquisitor. Although I, poor Domenego Scandella prisoner, have

---

[75] Bishop from 28 August 1585 to 1615; he died 14 September 1622: Degani, *La diocesi di Concordia,* 247–48; Del Col, "La storia religiosa del Friuli," 41–45.

[76] Fra Evangelista Pelleo of Force, inquisitor in Friuli from 14 June 1584 to 17 July 1586. He preached at Padua in 1581, was elected vicar general of the order on 5 July 1586 and minister general 7 May 1587; he was bishop of Sant'Agata dei Goti from 17 December 1588 until his death in 1595: Del Col, "La storia religiosa," 72; L. Chudoba & A. Sartori, "La predicazione francescana al Santo," in *Liturgia e pietà al Santo* (Vicenza: Neri Pozza, 1978), 347; F. Pennacchi, "Bullarium pontificium quod extat in archivo sacri conventus S. Francisci Assisiensis," *Archivum Franciscanum Historicum* 12 (1919): 530; G. van Gulik, C. Eubel & L. Schmitz Kallenberg, *Hierarchia catholica medii et recentioris aevi* (Münster, 1923), 3: 97.

[77] It emerges from the register that the bishop commenced his visitation on 26 May 1586 in the cathedral of Concordia, then moved on 2–4 June to the churches of S. Andrea, S. Gottardo, S. Nicolò and S. Cristoforo of Portogruaro. There is no mention of a visit to the convent of the minor observants S. Agnese: cf. AVPn, *Visite,* b. 2, reg. "Sacrarum visitationum sub illustrissimo Mathaeo Sanudo ...," fols. 2r–36r; Degani, *La diocesi di Concordia,* 301.

on other occasions beseeched the Holy Office of the Inquisition, and was not judged worthy of pardon, perhaps to permit me to do more penance for my error, now compelled by my extreme need I return to implore you to consider that more than two years have passed since I was taken from my home[78] and condemned to such a cruel prison. I do not know why I did not die because of the foulness of the air, deprived of being able to see my dear wife due to the distance from here, burdened with family, with children who because of their poverty will be forced to abandon me, so that I will necessarily have to die. Therefore, I, repentant and grieving over my great sin, beg forgiveness, first from our Lord God, and then from this holy tribunal, and ask them for the gift of my release. I offer proper guarantee that I will live in the teachings of the Holy Roman Church, and also that I will do whatever penance shall be imposed on me by this Holy Office, and I pray to Our Lord for their every happiness."

The most reverend and most illustrious bishop and the father inquisitor decreed, after hearing the supplication, to gather information concerning matters described in it, and they ordered, therefore, that the forenamed Domenico be questioned again to ascertain the presence of signs of his true repentance, change and correction. For this purpose they ordered that the jailer who had daily contacts with Scandella be questioned. Procedures were followed according to the requirements of the law.

19 January 1586

Before the most reverend and illustrious lord Matteo Sanudo, bishop, duke, count and marquis of Concordia, and the most reverend lord Evangelista Pelleo, inquisitor general for the diocese of Concordia, and the reverend and most excellent lord vicar,[79] in Portogruaro, in the episcopal palace, there appeared Ser Giovanni Battista de Parvis, guard and jailer of the episcopal prison in Concordia. After taking an oath from the hands of the reverend lord inquisitor, with his hand on Scripture, questioned, he replied: "I have had Ser Domenico Scandella in my custody from the day of his sentencing until today in the prison of the bishop of Concordia, which is between two cellars through which one reaches the prison, which is strong and secure, with three

---

[78] The arrest occurred on 3 February 1584, thus not even two years had elapsed.

[79] Giovanni Battista Maro.

stout and safe doors, in which all offenders, even murderers, have always been placed, and no other prison stronger or more severe than it can be found in the city of Concordia."

Questioned, he replied: "Domenico Scandella has never left this jail, nor did he try to, except when I conducted him to church to make his penances imposed by the sentence, that is, soon after the sentence, when he stood at the doors of the cathedral church of this city with a candle in hand; and he also did this the feast day of St. Stephen, and other times still I took him to hear Mass and receive communion, but usually I had him receive communion in prison since I did not have enough guards to take him to church."

Questioned, he replied: "I know that he fasted many Fridays, except when he was so sick that we thought he would die, and from then on it seems to me that he did not fast, but many times, on the other fast days, he would say to me: 'Tomorrow bring me only some bread, because I want to fast, and no meat or anything else fat.'"

Questioned, he replied: "From certain signs I recognized that he was very penitent of his error, because many times I quietly went up to the door of his cell to hear what he was doing or saying, and I heard him praying, and other times I saw him reading a book that had been given him by the priest Ludovico, and I know that your reverence saw it when you went to the prison to see and visit him. And he also has an *Office of the Madonna,* which has the seven psalms and other prayers, and he also asked me many times to find him an image before which he could say his prayers, and so his son bought him one."

Questioned, he replied: "I know that he has supported this penance of his patiently, saying that he always resigned himself to God, and recognized that he was suffering for his sins and errors and that God had helped him, because he did not believe he could survive fifteen days suffering as he did in prison, and yet he had come this far. And he told me this just a few days ago."

Questioned, he replied: "Many times he spoke to me about those follies of his that he had believed in previously, saying that he knew well that they were really follies, but he had never held them so deeply that he firmly believed them, and that it was through the temptation of the Devil that such extravagant thoughts had come into his head."

Questioned, he replied: "The hearts of men are not so easily known except by God, but from what I have seen in him, it is my opinion that he has repented his error and that in the future he will persevere in this good resolve."

The same day

There appeared Ser Domenico Scandella before the same persons as above, who as soon as he was conducted before the most reverend and most illustrious bishop, and the most reverend inquisitor general, and the reverend and most excellent vicar, prostrating himself on the ground tearfully beseeched pardon for his errors with humble words and supplications. And when he was questioned by the reverend inquisitor, he replied: "My son presented that petition, about which you ask me, in my name, and again with my own voice I beseech you for what it contains, resigning myself always to God's mercy and to the mercy of this Holy Office."

Questioned, he replied: "I am deeply repentant that I have offended my Lord God, and I wish now that I had not said the foolish things that I said, into which I stupidly fell blinded by the Devil and not understanding myself what he was telling me."

Questioned, he replied: "Not only have I not regretted doing the penance that was imposed on me and being in that prison, but I felt such a great happiness, and God comforted me always while I was praying to his divine majesty, that I felt I was in heaven."

And when he was asked: "If it should please the Holy Office that you continue to make your penance in prison, would you stay willingly?" he replied: "I would do whatever was pleasing to our most holy majesty." And these were his actual words: "If I did not have a wife and children, whose love pulls at me, since I, if I remain in this place, will be their ruin, I would willingly stay as long as I live to do penance for my offenses to the Lord Jesus Christ." And he said this clasping his hands and raising them from his eyes to heaven.

Questioned, he replied: "If I should be granted this grace, if I am worthy of it, of returning home to my little family, I will not hesitate to stick firm to this resolution to be a Catholic and a true Christian and to perform all those penances that this reverend tribunal will impose on me."

Questioned, he replied: "Two years have passed and I now begin a third year in prison."

Questioned, he replied: "I am fifty-three years old, going on fifty-four and have seven children, boys and girls, and my oldest son has a wife and children, and my wife is about fifty years old. As for my possessions, I am very poor and only have two rented mills and two fields which I lease and with these I supported and support my poor family."

Questioned, he replied: "The prison in which I am confined is harsh, earthen, dark and humid, so that I was very sick this winter and lay four months without getting out of bed. And this year I had swollen legs, and I also swelled up in the face, as you can see, and I almost lost my hearing, and became weak and almost beside myself." And truly while he was saying this he was very pale in appearance, and an invalid in his body, and in a poor way. This testimony having been received, he was dismissed, etc.

Same day and place, as above

The full congregation was convoked, consisting of the most reverend and illustrious bishop, the reverend father inquisitor, and the reverend vicar, assisting the most celebrated Iacopo Pizzamano,[80] the *podestà*, with the participation of the most excellent Giovanni Frances-co Palladio degli Olivi,[81] Valerio Trapola dai Colli and Girolamo Pigozzino, doctors of law. After considering the supplication presented on behalf and in the name of Domenico Scandella, and having examined the testimony of the jailer and of Domenico himself, perceiving signs of true repentance in the aforesaid Domenico, upon the advice of their board of experts, determined that they should mitigate and commute the sentence previously emitted against Ser Domenico, mitigating and commuting it as follows:

in the place of perpetual imprisonment they assigned the aforesaid Domenico the village of Montereale, which he was to consider as his prison and never attempt to leave without the permission of the Holy Office;

similarly that he was to offer a suitable security of two hundred ducats as guarantee that he would not leave the place assigned to him as a prison and present himself as often as required, and in the event that he should fail to meet this obligation, half of the fine was to be applied to the Arsenal of the most illustrious Dominion, and the other half to the expenses of the Holy Office;

---

[80] It is not possible to indicate the dates of Pizzamano's term in office since the register for these years is missing in ASVe, *Segretario alle voci, Elezioni del Maggior Consiglio*. His presence in 1587 is recorded by Cicogna, *Documenti storici*, 116.

[81] Giovanni Francesco Palladio degli Olivi, jurist, assessor and judge, son of Camillo, was born at Portogruaro in 1540 and died in 1590. He is not to be confused with the historian of the same name, son of Alessandro, author of the *Historia della Provincia del Friuli*, who died in 1669: G. G. Liruti, *Notizie delle vite ed opere scritte da' letterati del Friuli* ... (Venice: Tip. Alvisopoli, 1830), 4: 456–59; Ginzburg (95, 138) conflates them.

similarly that the aforesaid Domenico in the future was never to speak of or mention his wrongheaded opinions, except detesting them and reproaching himself for his frivolity and vacuity;

similarly that he should be obligated to wear continually and publicly over his other clothing the vestment described in the sentence;

similarly that, instead of the fast imposed on him as penance, since he is old and ill he should dispense alms every Friday according to his own possibilities;

similarly that he should be obligated six times yearly to confess his sins and receive the most holy Eucharist, namely on the day of the Resurrection of our Lord, Pentecost, Assumption of the Blessed Mary, the first Sunday of Advent, Christmas and the first Sunday in Lent; and that at the end of each year he is obliged to inform the above named judges, or one of them, by means of an attestation provided by the priest of the place.

The above sentence was promulgated by the forenamed judges on the day and at the place given above, and was read and published in their presence by me, Terenzio Placentino, co-adjutor in the episcopal chancery, in the presence of the following witnesses present at the publication of the sentence: the aforesaid Domenico and the witnesses Alvise Cumino, carpenter, son of the deceased Sebastiano of Udine, Francesco, son of the deceased Pietro Celi, and Giovanni, son of the deceased Pietro Biason of the castle at Sesto, inhabitants of the city of Portogruaro.

And there, after the publication of the above sentence, Domenico Scandella, in compliance with it, offered as surety two hundred ducats, as specified, through his bondsman Daniele de Biasio, presently a resident of Fanna. This Daniele de Biasio presented himself as bondsman for the sum of two hundred ducats on behalf of Domenico in case the sentence was contravened, and in compliance with the sentence. This was agreed to through the prayers and petitions of Domenico and Giovanni, his son, who together obliged themselves to Daniele to preserve him from any loss, pledging all their possessions, mobile and fixed, now and in the future, in the presence of those named above.

Second Trial Against Domenico Scandella

Porcia, 7 March 1596[*]

Leonardo Simon to Fra Giovanni Battista Angelucci[1]
Porcia, 7 March 1596

Most magnificent and reverend, my highly esteemed lord. Having heard the bull concerning heresy,[2] I cannot fail but to write these few words for the sake of my soul and also to wash away these sins. I found myself in Udine one day and conversing with a person called Menocchio, a miller of Montereale, he spoke these words to me, since he had heard that I wanted to become a monk: "I hear that you want to go and become a monk." And I said to him: "What do you think, wouldn't it be a good thing?" And he replied: "No, because it is a beggarly business, and those who die for love of God, we do not even know if they go to heaven or hell. It is true that God is master and can make and unmake." And then I told him that even Jews and Lutherans believe that he can make and unmake, but they do not believe that he was born from the Virgin Mary, and he replied that this is something we cannot know. And then I told him that we should not be probing what is hidden by God, because the Gospel says: "Blessed are those who have not seen and yet believe",[3] and he retorted: "Who do you think made these Gospels? No one else but monks, who have nothing better to do and write what they please." And I told him: "So, then, you do not believe in the Gospel?" and he replied, "No, I do not believe in it."

---

[*] AAUd, *S. Officio*, b. 1h, fasc. 285.

[1] Fra Giovanni Battista Angelucci of Perugia was appointed vicar of the Inquisition for the dioceses of Aquileia and Concordia on 17 July 1586 and then served as inquisitor until his death in Udine c. January-February 1598: Del Col, "La storia religiosa del Friuli," 72.

[2] It probably refers to the edict issued by the patriarch Francesco Barbaro and by the inquisitor Angelucci on 3 July 1595, reprinted in *1000 processi dell'Inquisizione*, 90.

[3] Jn 20: 29.

I should have written many days ago, perhaps a month ago, but I did not know him well, and many cares interfered so that I did not write. But now a Jubilee has come and I want to absolve myself with God's help. Nothing more. I kiss the hand of your most reverend lordship.

Porcia, 1596, 7 March

Of your most reverend lordship, Lunardo Simon.

Fra Girolamo Asteo to Fra Giovanni Battista Angelucci Pordenone, 3 April 1596

Most reverend and worshipful father. I have conducted the examination as I was instructed by your reverence and hereby send it to you. If I have served you well I shall be very content, and if I have not at least accept my good intentions, since I shall always be ready to serve you even beyond my capacities. Father Carpi kisses your hand and I respectfully bid you farewell and commend myself to your good grace. I have attached the accuser's letter to the examination.

Of your very reverend paternity your most devoted servant, Fra Hieronimo Asteo.[4]

3 April 1596

In the castle of Pordenone, customary residence of the most illustrious *provveditore* and captain, before me, Fra Hieronimo Asteo of Pordenone, vicar of the Holy Office especially delegated by the very reverend father master Giovan Battista of Perugia, most worthy inquisitor for the Friuli, with the presence and participation of the most

---

[4] Fra Girolamo Asteo was born in Pordenone in 1562, joined the order of minor conventuals and took his vows on 2 July 1581. He received a degree in theology and philosophy from Padua, became inquisitorial vicar for the dioceses of Aquileia and Concordia in 1591, was named inquisitor on 4 March 1598 and remained in that post until 30 December 1608, while also serving for a number of years as minister for the province of Sant'Antonio. He became bishop of Veroli on 17 November 1608, went to reside in his diocese, where he worked to realize the Tridentine reforms and died in 1626. He left numerous manuscripts of his writings and two printed works: *De iurisprudentiae methodis* (Brescia, 1614) and *De reo et actore commentarium in l. diffamari* (Padua, 1617): G. G. Liruti, *Notizie delle vite ed opere scritte da' letterati del Friuli* (Udine: Gallici, 1780), 3: 325–30; Chudoba & Sartori, *La predicazione francescana*, 348; *Dictionnaire d'histoire et de géographie ecclésiastique*, 4: col. 1156–57.

illustrious lord Alvise Pisano,[5] most worthy *provveditore* and captain of Pordenone, there appeared Lunardo de Simon of Roveredo below Porcia, who, cautioned, sworn in and questioned, replied as follows:

asked if he knew anyone who was suspect in the faith, he replied: "Finding myself in Udine at carnival time this year, four or six days before Santa Agnese,[6] in the square before the palace, I ran into a certain Menocchio, a miller of Montereale, who said to me: 'I understand that you want to become a monk, is that true?' I answered 'Is it not a good thing?' 'No,' answered Menocchio, 'it is a beggarly business.' I told him that I was not becoming a monk so that I could go around begging, and he replied: 'Of all the holy hermits and others who have led a saintly life, no one knows where they all went.' I said to him: 'The Lord God does not want us to know these secrets now.' To which he replied: 'If I was a Turk, I would not want to become a Christian, but I am a Christian and so do not want to be a Turk.' I told him: 'Blessed are those who have not seen and yet believe,'[7] and he replied: 'I do not believe if I do not see.[8] I do believe that God is the master of the whole world and can make and unmake.' Then I said: 'Even Turks and Jews believe, but they do not believe that God was born from the Virgin Mary.' He replied: 'What do you make of the fact that when Christ was on the cross and the Jews told him, If you are Christ, come down from the cross,[9] he did not come down?' I replied: 'This was so as not to show obedience to the Jews.' He said: 'It was because Christ could not.' 'So,' I told him, 'you do not believe in the Gospel?' And he replied, 'No, I do not believe.' And he added: 'Who do you think it is who makes these Gospels, if not priests and monks, who have nothing better to do? They think up these words and string them together one after the other.' I replied that the Gospels are not made by priests or monks, but were made before now. And so I left him thinking that he was a heretic, and this was in Udine, in the

---

[5] Alvise Pisan served as *provveditore* and captain of Pordenone from 13 August 1595 to November 1596: ASVe, *Segretario alle voci, Elezioni del Maggior Consiglio*, reg. 8, fols. 205v–206r.

[6] The feast days of sant'Agnese fall on 21 and 28 January.

[7] See note 3.

[8] An echo of Jn 20: 25.

[9] See Mt 27: 40 and Mk 15: 32.

square, in front of a house propped up by timbers, where they say the present vicar was born."[10]

Asked who was present at this conversation, he replied: "No one, just the two of us."

Questioned, he replied: "It might have been the hour of Vespers."

Questioned, he replied: "When I went to Porcia I talked about the matter with the father of the Servites of Porcia,[11] who urged me to write this information to the reverend father inquisitor, and so I did write to him."

Questioned: "Would you recognize the letter that you wrote to the very reverend father inquisitor?" he replied: "Seeing it I would recognize it." And when this letter was shown to him, he inspected it with care, and said: "It is the very same one."

Questioned: "How well do you know that person?" he replied: "At holiday time I used to play the violin in Griz and Malnis, and because this Menocchio plays the cithara we know each another."

Asked if that person also has another name, he replied: "I do not know, but he is a man about fifty years old, with a gray beard and rather tall."

Asked if the person was speaking seriously or in jest, he replied: "In my opinion, he was speaking seriously."

Questioned, he replied: "He spoke those words to me only once and I immediately left him feeling very scandalized."

Questioned, he replied: "I have heard from other people that this person, on another occasion, four years ago,[12] was imprisoned by the Holy Office as a Lutheran."

Asked about possible enmity, he replied properly: "God help me if I bear ill will to anyone."

At the conclusion, he signed with his own hand.

I, Lunardo de Simon of Roveredo, confirm the above with my own hand.

---

[10] The vicar general was Valerio Trapola.

[11] In 1599 Fra Alessandro da Ferrara was vicar of the convent of Santa Maria Maddalena in Porcia: Biblioteca Apostolica Vaticana, Vat. Lat. 11270, fols. 403r–404r, where the books of the convent are recorded. I owe this information to the courtesy of Sergio Bigatton.

[12] In reality not in 1592, but in 1584–1586.

Attestation of Giovanni Daniele Melchiori
Montereale, 22 January 1597

To my superiors reverence, to my equals honor, to my inferiors greetings in the Lord.

At the request of signor Domenico Scandella, I Giovanni Daniele Melchiori, parish priest of Montereale, say, believe and attest before all the magnificent and most reverend magistrates, that if one can deduce interior things from externals, the above named Domenico conducts a Christian and orthodox life, and therefore I humbly beseech you, when he appears before you, to receive him with kindness and charity, and for this reason I have written the present letter in my own hand and sealed it with my own seal.

Montereale, 1597, 22 January.

Sealed. The above named.

Fra Giovanni Battista Angelucci to Valerio Trapola
Udine, 26 January 1597

Most magnificent and most reverend my lord. There has come to me Domenico Scandella of Montereale, who some years ago abjured as a penitent heretic in the Holy Office, asking to be dispensed from the penitential garment which he is obliged to wear always. And because such a dispensation should not be decided lightly without the advice of the Holy Apostolic See, therefore for now I am content to dispense him from his place of incarceration, namely the village of Montereale, so that he can be free to do business everywhere, except in suspect places, and thus alleviate in some way his poverty and that of his family. I therefore beseech you to grant him this grace for now. With this I kiss your hands and pray the Lord for your happiness.

Udine, 26 January 1597.

Of your magnificent and reverend lordship, your affectionate servant, Fra Giovanni Battista da Perugia, inquisitor for the Friuli.

28 October 1598

In the Congregation of the Holy Office, recorded in the register of its acts,[13] it was decided to summon the accuser anew to ask him if the person denounced was Domenico Scandella, called Menocchio, and then to proceed to an inquisition as prescribed by the law.

---

[13] AVPn, *Processi*, reg. "Nonnulli processus ab anno 1584 usque ad annum 1586," first internal fascicle, fols. 8r–11r.

11 November 1598

In the palace of the illustrious lord Giovanni Foscari,[14] *provveditore* and captain of Pordenone, before the reverend father inquisitor general of Aquileia and Concordia, father Girolamo Asteo, with the participation of the worthy *provveditore* and captain himself, there appeared as witness the most reverend lord Ottavio of the counts of Montereale,[15] sixty-eight years of age, as he stated, and, cautioned, sworn in, and interrogated under oath, he replied: "In the village of Montereale, where because of dealings over many years I know almost everyone, I would not be able to say that there was anyone else who is suspect in matters of the faith except a certain Domenego Scandella called Menocchio, who was before the Holy Office some years ago."

Asked in what way this Domenico or Menocchio was suspect, he replied: "Over the entire place of Monte Reale he had the reputation of holding bad opinions, and since these were said publicly I informed the priest Odorigo that he was obliged to denounce him to his superior, and he did denounce him. Because of it the priest has been persecuted by the relatives of Menocchio and chased out of Montereale. As I understood it then, this Menocchio had learned his heresies from a messer Nicolò, a painter of Porcia, who painted in the home of my brother-in-law, signor Girolamo de Lazaris."

Asked if there are any other Menocchios in Montereale, he replied: "I do not know or believe that there is any other Menocchio in Montereale besides this one, who is a miller about 60 years of age, tall like myself, but thin, who goes around playing the cithara on feast days, has children, but I do not know their names, and just recently he lost his eldest son."[16]

Asked about Menocchio's reputation at that time, he replied: "After his case was settled by the Holy Office, it was and is thought

---

[14] Giovanni Foscarini was *provveditore* and captain of Pordenone from 19 April 1598 to July 1599: ASVe, *Segretario alle voci, Elezioni del Maggior Consiglio*, reg. 8, fols. 205v–206r.

[15] Priest Ottavio of the counts of Montereale, as deacon, became titular in 1566 of the altar of the Sacrament, under the hereditary patronage of the family, in the church of San Marco in Pordenone, with the obligation to say three Masses weekly, receiving an annual income of 100 ducats in 1584, the year that the Masses were being celebrated by the priest Nicolò de Fabris, one of the two vicars of San Marco: AVPd, *Biblioteca capitolare, Visite*, b. 6, fol. 102v.

[16] Giovanni Scandella.

that he still has the same false opinions that he had before, and I have heard many say that he himself has stated that he has heretical ideas."

Asked from whom he heard this and when, he replied: "I heard it from many people two or three years ago, but I cannot say from whom because I have had dealings with many whom I do not remember now. But your paternity will find a multitude of people who will be able to inform you much better."

Questioned, he answered: "That person goes to Mass, but I do not know whether he goes to confession or takes communion."

Questioned, he replied: "I do not know of any particular opinion held by this Menocchio because I have not had business with him, even if I am from Montereale."

Asked who can inform the court about it, he replied: "I believe that the priest and chaplain of Montereale[17] may know something."

About generalities, he responded properly, confirmed the proceedings when they were read back to him, took the oath to observe silence, and signed.

I priest Ottavio Montereale ratify the above.

28 November 1598

Before the reverend father inquisitor general, in his residence in Pordenone, there appeared Leonardo Simon of Roveredo; summoned, cautioned, sworn in with his hands on Holy Scripture, questioned, he replied: "I was already questioned some years ago by your reverence about a denunciation I had made against Menego, called Menocchio of Montereale."

Asked if this Menego has a last name, he replied: "If I remember, he is of the Scandellas, but since I do not know him well I cannot say for sure."

Questioned, he replied: "This Menocchio is a miller, married, but his wife is no longer alive."

Asked if Menocchio has children, he replied: "Yes father. Some years ago one died named Giacomo,[18] and now he has one called Stefano, who may be twenty-eight years old."

Questioned, he replied: "Since I was examined by your paternity, I have seen this Menocchio on various occasions, but I did not speak

---

[17] They were the priests Giovanni Daniele Melchiori and Curzio Cellina.
[18] Actually Giovanni: cf. note 16.

to him, because since he is a man with bad ideas, I did not want to have anything to do with him."

About generalities, he responded properly, confirmed the proceedings when they were read back to him, took the oath to observe silence, and signed.

I Lunardo de Simon ratify the above.

16 December 1598

The above named father inquisitor, in the parish of Aviano, in the home of signor Antonio Menegozzi, for the just reasons that influenced his decision, appointed as his commissioner and vicar the reverend Tommaso Ferro,[19] priest of the parish, with instructions to go to the castle of Montereale and interrogate under oath the witnesses named above and anyone else who would seem appropriate to the above named commissioner, empowering him, if the necessity arose, to impose any penalty and censure with the authority of the reverend father inquisitor himself, in fact, with apostolic authority. Thereupon the father inquisitor administered an oath to the commissioner to serve faithfully and to maintain silence in all the business of this Holy Office, as is the custom.

17 December 1598

Held in the village of Malnisio, under the jurisdiction of the lords of Montereale, in the sacristy of the church of that place. In the presence of the above named reverend commissioner, there appeared Giovanni Daniele Melchiori, priest of Montereale, who, cautioned, sworn under oath, and questioned, stated: "I know and believe that it is Domenego Scandella who is suspected of heresy, because he has been condemned by the Holy Office in the past."

Questioned, he replied: "I believe he is suspected of heresy because I hear that he does not observe his sentence. In his sentence he was condemned to wear a vestment with a cross and this Menocchio does not wear such a garment and also leaves Montereale, even though he is not supposed to, but he does go to confession and communion many times a year."

---

[19] Tommaso Ferro of Venice was parish priest of San Zenone di Aviano from 1576 to 1605 and was elected vicar *foraneo* by the apostolic visitor Cesare de Nores in 1584: Degani, *La diocesi di Concordia*, 517; AVPn, *Visite*, b. 2, reg. "Sacrarum visitationum Nores . . . ," fols. 40v, 138r.

Asked about the reputation of this Menocchio, he replied: "As for me, I consider him to be a Christian and an honorable man as far as one can judge externally."

Asked what reputation he had among the other people of the village, he replied: "I do not know."

Asked when he had seen Menocchio without his penitential vestment, he replied: "For the last few years, and I saw him in many places, and I even saw him this way outside Montereale, especially in Malnisio and elsewhere."

About generalities, he responded properly, confirmed the proceedings when they were read back to him, took the oath to observe silence, and signed.

I Giovan Daniel Melchiori, parish priest, confirm what is written.

Day and place as above

In the presence of the above mentioned etc. there appeared the reverend Curzio Cellina[20] of Montereale, chaplain of that place, and cautioned, sworn in and asked whether he knew anyone who was suspected of heresy in Montereale, replied: "I do not know of anyone except for a certain Domenego Scandella called Menocchio, a man about 60 years of age, a tall man who is a miller, a widower at present who has a grown-up son married to a person from Grizzo, who lived in Montereale and is called Stefano, but I do not know the names of the others."

Asked how he knows that he [Menocchio] is a suspect and from whom had he heard it, he replied: "I know him and that he was in the Holy Office in the past on this charge and that he was condemned by the Holy Office."

Asked what ideas this Menocchio now had about the faith, he replied: "This Menocchio has certain humors so that when he sees the moon or stars or other planets and hears thunder or something, he immediately wants to give his opinion on what has just happened. In the end he submits to the opinion of the majority saying that the whole world knows more than he alone. And I believe that this humor

---

[20] From roughly 1575 priest Curzio Cellina was chaplain of the altar of saints Rocco, Sebastiano and Francesco, which had an annual revenue of 40 ducats in 1584 and was left to the care of priest Andrea Ionima for 20–25 ducats: see the introduction, p. xxi. Notarial acts drawn up by Cellina in Montereale between 1595 and 1602 are preserved in ASPn, *Notarile*, b. 488, n.c. 3785–96.

of his is wicked, but that he submits to the opinions of others out of fear."

Asked about the reputation of this Menocchio, he replied: "I consider him a Christian because I have seen him confess and receive communion."

Asked if he fulfilled the penances imposed upon him by the Holy Office and wore the garment of the Holy Office, he replied: "I know that for a long time he wore a vestment with a cross on it given to him by the Holy Office, and he wore it secretly under his clothing."

Asked if he now wore the habit of the Holy Office, he replied: "I do not know if he is wearing it now, but I do know that Menocchio told me that he wanted to go and visit the Holy Office to obtain permission not to wear it, because he used to say that as a result of his having that garment with the cross men did not want to associate and speak with him, but I do not know if he obtained this permission."

Asked if he went out of Montereale, he replied: "I know that he goes to the country at haying time, but I do not know if he went to other places."

Asked who can inform the court about him, he replied: "I do not know, because I see him dealing with many and I believe he is everybody's friend."

Asked if he thought that Menocchio believed that the planets can constrain men and their free will and if they necessarily influence events, he replied: "I do not know because I do not remember what words he used in these discussions, but I do know that when he was heard talking about these things, he was told to be silent."

Asked if he knew whether this Menocchio was speaking truthfully or in jest, he replied: "I think that he was speaking seriously and that he had an evil humor, but about the faith or about things pertaining to the faith, I do not know that he said anything."

Asked when and where he had heard him speak about these things, and who had been present, he replied: "I heard him often in Montereale, where many were present, but who they might have been I do not remember now."

About generalities, he responded properly, confirmed the proceedings when they were read back to him, and took the oath to observe silence. Then he added of his own accord: "I am not related to this Menocchio nor do I feel for him either a close friendship or enmity, but I love him as a Christian and I deal with him as I do with others, when I have some task for him."

And I, priest Curzio Cellina, confirm that what was said above is true.

2 January 1599

In the congregation of the Holy Office assembled in the episcopal palace at Concordia, it was decreed to summon the suspect to respond, as it is contained in the register of the acts.[21]

Denunciation made by Gregorio Ferro
Pordenone, 2 May 1599

Since I Gregorio Ferro do not want to be subjected to any ecclesiastical censure, for the sake of my conscience I state and testify that about four or five months ago in Aviano, if I remember correctly, in my house, I do not know how it came up, we began a discussion. It turns out that a Ser Michiel del Turco, nicknamed Pignol of Aviano, began a conversation with an old man who lives in Montereale, a certain Menocchio who, I believe, is of the Scandella family, a man who in my judgment may be about 60 years old. And this Michiel told me that he heard these words from the mouth of this Menocchio: "If Christ had been the Son of God, he would have been ... to let himself be crucified," but he told me nothing else, about when or where this happened. And this is as much as I know.

2 May 1599

Before the reverend father, master Girolamo Asteo of Pordenone, in his own habitation, there appeared spontaneously the magnificent lord Gregorio Ferro of Pordenone who consigned the present paper and explained what was contained in it. He had been made to take an oath by the same reverend father, and he swore touching Holy Scripture, and, asked if the things he had denounced were true, he replied: "It is absolutely true that the above named Michiel told me what I have testified to you."

Asked why he had not testified about these matters sooner in accordance with the regulations of the Holy Office, he replied: "Since I had not heard them from the mouth of the suspect, but from others, I did not think I had to denounce him."

---

[21] AVPn, *Processi,* reg. "Nonnulli processus ab anno 1584 usque ad annum 1586," first internal fascicle, fols. 8r–11r.

Then when the reverend father advised him that in the future he had to obey the obligation to make denunciation, he nodded in agreement, and the reverend father inquisitor absolved him from the sentence of excommunication and imposed a salutary penance.

About generalities, he responded properly, confirmed the proceedings when they were read back to him, took the oath to observe silence, and signed.

I Gregorio Ferro ratify the above.

The fifth day of May fifteen hundred ninety nine

When the reverend father master Girolamo Asteo, inquisitor, heard that Michele del Turco, known as Pignol, of Aviano, a witness as above, was presently in the parish of Aviano, he ordered that he should be questioned, and he ordered a horseman in the entourage of the most illustrious governor Stefano Viari[22] to summon the above named before the Holy Office under pain of excommunication, and the emissary reported back that this was done.

The sixth of the same month

Before the reverend father inquisitor named above, in Polcenigo, in the convent of San Giacomo in the room of the reverend father provincial on the ground floor, there appeared Michele del Turco, called Pignol, of Aviano, forty-six years of age, as he said, who, having been cautioned and sworn in, after having laid his hands on Sacred Scripture, and asked if he knew the cause of his being summoned, replied: "To tell the truth, I do not know."

Asked if he had heard anyone utter heretical words, or matters pertaining to the Holy Office, he replied: "I do not know that I heard anything heretical, but if your paternity would recall something for me, perhaps I could remember."

Questioned: "Have you ever heard anyone say that if Christ had been the Son of God, he would not have done a certain thing?" he replied: "About this I remember that I once heard Menocchio of Montereale say these or similar words: 'If Christ had been God, he

---

[22] Stefano Viari was the Venetian governor (*luogotenente*) for the *patria* of the Friuli from 17 May 1598 to September 1599. He made his report to the senate on 4 November 1599: ASVe, *Segretario alle voci, Elezioni del Maggior Consiglio*, reg. 8, fols. 147v–148r; *Relazioni dei rettori veneti in terraferma. I. La Patria del Friuli (luogotenenza di Udine)*, ed. A. Tagliaferri (Milan: Giuffrè, 1973), 113–20.

would indeed have been an . . . ,' and he did not say what Christ would have been but I gathered that he meant to say that Christ would have been an ass (*coglione*), to use that ugly word, 'to have allowed himself to be put on the cross.'" And he added, on his own: "And I heard many people repeat these words in my house and elsewhere."

Asked from whom he had heard them, he replied: "I do not remember who told me they had heard these words of Menocchio's, which I have just repeated, but I think that when you question people in Montereale there will be many who will have heard them from his very mouth and thus that he still persists in those old opinions of his."

Asked where he had heard Menocchio utter these words, he replied: "It was in Malnisio, where we had eaten with Giovanni Vicenzo del Gastaldo, and having left Giovanni Vicenzo's house were coming down a path toward the square of Malnisio."

Asked who might have been present, he replied: "I do not believe there was anyone else but the two of us."

Asked when this was, he replied: "I do not remember precisely, but it may have been seven or eight years ago."

Asked if at that time Menocchio wore the garment commonly called the *abitello*, he replied: "He has not worn it for many years, as far as I know, in fact, I can state that I have never seen him with the *abitello*."

Asked what day it was, he replied: "It was the day of St. John, in June."[23]

Asked what had been the occasion for their conversation, he replied: "At the time that we ate together, we began to talk about Christ and he said what I reported above." He added on his own: "When I heard these words my hair stood on end, and I changed the subject immediately so as not to hear these things, because I consider him to be worse than a Turk."

Asked what trade Menocchio had, and what was his condition and age, he replied: "This Menocchio is a man of medium height, who was a miller and I do not know if he still is one now. He has sons who go around dressed like millers, and he is an old man, about sixty or more in my opinion, who some years ago was in the custody of the Holy Office, and, as we were saying, was condemned to wear a certain vestment, which I never saw him wear."

---

[23] 24 June, day of the festival of the *sagra* at Malnisio: cf. xci.

When the present witness was asked if he had repeated these words to anyone else, and to whom in particular, he replied: "I do not remember, but I am sure that I told others since it is a strange thing."

Asked why he had not reported it to the Holy Office, he replied: "I never knew about this obligation to denounce him, until now from your paternity, and I am very glad to learn it so that in the future I can do my duty immediately."

Asked if he had been to confession this year, he replied: "Yes father, I have gone to confession, and do so every year."

Questioned, he replied: "This year I confessed myself to father Bonifacio,[24] priest at the castle of Aviano, but he said nothing about this obligation to denounce."

Asked if the above named Menocchio when he proffered those words was inebriated or spoke jestingly, he replied: "It was well after we had eaten, but I saw no sign that he was drunk, nor was he speaking in jest."

At the completion of the questioning, he answered properly about generalities, confirmed the proceedings when they were read back to him, took the oath to observe silence, and said that he did not know how to write.

These proceedings took place on the day and place noted above, before the same named above, in the presence of the reverend father Fra Giuseppe Vianna of Polcenigo, custodian of the *custodia* of the Friuli, priest and Fra Giovanni Antonio Pisani of Belluno, deacon and Fra Tommaso Rizzi of Venice, members of the order of minor conventuals, who all took the oath to observe silence.

12 May at Pordenone in the residence of the magnificent lord Sartorio Altan, where the most illustrious and reverend lord bishop and the very reverend father inquisitor, in the presence of the most excellent vicar, after having carefully considered the evidence accumulated in the present trial, decided to invoke the assistance of the secular arm for the arrest of Domenico Scandella and his transfer to the custody of the Holy Office. For this purpose the most illustrious and

---

[24] Priest Bonifacio Canario was chaplain of the altar consecrated to the Body of Christ from 1581 to 1583, and from 1584 he was titular of the parish of saints Maria e Giuliana in Castello d'Aviano, which ecclesiastically was under the jurisdiction of the patriarchate of Aquileia: Degani, *La diocesi di Concordia*, 520–22.

reverend bishop wrote to the magnificent captain of the castle in Aviano requesting that he come to Pordenone on this business.

The captain arrived in Pordenone on 15 May, and having been asked for the assistance of the secular arm by the most illustrious and reverend bishop and the reverend father inquisitor, freely promised it.

28 May 1599

Before me, Father Tiberio Asteo[25] of Pordenone, apostolic notary public of the Holy Office for the most illustrious patriarch of Aquileia and the most illustrious bishop of Concordia, there appeared messer Michiel del Turco of the parish of Aviano, innkeeper in that village, who testified in my presence and that of the magnificent and noble signor Gregorio Ferro of Pordenone, as follows:

"On 6 May 1599, in my house in Aviano, in the course of discussing various matters with Andrea Patesio of Aviano, who resides in Cal Maior,[26] or in Concignon, this Andrea started a conversation and told me that he had heard from others that a certain Domenego Menocchio of Montereale, a man about sixty years of age, of average height, had uttered these words: 'Oh, how can you believe that Christ or God Almighty was the Son of the Virgin Mary if the Virgin Mary was a whore?' Andrea adding, 'Now I do not remember from whom I heard this, but if necessary, I could think about it and try to remember.'"

Questioned, he replied: "There were many people present when the aforesaid Andrea spoke those words, but now I do not remember who they were, nor the reason why we began to speak of this Menocchio. Moreover, I can say that on the same day finding myself in Polcenigo in the inn of Zan della Zotta, and talking with Zan, son of Lenardo de Mellina[27] of Piedemonte di Aviano, who is now an official in Polcenigo, I asked him if his wife was with him, and the host's wife answered: 'How do you expect her to be with him if he threw her into the Gorgazzo?' Hearing these words Zan Mellina replied: 'She lies through her teeth, even if it were the Son of God saying it.' And many

---

[25] A secular priest, brother of the inquisitor Fra Gerolamo, and appointed notary of the Holy Office by him on 17 September 1598: ASPn, *Congregazioni soppresse*, b. 6, fasc. 29. The notarial archive does not possess any acts drawn up by him.

[26] Calmaur, a place adjacent to Marsure in the map of Montereale Valcellina prepared by the *Istituto geografico militare*.

[27] See the introduction, cvi–cviii.

were there to hear these words: the innkeeper's wife, the knight of Polcenigo, Piero Bel of Caneva and two other officials of Polcenigo,[28] whose names I do not know, but if the reverend father inquisitor would like their names, he can get them from Antonio, knight of Polcenigo. And everything that I have said is the truth and I only say it for the good of my conscience and in obedience of the holy Church which commands it of me, and so as not to incur any censure by not denouncing. I do not remember anything else."

And with his own hand the above named magnificent signor Gregorio Ferro, who was present as I have said, confirmed all this.

And I Gregorio Ferro was present at what was testified to above by the aforenamed Ser Michiel.

Tiberio Asteo to Fra Girolamo Asteo
Pordenone, 2 June 1599

Very reverend father, my most respected brother. I send to your lordship the enclosed denunciation made by Ser Michiel del Turco, innkeeper and resident in the parish of Aviano, who having used as intermediary signor Gregorio Ferro to bring the said denunciation to my attention, I wanted signor Gregorio himself to be present at Michiel's deposition. And since Michiel did not know how to write, I arranged for signor Gregorio to sign it, and if the writing is poor, blame the pen, paper and ink.

In addition, I am sending the enclosed from priest Donato. The most illustrious monsignor and monsignor the vicar greet you warmly, and I believe will set out tomorrow.[29]

I should like to be of service to the magnificent signor Posarello, but we have neither red nor gray cloth, but only some white material and [... *doi bizzari alti*]. Messer Orazio has arrived and I think that tomorrow we shall make the deposit for the spices. I am well and hope the same for you and commend myself to you.

Pordenone, 2 June '99.

---

[28] They are respectively Ordaura, Antonio Fachineto da Ceneda, Piero Bel, Pasqualin de Zanuto and Francesco de Iuri, who are interrogated by the inquisitor the same day and the next day at Polcenigo: AAUd, *S. Officio*, b. 14, fasc. 285, fols. 13r–15r.

[29] The bishop and monsignor Trapola remained in Pordenone from 19 May to 3 June 1599 for the pastoral visitation to the city and the neighboring parishes: AVPn, *Visite*, b.3, reg. "Sacrarum visitationum sub illustrissimo Sanuto episcopo annorum 1599–1600," fols. 56v–75r.

Of your very reverend paternity, your affectionate brother, priest Tiberio Asteo, in great haste.

21 June 1599

Gregorio Pinuculo, a guard attached to the episcopal court of Concordia, reported that he went today with his squad to the castle of Aviano and, at the order of the most illustrious and reverend bishop, who was on a visitation to the parish of Aviano,[30] carried out the arrest of Domenico Scandella, called Menocchio, and conducted him to the prison in Aviano.

The most illustrious and reverend bishop ordered the same guard to transfer the prisoner, observing every care, to the prisons in the city of Concordia, and secure him closely, with the intention, etc.

23rd of the same [month]

The aforesaid guard Gregorio reported, in execution of the above order, that he conducted the above mentioned Domenico Scandella to the prisons of Concordia and arranged that he be kept under close watch.

Report on the confiscation of books
Montereale, 4 July 1599

I report on the commission executed by me, Fra Zanantonio Pisano of Belluno, at the request of the very reverend father inquisitor, whose assistant I am, in the presence of Bastian de Martin, the *podestà*, and of Biasio de Caligo and of the reverend parish priest. I went with the aforenamed reverend to the house of Domenico Scandella, called Menocchio, and after summoning the above named witnesses, I had all the chests opened and took all the books and writings that I could find to the reverend father. Among them was a book entitled *Lunario al modo di Italia calculato, composto nella città di Pesero da l'eccellentissimo dottore, maestro Camilo de Leonardis.*[31]

---

[30] The parish of Aviano was visited on 20 June, after Polcenigo and Dardago, which were visited on 17 and 19 June. On the 21st it was the turn of Marsure, on the 22nd Giais, the 23rd Montereale, the 24th Grizzo and Malnisio and on the next three days San Leonardo Valcellina, San Martino di Campagna and San Foca. The visitation of the diocese resumed 7 June 1600: Ibid. fols. 115r–32v.

[31] Camillo de Leonardis, *Lunario al modo d'Italia calculato, composto nella città di Pesaro:* see Sander, *Le livre à figures italien,* nos. 3936–43; Ginzburg, 29.

5 July 1599

In the parish of Aviano, in the residence of the magnificent lord Antonio Menegozzi, there appeared Michel del Turco of the parish of Aviano before the very reverend father master Girolamo Asteo, inquisitor, and questioned under oath if the above cited writing[32] was done in his name and if everything it contained was true he replied: "Reverend father, yes, this is the document that I had drawn up by the reverend messer priest Tiberio Asteo in Pordenone for the sake of my conscience, and everything that I have said in it is the truth."

About generalities, he responded properly, confirmed what was read back to him, took the oath to observe silence, but did not sign since he said that he could not write.

5 July 1599

In the parish of Aviano in the home of Signor Antonio Menegozzi, before the reverend father inquisitor, there appeared as witness Ser Andrea Patesio of Aviano, a lumber merchant, forty-seven years of age, as he said, and cautioned, sworn in under oath after laying his hands on Holy Scripture, asked if he knew of anyone who had done or spoken anything against the holy faith, he replied: "Last year when we were threshing oats here in the parish in the house of the priest,[33] I found myself by chance with three peasants threshing, whom I think are from Malnisio,[34] and I do not know how but we began to talk about Menocchio of Montereale, an old man who in the past had been before the Holy Office, whom I used to see at feast days playing his cithara, and he is a miller, and one of those three peasants said: 'I was once threshing in the house of that Menocchio who said that the Virgin Mary had given birth like other women and not through the Holy Spirit.'"

Asked the name of this peasant who had reported these words, he replied: "I do not remember, I did not pay any attention because I did not know about this obligation to denounce, but your paternity can learn from monsignor priest or from his familiars who those three peasants of Malnisio were who came to thresh his oats last year or the

---

[32] The deposition of 28 May at 119–20.

[33] The priest Tommaso Ferro.

[34] The three peasants of Malnisio who participated in the threshing in 1597 were Bernardo, forty to forty-five years of age, Battista di Piero Giacomello, thirty, Domenico Gerbaso, twenty: see 124.

year before, because I would not want to say one thing for another."

Asked whether the peasant reported that Menocchio had said these words after his case had been concluded by the Holy Office or before, he replied: "I do not know, I do not remember."

Asked if that peasant had told him that Menocchio had said anything about the divinity of Christ our Lord, he replied: "I do not remember this, but Menocchio did say: 'How do you expect Christ to have been conceived by the Holy Spirit, if he was born from a whore?'"

He was asked about the bystanders when the peasant reported these words. [No answer is recorded].

About generalities, he responded properly, confirmed the proceedings when they were read back to him, took the oath to observe silence, asked pardon for not having made a denunciation to the Holy Office out of ignorance of this obligation, and the reverend father inquisitor absolved him, etc.

I, Andrea Patesio, ratify the above.

The same day

Before me, Fra Girolamo inquisitor, in the place as above, there appeared as witness Leonardo son of the deceased Battista da Croda of the parish of Aviano, servant of the reverend parish priest; cautioned, sworn in and questioned, he said: "I have been with the reverend priest for six years."

Questioned: "Who were the men who threshed oats for the reverend priest last year?" he replied: "Domenico da Malacassa and Mene Blancat of Aviano."

Asked if there were any others, especially from Malnisio, threshing, he replied: "No sir, but there were the year before."

Asked who they were, he replied: "There were three, who stayed here two or three weeks."

Asked about their names, he replied: "I do not know the names exactly, but I do know that one is called Bernardo, who is a large dark man, perhaps forty or forty-five years old. Another is a certain Battista, a young man about thirty years of age, and the third was a youth, who could not be more than twenty, but I do not know their surnames, although I do know that they are from Malnisio."

Questioned, he replied: "The reverend priest has another servant, called Mene da Bar, who is of this parish, but he is up in the mountains now."

About generalities he responded properly, confirmed the proceedings when they were read back to him, and took the oath to observe silence.

5 July 1599, at Polcenigo, in the convent of San Giacomo
The reverend father, master Girolamo Asteo, inquisitor etc., granted authority to the reverend father, Fra Tommaso Rizzi of Venice, of the order of minor conventuals, guardian of the aforementioned convent, to travel to the village of Malnisio and question the three above mentioned witnesses of Malnisio concerning the articles cited above, and any other deemed necessary, appointing him as his commissioner in these parts with the authority to carry out whatever the law requires. In faith of which, etc. Given as above.
Fra Girolamo Asteo, inquisitor, in his own hand.

Fra Tommaso Rizzo to Fra Girolamo Asteo
Polcenigo, 6 July 1599
Very reverend father. This morning, in accordance with your request, I went to the parish of Aviano and talked with the very reverend priest, who was not able to furnish me with the names of the three witnesses of Malnisio whom we are seeking, but the priest did direct me to the parish priest of Grizzo,[35] telling me that he would be able to inform me about those witnesses, because it was he who two years ago sent them to him to thresh the oats. And so I went to Grizzo to see its parish priest, who also has Malnisio under his cure, and he gave me three names, one Toni Massoto, who is the first one I questioned, who then called the other two, whom I also examined, and he is the one mentioned in the records as having heard the suspicious words from Menocchio. The other two named are: Dominico Gerbaso, a youth of about twenty, the other a certain Battista, son of Piero Giacomello, a man of about thirty, a redhead. I did not question the last two, because, beside the fact that Domenico is the brother-in-law of one of Menocchio's sons, I talked to both in general, and having seen that they do not know anything about these matters, and since the first is the one we were looking for, I did not question the others. And if your reverence feels that it has not been served as it wishes, pardon my ignorance and my being new at this work, to which I dedicate myself with all my heart, beseeching for you from the Lord every prosperity and happiness.

---

[35] The priest Nicolò Nadino.

Polcenigo, 6 July 1599

Of your most reverend paternity, your affectionate servant, Fra Tommaso Rizzo.

6 July 1599

In the village called Grizzo, in the residence of the reverend parish priest Nicolò Nadini of Manzano, there appeared before me Fra Tommaso Rizzi of Venice, commissioner of the above named father inquisitor, Antonio Massot, an inhabitant of the village, summoned as a witness, who, cautioned and asked under oath: "How long ago did you thresh oats for Menego Scandella, called Menocchio?" he replied: "A year before he was taken off to prison, about ten or twelve years ago."[36]

Questioned: "Who were your companions when you were threshing oats?" he replied: "There was a certain Marchiò Gerbaso of Grizzo, who is now banished."

Asked if he had ever heard anyone saying things against the holy faith, he replied: "I do not remember."

And when the father commissioner also asked if he had ever heard Menocchio say that the Virgin Mary gave birth to Christ like other women and not by the Holy Spirit, he replied: "It could be that he said it, but I do not remember."

And asked if he had heard Menocchio say, "How could Christ have been conceived by the Holy Spirit, if he was born from a whore?" he replied: "I do not know, but summon Daniel de Giacomel and Zan Antonio Fassetto, who will be able to say something, since they were talking about God together."

Asked: "Did you hear what they were saying?" he replied: "I do not know what they were saying, because I did not understand any of it."

The father commissioner then repeated to Antonio the words against the faith about which he was asked above, and the latter persisted in the same reply: "It could be that he spoke them, but I do not remember."

About generalities, he responded properly, confirmed the proceedings when they were read back to him, and took the oath to observe silence. Asked if he knows how to write, he replied: "No father."

---

[36] In 1583, namely sixteen years before.

The same day

Before etc., after being summoned there appeared Giovanni Antonio Fassetta of the same village; cautioned, and after having laid his hands on Holy Scripture, asked if he knew anyone who had done or said anything against the faith, he replied: "In this place of ours I do not know of anything, nor of anyone who has spoken against the holy faith. True, once I was questioned about Menocchio of Montereale and what you ask me, namely whether Menocchio said that the Virgin Mary gave birth like other women and not by the Holy Spirit, if I heard him say this, it is written down in the other trial."

Asked if he heard him say anything against the holy faith after he came out of prison, he replied: "I heard him make music. And for my part I believe that he was in a bad mood and did not dare to speak out of fear."

Asked if he heard him proffer or say anything, he replied: "He said: 'I should like to say a few words of the Pater noster before the father inquisitor and see what he would say and reply.'"

Asked how long ago he had said these words, he replied: "It may be three or four years ago."

Asked the time and place these words were said, he replied: "Walking about here and there."

About generalities he responded properly, confirmed the proceedings when they were read back to him, took the oath of silence, and signed.

I Zaneto Faseta ratify the above.

The same day

There was summoned and interrogated Daniel Iacomel of the same village, who cautioned, and after having touched Holy Scripture and asked if he knew anyone who had spoken against the holy faith, replied: "One day coming down from Malnisio with Menego Scandella, called Menocchio, of Montereale, he asked me: 'What do you think God is?' I replied: 'I know not.' And Menocchio said: 'It is nothing but air.'" And then he [Daniel Iacomel] added: "Finding myself once in the house of the wife of the deceased Piero Gastaldo, talking with one of her brothers called Giovanni Antonio Locatello of Gradisca, Menocchio said this about the passion of Christ: 'If he was God, how could he have let himself be crucified by the Jews.' And the man from Gradisca replied that he had suffered as a man, but not in his divinity."

Asked if he has heard this Menocchio or anyone else say that the Virgin Mary gave birth like other women and not by the Holy Spirit and : "How could Christ have been conceived by the Holy Spirit, if he was born from a whore?" he replied: "I did not hear such things said."

Asked if he remembered anything else about this Menocchio, he replied: "Once he said: 'What do you think? The inquisitors do not want us to know what they know.' And I also heard tell that this Menocchio said St. Christopher is greater than God, since he carried the whole world on his back."

Asked if he remembers who was present when Menocchio spoke these words, he replied: "I do not remember, but if they come to mind I shall not fail to report them."

Questioned: "How long ago did Menocchio say all the things about which you testified?" he replied: "Perhaps three years."

Asked if it was all in one day, he replied: "Yes sir."

He took the oath of silence and confirmed what was read back to him.

12 July
In the palace of the most illustrious *podestà* of Portogruaro, the reverend father inquisitor and the reverend vicar, with the participation of the most illustrious lord Pietro Zane,[37] decided that they would interrogate the arraigned Domenico Scandella, who was in custody, reserving to themselves the right to question again, if it should be necessary, the above witnesses and any others, in accordance with the law, etc. And they thus ordered the guard to conduct the aforenamed prisoner to their presence.

12 July 1599
Held in the palace of the city of Portogruaro. Before the reverend father master Girolamo Asteo, inquisitor etc. and the most excellent lord Valerio Trapola dai Colli, vicar general of Concordia, with the assistance of the most illustrious lord Pietro Zane, worthy *podestà* of the place, there was led forth from prison a certain old man, dressed in a gray vestment under a white one, as worn by millers in the country, and a cap of the same color, his beard gray and turning white, his hair

---

[37] Pietro Zane was *podestà* at Portogruaro from 31 May 1599 to August 1600: ASVe, *Segretario alle voci, Elezioni del Maggior Consiglio*, reg. 8, fols. 149v–50r.

already white, about sixty years of age. Asked about his name, his father, his home village and trade, under oath, laying his hand on Scripture, he replied: "I have the name of Domenego Scandella and am called Menocchio, of Montereale, and I am sixty-seven years old. My trade is that of miller, but I have been a sawyer and innkeeper, I have kept a school for children to learn the abacus and reading and writing and I also play the cithara on holidays."

Asked if he had ever been summoned to the Holy Office and why, he replied: "Fifteen years ago, in 1584, I was called before the Holy Office and was interrogated about the Creed and about other fantasies that had come into my head because I had read the Bible and because I have a keen mind. But I have always been a Christian and remain so."

Questioned, he replied: "The Holy Office condemned me to wear the *habitello*, which I am wearing even now, and condemned me to prison, but later granted me the grace of letting me stay in Montereale."

Asked if he had fulfilled the penance imposed upon him by the Holy Office, especially the last time, when the place of his imprisonment was changed so that he could remain in Montereale, he replied: "I performed the penance that was imposed on me."

Asked about his penance, he replied: "My penance was that I should confess six times a year and receive communion, and I did this, although on some occasions I could not take communion because the priest was absent. I was also obliged every Friday to fast or give alms, which I did."

Asked where were the priests' letters of testimony that he had gone to confession and received holy communion, he replied: "I have never known of this obligation to carry this certification, and so I never did."[38]

Asked if praying was among his penances, he replied: "I did not know that I was obliged to say prayers, but I said many on my own."

Asked if he had transgressed the geographical boundaries assigned to him by the Holy Office, and how often, he replied: "On the occasion of the death of one of my sons who supported me, I obtained

---

[38] The sentence commuting the punishment expressly contained this obligation: see 104. Menocchio, instead, was right in the next reply, because the injunction to recite daily the seven penitential psalms or the rosary was only contained in the first sentence: see 98.

permission from the reverend father inquisitor to go outside my confinement for two months, and as license the father inquisitor gave me a note, which I gave to messer Zuane Ghibillino, who is now deceased.[39] And that was the Lent when the reverend father inquisitor was preaching here in Portogruaro. I do not know what happened to that note, because I left it with the notary. Moreover, another time I went to see the father inquisitor in Udine to obtain a new license and he gave me a letter to bring to monsignor the vicar, which I did. And monsignor vicar told me that the father inquisitor in that letter was enlarging my boundaries and the vicar said that, if it was agreeable to the father inquisitor, he too was content and that letter should be in his [the vicar's] hands."

When he was told that in the Holy Office there was no trace of these so-called licenses and that he had made them up, he replied: "Monsignor the vicar must have them and he needs to find them."[40]

Asked if he always wore the penitential garment of the Holy Office, he replied: "I always wore it, but sometimes, when I had to work, I took it off."

Questioned: "Did you have it when you were taken?" he replied: "I was summoned early one morning to come to Aviano, so I mounted on horseback without putting it on, and then my son Daniele brought it to me two days later."

When he was told: "It appears from the trial records that you often did not wear it and kept it hidden," he replied: "I swear upon my faith that on feast days sometimes I wore it and sometimes not; and on work days in winter when it was cold I always wore it, but underneath."

And when he was asked why he had disobeyed the law, he replied: "I was losing many earnings not being called to do assessments and other jobs that I can do, because men considered me excommunicated when they saw the garment, and so I did not wear it."

When asked why he had not petitioned the Holy Office, he replied: "I did petition, but the father inquisitor would not give me permission to take off the vestment."

---

[39] He was the chief episcopal notary as well as notary of the Holy Office during the first trial. The document has not been preserved.

[40] It is the letter of 26 January 1597, published at 109, which was returned by the vicar general to the inquisitor on 13 July 1599, as the inquisitor wrote on the back of the letter.

Asked if after the conclusion of the trial he continued to have doubts about those questions for which he was condemned, he replied: "Many fantasies came into my head, but I never wanted to pay attention to them, nor have I ever taught anyone bad things."

Asked if he had ever discussed articles of the faith with anyone, and who they were, and on what occasion and where, he replied: "I sometimes spoke jokingly with some about the articles of the faith, but truthfully I do not know with whom, or where, or when."

Questioned: "How is it that you were joking about matters of the faith? Is it proper to joke about the faith? What do you mean by this word 'jokingly?'" he replied: "Saying some lie."

Questioned: "What lie were you saying? Come, speak up clearly," he replied: "I truthfully cannot say." And questioned often on this point, he persisted in his answer, saying: "I know not, someone may have misinterpreted it, but I have never believed anything that is against the faith."

And when he was told that in the sentence of the Holy Office he had been prohibited to speak about the faith with anyone, he replied: "I never learned what articles were contained in the sentence."

Informed that by a notarized statement he gave assurance that he would observe all the things contained in the sentence and, therefore, it is not possible that he does not know the articles contained in the sentence, he replied: "Sir, I do not know."

Asked if he had ever said that we do not know if saintly hermits and others who confronted death for God and led holy lives had gone to paradise, and to whom he had said it, how often, when, where and in whose presence, he replied: "I do not know that I talked about these things with anyone."

Asked if he had ever said that to become a religious is a thing for beggars, he replied: "I remember saying this, but I do not know to whom, perhaps I was just talking to myself: they are rich, they could give alms, so why become monks?"

Asked if he thought it was better to remain in the world than become a religious, he replied: "It is better to stay in the world than become a monk and then not observe the rules of the order, but for those who live properly, I believe it is better to enter an order."

Asked why, then, dissuade people from joining orders, he replied: "I do not know."

Asked whether he had said when the Jews told Christ hanging on the cross: "If you are the son of God, come down from the cross,"[41] that Christ did not descend because he could not descend, he replied: "I do not remember saying this, but if Christ's Father did not want him to descend, he could not descend."

Asked if Christ had the power to descend, he replied: "I believe that Christ had the power to descend."

Asked whether he had said that he did not believe in the Gospel, he replied: "I never said this, but I believe in the Gospel that which is the truth." Then he added of his own accord: "I believe that the Gospel is the truth."

When he was told, "It appears from the trial that you said you did not believe in the Gospel and that the Gospels were made by priests and monks, who have nothing else to do and imagine them and just put down one thing after another," he replied: "No sir, I never said this, but I did indeed say that priests and monks who had studied made the Gospels through the mouth of the Holy Spirit."

Asked to whom, where and when he had said this, he replied: "By my faith I do not know."

Asked if he believed that the Gospels had been written by the evangelists, and who were those monks who he said wrote the Gospels, he replied: "How should I know? Truthfully, no, I do not know this."

Questioned: "Why did you say it if you do not know it?" he replied: "Sometimes the Devil tempts me to say certain words," and then added: "Curse all this reading! I have read that various people have made Gospels, such as St. Peter, St. James and others, which justice has suppressed."

Questioned: "Where did you read this?" he replied: "I read it in the *Suplimento delle Croniche*,[42] a book that was given to me by messer Tomaso Moro of Malnisio, but then the pages became torn and the book was destroyed."

Questioned: "When you heard thunder and lightning, what did you use to say?" he replied: "I believe that God made all things, that is earth, water and air."

To this the most excellent lord vicar said, "But where did you put fire then, who made that?" and he replied: "Fire is everywhere, just as

---

[41] Mt 27: 40; cf Mt 27: 42; Mk 15: 30–32.

[42] Iacopo Filippo Foresti, *Supplementum supplementi delle croniche* ... (Venice, 1553), fols. 180r–v; Ginzburg, 104–5.

God is, but the other three elements are the three persons: the Father is air, the Son is earth, and the Holy Spirit is water." And then he added on his own: "At least this is how it seems to me; but I do not know if it is the truth, and I believe that those spirits that are in the air fight among themselves, and that the lightning flashes are their artillery."

Asked from whom he had learned this and to whom he had talked about it, he replied: "By my faith, I do not know."

Asked why he had said that air was the person of the Father, earth of the Son, and water of the Holy Spirit, he replied: "I believe that the Father is air, because air is an element higher than water and earth. Then I say that the Son is earth because the Son is produced by the Father; and since water comes from air and earth, so the Holy Spirit comes from the Father and from the Son." Then he added on his own: "But I do not want to believe these things."

Asked if he thought that God had a body, he replied: "I know that Christ had a body." And when the reverend father inquisitor then remarked: "You say that the Holy Spirit is water; water is a body; thus would it not follow that the Holy Spirit is a body?" He replied: "I say these things as similitudes."

He was told: "It appears in the records that you said God is nothing other than air," to which he replied: "I do not know that I said this, but I did really say that God is all things."

When asked, "Do you really believe that God is all things," he replied: "Sir, by my faith yes, I do believe it."

Asked in what way he understood it, he replied: "I believe that God is everything he wants to be."

Questioned: "Can God be a stone, a serpent, a devil and such things?" he replied: "God can be everything that is good."

Questioned: "Then God can be a creature, since there are good creatures?" he replied: "I do not know what to say."

Asked if he had said that he was born a Christian and so wants to live as a Christian, but that if he had been born a Turk, he would have wanted to remain a Turk, he replied: "Yes sir, I said it, but I do not know to whom." Then he added of his own: "I beg you, sir, listen to me. Once upon a time there was a great lord, who declared that his heir would be the person who had a certain precious ring of his, and when death was near, he had two other rings made just like the first, since he had three sons, and he gave a ring to each son. Each one of them thought that he was the heir and that he had the true ring, but since they looked alike one could not tell for sure.[43] In the same way God the Father has various children whom he loves, that is Christians, Turks and Jews, and he gave them all the will to live in his law, and we do not know which is the good one. Thus I said that, since I was born a Christian, I want to remain a Christian, and if I had been born a Turk, I should like to live as a Turk."

Questioned: "Do you believe then that we do not know which is the good law?" he replied: "Yes sir, I do believe that every person considers his faith to be right, and we do not know which is the right one. But because my grandfather, my father, and my people have been Christians, I want to remain a Christian and believe that this is the right one."

Asked to whom, when, and how often he had said this, he replied: "Sir, by my soul, I do not know."

Asked from whom he had learned the similitude of the three rings, he replied: "I read it in some book or other."

Asked if he had said: "If Christ was the Son of God, he was an (omitting that word) to let himself be crucified," he answered smiling: "By my faith, I do not know."

And cautioned to think carefully about a matter of such importance and that it was not possible that he could have forgotten such words, he replied: "I do not know that I said it."

Asked whether he had doubted the divinity of Christ, our Lord, he replied, a little lost in thought: "I have never doubted that Christ was God."

Questioned: "Do you believe that Christ is the Son of God, having allowed himself to be crucified?" he replied: "I believe yes, and that he was doing his Father's will."

Asked if he had ever said to anyone: "How can you believe that Christ who is God was the son of the Virgin Mary, if the Virgin Mary was a whore?" he replied: "I never said that, nor did my mind ever think it. I did say that the Madonna was married to St. Joseph."

Asked whether he had said that the Virgin Mary gave birth like other women and not by the Holy Spirit, he replied: "I never said it and never thought it."

Asked if he thought that the act of matrimony had been consummated between the most Blessed Virgin Mary and the blessed Joseph,

---

[43] G. Boccaccio, *Decameron*, third tale of the first day; Ginzburg, 50. This story was expunged from the expurgated editions.

he replied: "I know nothing about this, but he was old."

Informed that in his first trial he had been condemned on these grounds, which he abjured, he replied: "I believe what so many saints say, that St. Joseph did not touch the most Blessed Virgin, our lady."

Asked whether he had said: "How could Christ have been conceived by the Holy Spirit, if the Madonna is a whore?" he replied: "I never said this and whoever said this is an assassin."

Asked if he had said that St. Christopher is greater than God, since he carried the whole world on his back, after a short delay he replied, with a smile: "No sir, I did not say it."

Asked if he had said: "I should like to say a few words to the inquisitor about the Pater Noster and see a little what he would reply," and to whom he had said this, when and where, he replied: "Yes sir, I said it, but I do not remember to whom or when."

And asked what those words were that he wanted to propose, he replied: "I wanted to propose those words of the Pater Noster that say: 'and do not lead us into temptation, but liberate us from evil.' And thereby I would have asked for the grace to be released from these tribulations of mine." And he added of his own accord: "And I have also prepared a written statement on this matter, and here it is." And he presented two sheets.

Asked if he had said: "These inquisitors do not want us to know what they know," he replied: "It is true that inquisitors and our other superiors do not want us to know what they know; and so we should remain silent."

And cautioned diligently that he should consider better telling the truth, he said nothing other than what he had already testified, and was again cautioned to think better about telling the truth, etc. He confirmed the proceedings when they were read back to him and he signed.

I Domenego Scandella called Menocchio confirm the above.

And then the guard Pietro Dulceto was ordered to lead the above named Domenico back to prison and keep him under close surveillance.

Autograph petition of Domenico Scandella
[Portogruaro, 12 July 1599]

In the name of our Lord Jesus Christ and of his mother the Virgin Mary and of all the saints in paradise, I appeal for help and counsel.

Oh great, omnipotent, and Holy God, creator of heaven and earth, I beg you, in the name of your most saintly goodness and infinite mercy, to enlighten my spirit, and my soul, and my body so that it will think, and say, and do everything that is pleasing to your divine majesty: and so be it in the name of the most holy Trinity, Father, Son, and Holy Spirit, and Amen. I the wretched Menego Scandella who have fallen into disgrace with the world and with my superiors resulting in the ruin of my house, of my life, and of my entire poor family, no longer know what to say or what to do except to speak these few words: First, "Set libera nos a malo et ne nos inducas in tentazionem et demite nobis debita nostra sicut ne nos dimitimus debitoribus nostris, panem nostrum cotidianum da nobis hodie:"[44] and so I pray our Lord Jesus Christ and my superiors that out of their mercy they give me some help with little bother to themselves. And wherever I Menego Scandella shall go I shall beg all faithful Christians to observe everything commanded of them by our holy mother Catholic Roman Church and her officials, that is, inquisitors, bishops, vicars, priests, chaplains, and curates of her dioceses, so that they should profit from my experience. I Menego also thought that death would free me from these sufferings, so I would not bother anyone, but it has done just the opposite, it has taken away a son of mine who was able to keep every trouble and suffering from me; and then it has wanted to take my wife who looked after me; and the sons and daughters who remain to me consider me crazy because I have been their ruination, which is the truth, and if only I had died when I was fifteen, they would be without the bother of this poor wretch.

And if I have had some evil thoughts or said some word falsely, I never believed them or ever even acted against the Holy Church, because our Lord God has taught me to believe that everything I thought and said was vanity, not wisdom.

And this I hold to be the truth, because I do not want to think or believe except what the Holy Church believes and to do what my priests and superiors will command of me.

Monday, 19 July 1599

Held in the palace of the most illustrious *podestà* of Portogruaro, before the aforementioned reverend father inquisitor, in the presence of the most illustrious lord Pietro Zane, most worthy *podestà*, and of the reverend father Fra Giovanni Antonio Pisani of Belluno, of the

---

[44] The quotation is from the second part of the *Pater noster* with the order of the sentences practically reversed: cf. Mt 6: 11–13.

order of minor conventuals, as well as of the most reverend theologian, the excellent Medicis,[45] consultors, etc. Led out again from prison was Domenico Scandella, called Menocchio, diligently cautioned, examined and, under oath, having touched Sacred Scripture, asked if he has resolved to speak more forthrightly and better speak the truth, he replied: "Yes sir."

After being told, "Speak up, then," he stated: "I was wrong not to wear my vestment, and I also said some words foolishly and those words that I said about the faith, namely that everyone should remain within his own law, because I believed that the law of the Turk was good, I spoke badly, and I have regretted it."

And told that he should avow his errors clearly in every matter, he replied: "Just as if four soldiers were fighting, two in each band, and one of the soldiers joined the other band, would he not be a traitor? And so I thought that if a Turk abandoned his law and made himself a Christian, he would be doing an evil thing, and I also thought that a Jew would be doing an evil thing if he made himself a Turk or a Christian, and anyone else who abandoned his law. And I believed this because I had read it in a book that contains the similitude of the three rings."

And when he was told that the similitude is in a prohibited book, and he should say what the book is and who gave it to him, he replied: "I cannot remember."

Questioned: "To whom did you express this opinion or heresy that one would be doing an evil thing abandoning his law?" he replied: "Sir, I do not know to whom I said it, but I no longer hold this opinion, in fact I have repented it and beseech pardon."

Questioned: "The last time that you were before us, at the end of the session you stated that you thought you were a philosopher, astrologer and prophet, but that even prophets erred. How do you understand this matter about being a prophet and that prophets err?" he replied: "I thought that I was a prophet because the malignant spirit made me see vanities and dreams and was persuading me to see the nature of the heavens and similar things. And I now believe that the prophets spoke what angels dictated to them."

Questioned: "What did you mean when you stated in the first session that God had given everyone the will to stick to his law?" he

---

[45] The canons Domenico Marino, a theologian and Andronico Medicis.

replied: "I believed that the will to remain Turk was good and there-fore had been given by God."

Questioned: "How long have you had this opinion?" he replied: "I may have had this opinion for fifteen or sixteen years, when we began to reason and the Devil put it into my head."

Questioned: "With whom did you begin to reason?" after a long pause, he replied: "I do not know."

Questioned: "You also said in your first interrogation that, discussing matters of the faith, you told some lies and joked. State now what you said joking about the faith." He replied: "I do not know what to say."

Questioned: "Tell the truth about what you said and believed about hermits and the other saints who gave their lives for the love of Christ, whether they went to paradise, or not." He replied: "I believe that the saints went to paradise, but if I said otherwise, I erred and ask forgiveness."

Questioned: "To whom did you say it?" he replied: "I believe that I said it, that is I believe that I said 'I do not know if there is a para-dise.' And so I said that we cannot know if they went to paradise, but I do not remember to whom I said it or when."

Questioned: "Why did you think that paradise does not exist?" he replied: "I did not believe in paradise because I did not know where it was."

Questioned: "How long have you held this opinion?" he replied: "I never held this opinion, but I think I uttered it and I repent it."

Questioned: "In the other session you stated that you believed that priests and monks who have studied made the Gospels through the mouth of the Holy Spirit. Tell who you think are those priests and monks who have studied." He replied: "I meant the evangelists, who I believe all studied."

Questioned: "It emerges from the trial records that some person told you: 'Beati qui non viderunt et crediderunt,' and you stated 'I do not believe, if I do not see.'"[46] He replied: "I was only referring to the things of this world, which I do not believe, if I cannot see."

Questioned: "To whom did you say it?" he replied: "I do not know."

Asked if he had spoken those words, he replied: "I may have said them."

---

[46] Jn 20: 29; cf. 20: 25.

And informed that it emerges from the trial records that he was reasoning about the faith, he replied: "Those witnesses lie."

Questioned: "You also stated that when it thunders and there is lightning, these are spirits in the air and the thunder is their artillery. What spirits do you think they are?" He replied: "I believe that they are spirits created by God, who are in the air."

Questioned: "You also said that God is all things. How do you understand this matter that you confusedly talked about in the other session?" He replied: "I believe that God can become all things, as also happens in the consecrated host."

Questioned: "You also told different people, as appears from the trial records, that if Christ was God he was a ... to let himself be crucified. Tell clearly what you believe about this matter and if you deceived anyone." He replied: "If I said it, I said it because it is written 'My God, my God, why have you abandoned me?'[47] because Christ was human and did not have it."

Asked to explain how Christ "did not have it" and how had God abandoned him, he replied: "I mean that Christ did not have the power of the Father, since he had a human body."

Informed that he should speak clearly, that this was sheer confusion, he persisted in his answer: "I do not remember saying it and I am an ignoramus."

Questioned: "You also stated in the other session that you believed what was true in the Gospel. Tell us what is that part of the Gospel that you believe and that which you do not believe to be true." He replied: "I believe the whole Gospel is true."

Cautioned again to tell the truth about the divinity of Christ our Lord and about the other questions from the first session, he replied that to the best of his knowledge he had told the truth.

Asked if he wanted to defend himself and make his defenses, he replied: "I do not want to make any other defense except to ask for mercy. Yet, if I could have a lawyer, I would accept one, but I am a poor man."

Then the reverend father inquisitor assigned him eight days to prepare his defense. When the trial proceedings were read back to him, he confirmed them and signed.

And I Domenego called Menocchio ratify the above.

---

[47] Mt 27: 46; Mk 15: 34.

At the conclusion, the reverend father inquisitor ordered that the forenamed Domenico be conducted back to his cell and kept under close guard.

The same day
The reverend father inquisitor assigned to Domenico Scandella as his defender and lawyer Agostino Pisenti, in accordance with the provisions of the law.

Oath taken by Agostino Pisenti
[Portogruaro] 19 July 1599
I, Agostino Pisenti, doctor in both laws, selected as defense lawyer for Domenico Scandella called Menocchio of Montereale, humbly seek license from the Holy Office of the Inquisition, promising and testifying publicly that I shall defend him, inspired not by any error, but in accordance with the truth and the sacred laws. And I swear this in the hands of the most magnificent and reverend lord, the father inquisitor.
The same as above in his own hand.

The defense
[Portogruaro], 22 July 1599
It is found written in Holy Scripture that it is wrong to sin and emend the Gospel, and diabolical to persevere in so doing, as is demonstrated by the text of the law *consentaneum* and also in the apposite gloss, *Codex, quomodo et quando iudex sententiam*[48]; and that God does not desire the death of the sinner but his conversion, and that he should live, as is demonstrated in the chapter *quia divinitatis, de Poenitentia*, distinction 1, where one finds these formal words: "Since divine nature is mild and pious and more inclined to kindness than to vengeance, because it does not desire the death of the sinner, but that he should be converted and live, if someone should be converted to true penitence after his fall into sin, he shall immediately be pardoned by the merciful judge."[49] And this is affirmed even in the chapter *his a quibus*, 23 q. 8.[50] And judges before giving judgment should always have mercy before their eyes, since true justice is to have

---

[48] See C. 7, 43, 8, gl. perseveraverit: "malum est peccare, diabolicum perseverare."

[49] See. c. 73, De poenit., D. 7.

[50] See. c. 30, C. XXIII, q. 8: "cui tamen conmunio exeunti ex hac vita non est neganda propter Domini misericordiam, qui non vult peccatoris mortem, sed ut convertatur et vivat."

mercy for those who have erred: one reads this in the chapter *vera iustitia,* distinction 45;[51] and those who "believe that mercy should be denied to sinners, and assume their own justice, will die struck down by the Lord, because there will be judgment without mercy for those who do not want to show mercy to those who have erred, about which Solomon declares: 'Do not be too just, because it is the just man who perishes in his own justice:'" in the chapter *plerumque,* rubric *his ita,* II, q. VII,[52] and which can be read also in the chapter *serpens* and apposite gloss, *de poenitentia,* distinction 1,[53] that we must not be too just, because the one who is too just often perishes in his own justice: chapter *de his,* II, q. VII.[54] In fact, if justice was not tempered by mercy, God would be called the God of vengeance, not of mercy,[55] which is what he is, and one could speak these words: if every time that men sinned, Jove sent his thunderbolts, in a short time there would be no one left.

Therefore, as the legitimate defender of the poor Domenico Scandella, known as Menocchio, trusting in these arguments and after having examined the trial against Domenico prepared by the Holy Office of the Inquisition on the grounds that he dared on diverse occasions to speak against the holy Catholic faith and the Roman Church, as well as against Sacred Scripture and the Gospels, as is stated in the trial records, to which we must always refer positively for the favorable aspects, and contesting the other aspects, it is our desire to exculpate and defend him legitimately, on the basis of the legal premise that he is defending the man, not the error, and states and denies that the matters described are true or even possess the slightest truth in them. Nor will it emerge that the poor prosecuted Domenico did or committed what was falsely asserted in the denunciation presented against him, despite the witnesses questioned on the matter or the interrogations of the defendant himself, so that he can be punished according to the law and all this can be proved. In fact, the trial not only should not have been formed on the basis of denunciations of this kind, according to the opinion of all the doctors, but the accused himself should not have been proclaimed, as was done against the law

---

[51] See c. 15, D. 45: "vera iusticia compassionem habet."

[52] See c. 27, C. II, q. 7.

[53] See c. 47, De poenit., D. 1: "et Salomon ait: Noli esse nimis iustus."

[54] See c. 27, C. II, q. 7.

[55] Echo of Mt 9: 13; 12: 7.

which provides for the punishment of the person who does not observe it, according to the law 1, *Digest, de iis quae pro non scriptis habentur*,[56] there not being the slightest evidence against him. All these elements render null and void the trial and even the arrest of the accused.

In criminal cases one proceeds either through inquisition or accusation. If through the former, which is adopted to cleanse cities of evil men, the judge can proceed when he receives strong information from honest people who are not themselves under suspicion, often and repeatedly. And for this reason the words "often and repeatedly" are placed in the inquest, as asserted by Angelo [Gambiglioni], *De maleficiis*, in his commentary on the word, not one time only, for substantiating the report itself, since one voice alone is not at all sufficient, but the repeated voice of people or of a commune is needed, as noted by Bartolus in his comment to the law *de minore*, rubric *tormenta, Digest, de quaestionibus*[57] and in the chapter *qualiter et quando debeat, II, Liber extra, de accusationibus*. It is stated there that it can be found in the Gospel that an administrator, who had been accused before his lord of having squandered his goods, and was asked by him "What is this that I hear about you? Give an accounting of your service, because you will no longer be able to serve as my steward." And even in Genesis the Lord declares: "I will go down to see whether they have done altogether according to the outcry which has come to me."[58] And the omnipotent God said: "I shall come down and look about me as a judge, because as God all certain things are known to me and in my sight",[59] from which it can be deduced that if the judge becomes aware of a crime, he should not proceed against it until a denunciation and claim of defamation should arise against it. "No one is ever con-

---

[56] See D. 34, 8, 1.

[57] Angelo Gambiglioni, *De maleficiis. Repertorium primi voluminis maleficiorum* ... (Lyons: apud Iacobum Giuncti, 1542), fols. 334v–39v, where reputation is talked about, especially at fol. 337v: "toties fama contra aliquem orta inquisitionem et praesumptionem inducit quoties contra eum fuerit scandalum vel clamor generatus per villam, parochiam aut alicuius viciniae maiorem partem"; Bartolo da Sassoferrato, *Secunda Bartoli super Digesto Novo* ... (Lyons: per Ioan. Dominicum Guarnerium, 1545), fol. 196r (commentary on D. 48, 18, 10 [3]): "Fama totius civitatis, quod requiratur in negotiis magnis, in parvis vero sufficit fama viciniae."

[58] See c. 24, X, V, 1; cf. c. 17, X, V, 1. The Biblical citations are to Lk 16: 1–2; Gn 18: 21.

[59] I have not been able to locate this sentence in the Bible.

demned without an accuser, according to a saying by our Lord: 'If no one accuses you woman, nor will I condemn you,'" as stated by Egidio Bossi under the rubric *de accusatione,* no. 1.[60] But where there has been no denunciation, then judges should abstain from investigating, except in the case of grievous crimes. One should not investigate frivolous cases because then we would be prosecuting peccadilloes rather than crimes and God condemns those mean judges who investigate improperly, and they are obliged to pay all the expenses plus interest to the side that was unduly oppressed and especially when it was the fault of the judges, as per the text of the law *si filius familias* and the commentary by Bartolus in the *Digest, de iuditiis.*[61]

If, instead, one proceeds by means of accusation, then the accuser, after having made his charges, must prove them with witnesses or documentation, otherwise the defendant is absolved and the accuser is condemned to pay all damages, expenses and interest, both suffered and expected. This is so for two reasons. First, if the accuser does not prove his case, the defendant must be absolved according to the law: in the laws *qui accusare, Codex, de edendo* and *qui sententia, Codex, de poenis.*[62] But even more, the accuser must be condemned for defamation because his charges failed, as stated by Durant in the rubric *de accusationibus,* no. 24.[63] The second reason consists in the fact that in criminal cases proof must be clearer than the light at mid-day: see chapter *sciant cuncti,* II, q. VIII and the chapter *Epiphanium,* V, q. VI, and the chapter *veniens, Liber extra, de testibus,*[64] so that the judge

---

[60] See Egidio Bosso, *Tractatus varii* ... (Venice: apud Ioan. Bapt. Somascum, 1565), fol. 54v, col. 2, num. 1: "Haec est regula, quod nemo sine accusatione damnatur, iuxta illud Domini: Si nemo te accusat, mulier, nec ego te condemno"; cf. Jn 8: 10–11.

[61] See D. 5, 1, 15: "Iudex tunc litem suam facere intelligitur, cum dolo malo in fraudem legis sententiam dixerit (dolo malo autem videtur hoc facere, si evidens arguatur vel gratia vel inimicitia vel etiam sordes), ut veram aestimationem litis praestare cogatur"; Bartolo da Sassoferrato, *Bartoli prima super Digesto Veteri* ... (Lyons: per Ioan. Dominicum Guarnerium, 1545), fol. 153r.

[62] See C. 2, 1, 4: "Actore enim non probante qui convenitur, etsi nihil ipse praestarit, obtineat"; C. 9, 47, 16.

[63] See Guillaume Durant, *Speculi iuris* ... *pars tertia et quarta* ... (Basel: apud Ambrosium et Aurelium Frobenios fratres, 1574; reprint: Aalen: Scientia Verlag, 1975), 18: "In summa nota quod accusator in probatione deficiens, eo ipso calumniari praesumitur."

[64] See c. 2, C. II, q. 8: "vel indiciis ad probationem indubitatis et luce clarioribus expedita"; c. 4, C. V, q. 6: "Criminis ergo eius auctores volumus te perscrutari, et nisi qui eandem transmisit epistolam paratus fuerit hoc, quod obiecit, canonicis atque districtissimis probationibus edocere, nullatenus ad sanctae communionis ministerium accedat"; c. 10, X,

can make a proper judgment over the offender: in the final law, *Codex, de probationibus;* in the law *additos, Codex, de appellationibus;* in the law *absentem,* at the beginning, *Digest, de poenis*[65]; otherwise they are obliged to give an accounting principally for these reasons: first, because the greater the danger, the greater is the need to proceed cautiously: see in the law 1, rubric *sed et si quis, Digest, de Carboniano edicto;* in the final chapter, in the gloss on the word *personaliter,* at the end, *Liber extra, de officio delegati* and in the chapter *ubi maius, Liber extra, de electione* in the *Liber sextus,*[66] and not only (because) where a man's life is involved, much is at stake, as we find in the law *additos, Codex, de episcopali audientia,* but even where the slightest corporal punishment is at issue, we consider the risks to be greater than in any civil case: see the law in *servorum,* at the end, *Digest, de poenis*[67]; second, because judges must condemn the offender only when the proof is clearer than the light of day, because in occult matters only God's judgment counts, and earthly judges must judge on the basis of things presented and proven, and on the basis of that prudence which is man's, leaving the rest to the judgment of God, as we read in *Exodus,* chapter 21.[68]

In the trial formed by the Holy Office of the Inquisition against the aforesaid Domenico, nowhere is any proof adduced by any denouncer substantiated by the word of at least two witnesses, because every word must come from two or three persons: see the chapter *cum esses, Liber extra, de testamentis;* the chapter *licet, Liber extra; de iuditiis;* the chapter *quod vero,* II, q. IV; the chapter *licet, Liber extra, de testibus;* St. Paul, second epistle to the Corinthians, chapter 13 and in the

---

II, 20: " . . . nec unius testimonium ad condemnationem sufficiat alicuius."

[65] See C. 4, 19, 25: "Sciant cuncti accusatores eam se rem deferre debere in publicam notionem, quae munita sit testibus idoneis vel instructa apertissimis documentis vel indiciis ad probationem indubitatis et luce clarioribus expedita"; C. 7, 62, 29; D. 48, 19, 5: "Absentem in criminalibus damnari non debere divus Traianus Iulio Frontoni rescripsit. Sed nec de suspicionibus debere aliquem damnari divus Traianus Adsidio Severo rescripsit: satius enim esse impunitum facinus nocentis quam innocentem damnari."

[66] See D. 37, 10, 1 (5); c. 43, X, I, 29 ("de officio et potestate iudicis delegati"); c. 3, VI, I, 6: "Ubi periculum maius intenditur, ibi procul dubio est plenius consulendum."

[67] Cfr. C. 1, 4, 6; D. 48, 19, 10.

[68] There is no mention, directly or indirectly, of these sentences in this chapter which consists of legal provisions imparted by God to Moses.

law *ubi numerus, Digest, de testibus.*[69] To have the force of proof this evidence must be superior to any exception, as is noted by Baldus and Bartolomeo da Saliceto in their commentaries to the final law, *Codex, de probationibus*[70] and by Francesco Bruni in his treatise *De inditiis et tortura,* q. II of pt. 1, no. 7.[71]; but proof is not obtained even from other particulars in the trial, and he cannot through them be punished according to the law. That is because the judge cannot institute the trial nor receive accusations against anyone, unless there is verification that a crime has occurred, as affirmed by Bartolus in his commentary to the final law, in the first column and to law 1, rubric *qui quaestionem, Digest, de quaestionibus* and to law 1, rubric *item illud, Digest, ad senatus consultum Sillaniano.*[72] And even if the statutes of the most serene doge of Venice state that a contumacious person must be considered a confessed criminal, or need not be heard at all,[73] never-

---

[69] See c. 10, X, III, 26: "... quum scriptum sit: In ore duorum vel trium testium stet omne verbum"; c. 13, X, II, 1; "quod vero" is not the title of a canon, but the title of the first part of C. II, q. 4, which contains: "Item Paulus in epistola ad Corintios: In ore duorum vel trium testium stabit omne verbum"; c. 23, X, II, 20: "iuxta illud dominicum: In ore duorum vel trium testium stat omne verbum"; 2 Cor 13: 1; D. 22, 5, 11: "Ad fidem rei gestae faciendam etiam non rogatus testis intelligitur"; cf. Mt 18: 16.

[70] See Baldo degli Ubaldi, *Baldi de Perusio ... super quarto et quinto Codicis Iust. lib. commentaria ...,* (Lyons, 1593) [colophon: printer's mark of Melchior and Gaspar Trechsel], fol. 42v, col. 2: "accusator debet accusationem suam probare per idoneos testes vel apertissima documenta et indicia indubitata et luce clariora" (commentary to C. 4, 19, 25); Bartolomeo da Saliceto, *Ad I. II. III. et IIII. Lib. Codicis commentarii ...* (Lyons: excudebat Claudius Servanius, 1560), fol. 288v, n. 3: "Item recipe aliud exemplum quod in criminalibus testes debent esse omni exceptione maiores" (commentary to C. 4, 19, 25).

[71] See F. Bruni, *Tractatus de indiciis et tortura ...* (Venice: in aedibus Francisci Bindoni, 1549), fols. 2r–7v, especially fols. 3v–4r: § 3 "(...) testis singularis de visu faciens indicium debet esse omni exceptione maior," "7. Testes in criminalibus debent esse omni exceptione maiores."

[72] See Bartolo da Sassoferrato, *Secunda Bartoli super Digesto Novo ...* (Lyons: per Ioan. Dominicum Guarnerium, 1545), fol. 200r: "antequam ad investigationem aliquam procedatur, debet constare de maleficio" (commentary to D. 48, 19, 22); ibid, fol. 194v: "respondeo: in hac inquisitione generali debet prius constare maleficium esse commissum ..." (commentary to D. 48, 19, 1 [21]); Idem, *Prima Bartoli super Infortiato,* fol. 193r: "ex isto sumitur practica quod curia mittat notarium ut videat mortum et describat vulnera, quae cum constat curie poterit postea procedere ad investigationem" (commentary to D. 29, 5, 1 [24])

[73] See *Statuta Veneta,* M. D. XLVIII [colophon: Venice: apud Cominum de Tridino Montisferrati, Anno M. D. XLVIII], fol. 10v (l. 1, c. 6): "si vero non venerit, tunc iudices audiant rationes partis praesentis et si liqueat eis de causa, iudicabunt ...";fol. 25v (l. 1, c. 45): "et si vocatus ad placitum non venerit, pro actoris sacramento absens condemnetur;

theless these provisions are not applied in cases where the commission of a crime has not been determined to the satisfaction of the judge. His first responsibility is to concern himself with the crime[74] and only later with the criminal, as we read in law 2, *Codex, de iureiurando propter calumniam,* and in the commentary by Bartolus and in the law *raptores, Codex, de episcopali audientia,* where it is demonstrated that the criminal must be convicted of the crime, and that the crime must be proven as stated above through two or three witnesses who testify that what they have heard comes directly from the mouth of the accused, not from others, because in the latter case they would not provide proof, since they would not be testifying from what they had heard first hand, as required by the gloss to the law *testium,* at the word *praesto, Codex, de testibus,* and by Felino Sandeo and Francesco Accolti in their commentaries to the chapter *tam litteris (Liber extra), de testibus.*[75]

And since in this trial no crime has been verified, we must conclude then that the aforesaid defendant can in no way be punished according to the law because of the words contained in the denunciations. In fact, he should be absolved and freed from this false charge and reimbursed for his expenses as is proper and fitting.

This fact is not invalidated by the denunciation since it is lodged by a person whose name is unknown, and hence must be treated as if it contains nothing certain. It lacks the denouncer's name, as well as the requisite elements required by the law, without which the trial not only becomes null and void, but also becomes impossible to pursue

---

(...) si autem in termino sibi statuto non apparuerit in curia coram iudicibus, stridetur in curia et facta stridatione si non apparuerit, procedatur in causa."

[74] See C. 2, 58, 2; Bartolo da Sassoferrato, *Prima Bartoli super Codice,* fol. 106r; ibid, fol. 30r: "ex quo habes quod si aliquis fugit et est captus, propter illam fugam non habetur pro confesso:" (commentary to C. 1, 3, 53, which is entitled "de episcopis et clericis," not "de episcopali audientia"). Nevertheless, in the edition that I have consulted, the running head already has the latter title.

[75] See C. 4, 20, 18, gl. praesto: "Sic ergo de sua scientia debent reddere testimonium, ut hic et statim subiicit, sua praesentia (...). De auditu autem alieno non nisi in casu aquae pluvialis arcendae ..."; Felino Sandeo, *Commentaria ad V. Decretalium libros secunda pars ...* (Venice: in aedibus Gregorii de Gregoris, 1521), fols. 134r–v; F. Accolti, *In Secundi Decretalium titulos ... commentaria* (Venice: apud Iuntas, 1581), fols. 119r–20v, in particular 120r: "quia testimonium de auditu auditus minus est validum, facultas probandi totaliter non est in unum relaxanda (...). Sed queritur pro intellectu huius articuli, numquid si testes deponunt se audivisse ab uno sufficiat ..." (commentaries to c. 33, X, II, 20).

further. And if the judges insist on continuing with it, they are not following the order of the law and thus are acting unjustly, as noted by Ippolito Marsigli in his commentary to law 1, no. 86, *Digest, ad legem Corneliam de sicariis*.[76] To be valid, summons must contain first the name of the judge, second the name of the accused, third the name of the person at whose instigation the summons is issued, fourth the reason for the summons, fifth the place where he must make his appearance, and sixth and last the length of time within which he must make his appearance. This is how it is stated by Roberto Maranta, in the title *de ordine iuditiorum*, pt. 6, no. 63, fol. 148 of the edition in my possession.[77] Thus, the denunciation which takes the place of the summons, must conform to the law in every particular, otherwise it is rendered null and void, because the argumentation proceeds from like to like, every time there is a likeness, as in the proposed case, as stated in the text of the law *non possunt, Digest, de legibus* and in the chapter *in causis, Liber extra, de re iudicata*.[78]

Nor do the witnesses examined for the prosecution constitute an obstacle. In fact, the first one examined said one thing, the second something else, so that they were in disagreement between themselves, and thus according to the law no credence needs to be accorded them, as stated in law 1, at the beginning, *Codex* and *Digest, de testibus*, and

---

[76] See Ippolito Marsigli, *Brassea Excellentissimi . . . D. Hippolyti de Marsilijs commentaria super titu. ff. ad legem Corneliam de siccariis* (Venice: per Franciscum Caronum, 1526), fol. 5r, n. 86: "Quando autem iudex seu officialis dicatur iniuste facere, dicas quod tunc quando non servat ordinem iuris."

[77] See Roberto Maranta, *Speculum aureum et lumen advocatorum in practica civili . . .* (Venice: apud Andream Baba, 1615), 315: Tractatus de ordine iudiciorum; sexta pars: iudicium trifariam partitum; De citatione, primo membro iudicii, n. 63: "citationes, de quibus infra dicam, debent continere sex requisita ad hoc ut valeant. Primum scilicet nomen iudicis citantis. Secundum nomen eius qui citatur. Tertium nomen eius ad cuius instantiam fit citatio. Quartum est causa ob quam citatur. Quintum est locus in quo debet comparere. Sextum est tempus infra quod debet comparere. Additur etiam septimum requisitum, quando citatio fit in scriptis, scilicet ut contineat verbum peremptorie. Haec omnia probantur. . . ."

[78] See D. 1, 3, 12: "Non possunt omnes articuli singillatim aut legibus aut senatus consultis comprehendi: sed cum in aliqua causa sententia eorum manifesta est, is qui iurisdictioni praeest ad similia procedere atque ita ius dicere debet"; c. 19, X, II, 27: "cum in similibus casibus ceteri teneantur similiter iudicare. . . ."

in the law *qui falsa vel varia, Digest, de testibus*.[79] The third, sixth and seventh witnesses testified that they were reporting the information of others, and to these no credence needs to be accorded, because they are not testifying about what they had heard at first hand, as noted in the gloss to the law *testium* at the word *praesto, Codex, de testibus,* and also in Felino Sandeo and Francesco Accolti in their commentaries to the chapter *tam litteris, Liber extra, de testibus*.[80] The fourth and fifth witnesses contradict each other in their testimony and thus do not produce proof in the case, as noted by Durant in the title *de teste,* rubric 1, verse *item quod testis*.[81] The eighth witness talks in one way at the beginning of his interrogation, and differently half way through and at the end, so that not only is he vacillatory and contradictory, but his testimony is also too hostile and biased so that it cannot be given any credence according to the law, as stated in chapter 2, *Liber extra, de in integrum restitutione* and in the chapter *accedens, Liber extra,* so that if the case cannot be proven through their testimony, one does not proceed to the acceptance of the witnesses.[82] The ninth, tenth, and eleventh witnesses also testified what they had heard from others, and no credence should be accorded their testimony, as stated above, also because there are discrepancies in their testimony and thus it is not to be relied upon, as noted by the doctors in their commentaries to the law *ex libero, Digest, de quaestionibus*.[83] In fact, variability in a witness is of such force that the judge cannot pronounce sentence on what has been testified to, as asserted by Innocent IV in his commentary to the chapter *praeterea, Liber extra, de testibus cogendis,* and by Angelo degli Ubaldi in his *consilium* 233, which begins "Domina Margareta."[84]

---

[79] See C. 4, 20, 1: "Contra scriptum testimonium non scriptum non profertur"; D. 22, 5, 1: "Testimoniorum usus frequens ac necessarius est et ab his praecipue exigendus, quorum fides non vacillat"; D. 22, 5, 16: "Qui falso vel varie testimonia dixerunt vel utrique parti prodiderunt, a iudicibus competenter puniuntur."

[80] See note 75.

[81] See Durant, *Speculum iuris,* 294, vers. 50: "Item quod testis obscure vel confuse dixit, IIII, q. III, versi. in testib. II, unde non valet, nisi iterum deponat et dictum suum declaret, quod facere potest."

[82] See c. 2. X, I, 41; c. 2, X, II, 6, where there do not appear to be references regarding arguments for the defense.

[83] Commentaries to D. 48, 18, 15 are being generically referred to.

[84] See Innocent IV, *In V. libros decretalium commentaria, a d. L. Paulo Rosello adnotationibus ... ornata ...*(Venice, 1570), 327: "Et nota quod varians dicitur qui primo dixit aliquid et postea eius contrarium, nullam causam variationis assignans (. . .); vacillans dicitur

The twelfth witness testifies that he was examined in a previous trial against the denounced, but that he had subsequently heard nothing about what the denounced might have said about the faith and that it was his own opinion that the aforesaid offender had wrong beliefs about the faith, but had heard nothing. Thus, his words should not be held in any account because a witness who testifies on the basis of his own opinion without furnishing a reason through an appropriate bodily sense, proves nothing, as is the case with the witness in question, as demonstrated by Giovanni d'Andrea in the additions to the *Speculum* under the title *de teste,* rubric *nunc autem tractandum,* towards the end.[85] In fact, in the above cases the witnesses seem to be emitting a judgment and thus exceeding the proper limits of testimony, thereby not providing any sort of conclusive evidence, as stated especially by Bartolus in his commentary to the final law, *Codex, de usuris.*[86] The thirteenth and last witness states at the beginning of his deposition that he had heard words about the faith spoken by the denounced, and at the end he asserts that he heard other words spoken by others. But he does not remember their names, thus his testimony must not be given heed, because it is one person's only, and also because he is relating what he has heard from others and does not give a reason for his affirmations. There are two reasons for this. First, single witnesses whose testimony is based on what they have heard from others cannot be bunched up together to form evidence or provide proof, as is asserted by Alessandro Tartagni in his *consilium* 82, col. 2, vol. 1, verse *praeterea,* and by Fulgosio in *consilium* 182, col. 2[87]; and second, because witnesses who testify on a matter and do not provide a reason

---

qui dubitando et timendo loquitur; item et qui varie loquitur (. . .), horum autem testimonium non valet, imo puniuntur"; Angelo degli Ubaldi, *Responsa Angeli de Ubaldis . . . quae vulgo Consilia dicuntur, acutissima . . .* (Turin: Apud haeredes Nicolai Bevilaquae, 1582), fols. 94v–95r: "Punctus est quaedam domina Margareta. . . ."

[85] See Durant, *Speculum iuris . . . pars prima et secunda,* 328, § 7, "Nunc tractandum qualiter in testium examinatione," addition g: "Adde tu, quod testis deponens quoad oculum intellectus, nisi reddat rationem eius, quod per sensum percipitur, non probat."

[86] See Bartolo da Sassoferrato, *Prima Bartoli super Codice,* fols. 170v–171r (commentary to C. 4, 32, 28).

[87] See Alessandro Tartagni, *Consiliorum liber primus . . .* (Venice: ex off. Damiani Zenari), 1578, fol. 91r, last line; Raffaele Fulgosio, *Consilia sive responsa . . . Raphaelis Cumani nempe et Fulgosii . . .* (Venice: apud Gasparem Bindonum, 1575), fol. 224r: "Et licet videantur hi testes singulares, quia de diversis confessionibus attestentur, ideoque nec probare (. . .), potest tamen probabiliter pro defensione veritatis attentari. . . ."

behind their statements do not produce proof of any kind because it is reason that validates or invalidates the testimony of a witness, as asserted by Baldus in his commentary to the law *conventiculam, Codex, de episcopis et clericis* and again in his commentary to the law *edita*, in *repaetitione Patavina, Codex, de edendo*, where he states that the witness who testifies without reasoning is said to be testifying like a beast,[88] not like a man, especially in criminal law, where witnesses, even without being asked, must give a reason for their statements, otherwise they prove nothing, as affirmed by Bartolomeo da Saliceto in his commentary to the final law, *Codex, de probationibus*, and Alessandro Tartagni in his commentary to the law *ait praetor, Digest, de iureiuran-do*.[89]

Nor, second and last, does the testimony rendered by the defendant himself militate against this: in fact, if it is examined properly, all that can be deduced from it are his simplicity and ignorance, and all this exempts him from punishment and from justice, for the many reasons explicated in the law. First, because simplicity is the characteristic of the dove, which is without guile: see the chapter *ex merito* and the chapter *si cupis*, VI, q. 1,[90] that excuses only for deeds committed, and also the chapter *tanta nequitia*, towards the end, distinction 86, and in the chapter *de Petro*, distinction 47, and one should pardon and

---

[88] See Baldo degli Ubaldi, *Super primo, secundo et tertio Codicis commentaria* ... (Lyons: apud Melchiorem et Gasparem Trechsel fratres, 1539), fol. 37v, col. 2: "Et de hoc do regulam: quod ubi testis in dicto minus probat, sed in ratione probat efficacius, semper attenditur ratio, nam ratio in teste est quae dat esse rei, id est testimonio" (commentary to C. 1, 3, 15); ibid, fol. 88v: "Sequitur eiusdem legis repetitio in Studio Patavino per eundem dominum Baldum facta," in particular fol. 93v, col. 1, n. 103: "quia tunc homo deponit ut homo, cum deponit ut ipsa ratio (...) est hominis forma intellectiva; qui enim non deponit per rationem, interrogatus de ipsa, non deponit ut homo, sed ut pecus (...), ipsa positio interrogat tacite testem de ratione et ideo nisi reddatur ubi positio est de invisibilibus et insensibilibus ex se, quia a teste reddenda est, alias non probat dictum" (commentary to C. 2, 1, 3).

[89] See Bartolomeo da Saliceto, *Ad I. II. III. et IIII. Lib. Codicis commentarii*, fols. 288v–289r: "1. Accusator debet actionem suam probare per idoneos testes vel apertissima documenta seu indicia indubitabilia, luce clariora (...). 3. (...) Quero in criminalibus probationes debent esse clariores quam in civilibus ..." (commentary to C. 4, 19, 25); Alessandro Tartagni, *In I et II Digesti Veteris partem commentaria* ..., (Venice: apud Iuntas, 1570), fols. 149r–150v.

[90] See c. 13, C. VI, q. 1: "Habeant omnes simplicitatem columbae, ne cuiquam machinentur dolos et serpentis astutiam"; c. 5, C. XVI, q. 1: "Habeto simplicitatem columbae, ne cuipiam machineris dolos et serpentis astutiam."

grant clemency, as is demonstrated in the chapter *scriptura, de consecratione,* distinction 2.[91] The second reason is because what is committed out of ignorance can be easily pardoned: see the chapter *unum orarium,* rubric *criminis,* distinction 25, and the sins of those who are cognizant are more serious than those of the ignorant: see the chapter *quaero,* VI, q. 1[92]; the third reason is that, in fact, sin is not called sin if it is not voluntary: see the chapter *sicut,* no. 32, q. 5[93]; the fourth and last reason is, as we have expounded above, that God does not desire the death of the sinner, but rather his conversion and life, as we read in the *Autentica ut non lussurientur homines contra naturam* at the beginning, and in the chapter *admonere,* XXXIII, q. 2.[94] The pure simplicity and unambiguous ignorance of the defendant emerge from his various interrogations; thus we have to conclude that according to the law he cannot be punished in any way, in fact, he must be absolved from the charges and reimbursed for his expenses; or, at least, this time he should be pardoned and considered absolved, keeping mercy always before one's eyes, as was demonstrated above through God's words "Judge not, and you will not be judged," and "For there will be judgment without mercy towards those who do not want to show mercy to sinners."[95]

In view of these matters the defense attorney requests that the aforesaid Domenico who has been arrested and is incarcerated in the prisons of the Holy Office of the Inquisition be absolved and freed from the charges directed against him, and reimbursed for his expens-

---

[91] See c. 24, D. 86: "Et quidem penae sententia in te fuerat iaculanda, sed quia simplicitatem tuam cum senectute cognovimus, interim tacemus"; c. 4, D. 47: "quia persona eius nobis ignota est, et utrum ita sit de simplicitate, quod ad nos perlatum est ignoramus"; c. 3, D. 2, de cons.: "Sed vide, frater karissime, si quis de antecessoribus nostris vel ignoranter vel simpliciter non hoc observaverit et tenuit, quod nos Dominus facere exemplo et magisterio docuit, potest simplicitati eius de indulgentia Domini venia concedi."

[92] See c. 3, D. 25, § 4: "Unde Beda super epistolam Iacobi: Peccata, que ex ignorantia vel infirmitate humana committuntur, dicit et precipit alterutrum confiteri, quia facile dimittuntur: quecumque vero fiunt ex deliberatione, non nisi per penitentiam"; c. 21, C. VI, q. 1: "secundum illam regulam, qua peccata scientium peccatis ignorantiae preponuntur, avarum conscientia vincit in scelere."

[93] See c. 10, C. XXXII, q. 5: "Sicut enim peccatum opus sine voluntate non facit, ita et iusticia ex opere non consummatur, nisi et voluntas affuerit."

[94] See Nov. 77: "quoniam et Dei misericordia non perditionem sed conversionem et salutem vult, et delinquentes qui corriguntur suscipit Deus"; c. 8, C. XXXIII, q. 2: "Non enim vult Deus mortem peccatoris, sed ut convertatur ad penitentiam et vivat."

[95] Lk 6: 37; Jas 2: 13.

es, and that it be thus stated in the best form prescribed by the highest claims of the law, safeguarding all his other rights and claims to defense which are legally his. And if there should be something defective in the above claims, and he does not believe that there is, he reserves the right to appeal to other clearer pronouncements of the law, as will seem opportune to the praise and glory of the omnipotent God and of the most Blessed Virgin, Mary, his mother and our advocate. Amen.

Admitted conditionally, 22 July 1599.

Fra Girolamo Asteo, Apostolic Inquisitor General.

30 July 1599

In the government palace, before the very reverend father inquisitor, in the presence of the most distinguished *podestà* of Portogruaro, Pietro Zane, and of his most excellent lordship Medicis, consultant, there was conducted from prison Domenico Scandella and ordered to be loosened from his bonds. He was then asked whether he wished to say or adduce anything else in his case either personally or through his attorney, orally or in writing, and add to his defense. He replied: "I do not want to make any defense beyond what I have already done, nor do I intend to say anything else, except to beg for mercy, and if I have sinned in any way, I have always thrown myself on the mercy of the Lord."

The court record was read back to him and he ratified and signed it.

And I, Menego Scandella called Menocchio, hereby confirm the above.

Thereby the reverend father inquisitor ordered the aforesaid Domenico to be led back to prison and kept under close surveillance, etc.

The same day

Before the reverend father, as above, etc. there appeared the most excellent Agostino Pisenti, Domenico Scandella's court appointed attorney, who was asked if he wished to make any additional arguments in Scandella's defense either orally or in writing. To which he replied: "I do not wish to make any further defense, so your paternity may conclude the case."

2 August 1599

Having assembled all the members of the court in the episcopal palace of Portogruaro, where the most illustrious and most reverend lord bishop and the most reverend father, master Girolamo Asteo, inquisitor general for all the patriarchate of Aquileia and the diocese of Concordia, in the presence of the most distinguished lord, Pietro Zane, worthy *podestà* of Portogruaro, and of the most excellent Valerio Trapola dai Colli, vicar general, Domenico Marino, theologian, Andronico de Medicis and Giovanni Raimondo, consultors of the Holy Office of the Inquisition, called and summoned, ordered me Orazio Crasso, notary, to read out the entire trial and the defenses. After I had finished reading, the most excellent individual consultors expressed their opinion, namely that the aforesaid Domenico Scandella was a convicted recidivist and should be considered as such, and that he should be tortured, not for the merits of his own case, but to extract the names of his accomplices and companions, with the understanding that he is to be considered a convicted criminal.

The most illustrious and most reverend Matteo Sanudo, Bishop of Concordia, and the most reverend father, master Girolamo Asteo, inquisitor general for the entire patriarchate of Aquileia and the diocese of Concordia, decreed and sentenced that the aforesaid Domenico Scandella was to be considered as and indeed had been ascertained to be a confessed *relapsus,* and was to be tortured, as stated above, for his accomplices and companions.

Denunciation lodged by Michele Carboni
Portogruaro, 3 August 1599

One day, when I, priest Michele Carboni had entered by chance in the house of the innkeeper *donna* Narda, I found there a certain man called Simon the Jew, I do not know from what place, who has become a Christian, and goes around begging in the diocese. And while I was standing there I heard him speak and ask about a certain miller who was in prison in Concordia, and if it was true that he was really being held. I told him yes, and then this Simon said that he once had spent the night with that miller and all through the night the miller said enormous things about the faith. For example, to the question "Who do you think made the Gospels," he himself replied: "God, from His own mouth." But, instead, the miller said: "They were done by monks and priests because they have nothing better to do." And he also said that he had read a most beautiful book, which he wanted to show him, but then regretted it. And going on, he said that the Madonna, before taking St. Joseph, had made two or three creatures, and for this reason St. Joseph did not want to accept her as his wife[96]; and he [the miller] knew that he would die for these things, but because a companion had posted surety for him, he would not flee, otherwise he would have run away to Geneva, and if his children wanted to do as he had, more power to them, and that at his death the Lutherans would come to know of it and come to collect his ashes. And I heard all this from that Simon.

3 August 1599, in Portogruaro

I, priest Michiel Carbo

3 August 1599, in the convent of San Francesco in Portogruaro.

The reverend priest Michele Carboni of Venice, residing in Portogruaro, chaplain at the altar of the Most Holy Body of Christ, presented the attached sheet, appearing spontaneously and testifying, in accordance with it. I, Fra Girolamo Asteo, inquisitor, administered the oath to him to speak the truth, and he stated: "Everything that I have written down is the truth."

Questioned, he replied: "Sir, I do not know where that Jew is from, but it was about 15 days ago that he came to Portogruaro and slept in the hospital of St. Thomas with four or five persons, Jews who became Christians." And he added of his own accord: "That book that the aforesaid prisoner said he had, that Jew thought that it must be the *Koran*."[97]

Questioned, he replied: "That Jew said it was at least a year ago when he went to Montereale, slept with the forenamed prisoner and went, as stated above."

About generalities, he responded properly, took the oath of secrecy, and signed. He confirmed his testimony.

I priest Michiel ratify the above.

Wednesday, 5 August 1599

In the palace of the most distinguished *podestà* of the city of Porto-

---

[96] Mt 1: 19.

[97] *L'Alcorano di Macometto* . . . ,[Venice, Andrea Arrivabene], 1547: cf. C. De Frede, *La prima traduzione italiana del Corano sullo sfondo dei rapporti tra Cristianità e Islam nel Cinquecento* (Naples, 1967).

gruaro, before the most illustrious and most reverend Matteo Sanudo, bishop of Concordia, and the most reverend father, master Girolamo Asteo, inquisitor, etc., with the participation of the most illustrious lord Pietro Zane, most worthy *podestà* of the place, the most excellent consultor, Valerio Trapola, and the most worthy Raimondo, the aforesaid Domenico Scandella was conducted from prison and first cautioned to state the truth more clearly, replied: "Most illustrious lord, I told you even the other day that I did not learn my errors from anyone, but got them out of my own head or read them in books. And that simile about the three rings I read in the book the *Cento novelle* of Boccaccio, which was given to me by Nicolò de Melchiori, now deceased."[98]

Questioned with whom he had conversed about his opinions, he replied: "I do not know that I spoke about them with anyone."

Then it was stated to his face that the Holy Office was seeking nothing more about his person or about his errors, considering him convicted, but would torture him to learn the names of his accomplices and of the persons with whom he had spoken. To this he replied: "Sir, I do not recall that I discussed with anyone."

The order was given that he should be stripped and examined to determine if he was capable of supporting torture, and the jailers were ordered to attempt to extract the truth from him. And while he was undressed, he was questioned, and replied: "I talked with so many people that now I do not remember."

Then he was ordered to be bound, and while he was being bound, he was again admonished to state the truth about his accomplices, to which he replied: "I do not remember."

He was ordered to be conducted to the torture chamber where a rope and pulley had been set up, and it was now 12:30 in the afternoon. He was again admonished to speak the truth about his accomplices, and he replied: "I have thought and tried to imagine with whom I might have talked, but I have not been able to remember."

Then he was ordered to be tied to the rope, and while he was being bound, he said: "Oh Lord Jesus Christ, mercy, Jesus, mercy. I do not know that I ever had discussions with anyone, may I die if I have pupils or companions, but I read on my own. O Jesus, mercy."

---

[98] See note 43. Nicolò de Melchiori was of Montereale, as can be deduced from his family name, and should not be confused with the Nicolò who was a painter from Porcia, who was still alive in 1606: cf. the introduction, liii; Ginzburg (22), conflates them.

Then he was ordered to be raised a little, and while he was raised, he said: "Oh Jesus, oh Jesus, poor me, poor me." Asked: "Tell us with whom you have had discussions," he replied: "Jesus, Jesus, I do not know anything." Again admonished to speak the truth, he replied: "I would tell it willingly, let me down so that I can think about it."

It was ordered that he should be lowered to the ground and unbound, and then he was asked to tell the truth and name his accomplices and companions, and he, in thought, replied: "I do not know that I had discussions with anyone, and I do not know that anyone has my opinions, and I certainly do not know anything."

He was ordered to be raised again, and he spoke: "Alas, poor martyred me, Oh Lord Jesus Christ." And once again admonished to speak the truth, he said: "Sir, let me down and I shall say something."

He was ordered to be lowered, and, asked once again about his companions and accomplices, he replied: "I told Signor Zuan Francesco Montereale that we did not know what was the true faith. And that book about the story of the three rings was brought to my house by Lunardo della Minussa of Montereale." Questioned again about individual articles and with whom he might have conversed about them, he replied: "Sir, I have not discussed any matter with anyone else."

Then he was ordered to be untied, and the torture had been conducted with moderation and he was never elevated beyond a certain point, and the interrogation was completed before the thirteenth hour, and he was ordered to be led back to prison and kept under close surveillance, etc.

Thursday, 6 August 1599

Before the very reverend father inquisitor, etc., assembled in the government palace, in the presence of the most celebrated lord Pietro Zane, *podestà* of Portogruaro, Domenico Scandella, led out from prison free of all bonds, was interrogated under oath and testified: "Everything that I said yesterday after I was released from the ropes is absolutely true. I only want to add this, that the above named signor Giovanni Francesco reprimanded me for my madness." Then he added, of his own accord: "Moreover, one night I slept with a Jew[99] and I discussed my heresies with him, as best as I can remember."

---

[99] Simon the Jew.

After the testimony was read back to him, he ratified it and signed.

I Domenego Scandella confirm the above.

Sentence against Domenico Scandella
Portogruaro, 8 August 1599

We, Matteo Sanudo, by the grace of God and of the Holy Apostolic See bishop, duke, marquis and count of Concordia and Fra Girolamo Asteo of Pordenone, of the order of minor conventuals, doctor of arts and of sacred theology and inquisitor general for the dioceses and cities of Aquileia and Concordia specially delegated by the Holy Apostolic See, became apprised, legitimately informed, that you Domenico Scandella, known as Menocchio, of Montereale in the diocese of Concordia, had already been denounced for heresy in the year of our Lord 1583 before this Holy Office. Through the testimony of witnesses and through your own statements made spontaneously during the proceedings under oath, you were found to have been infected by the stain of heresy with a hardened heart for about twenty years, and that you, as heretic, nay as heresiarch, often taught, discussed and proposed as truth, especially to simple and ignorant people, many heresies and errors, and equally that you committed by deeds many heretical acts, but especially these:

in fact, you believed and attempted to persuade others that in the most Holy Trinity the Son and the Holy Spirit do not have the same essence, glory, majesty, omnipotence and will as the Father; that only the person of the Father is from eternity, but not his power, intellect and will; that it was imperfect at first and then little by little and by stages acquired power, knowledge, etc.; that the person of the Father is greater than the Son and the Holy Spirit, but not at all omnipotent; that the Son and the Holy Spirit are creatures and did not always exist, and the Holy Spirit is greater than the Son.

Christ is not the natural Son of God, but is the son by election; Christ is pure man made from corruptible substance and is not different by nature from other men; the Son proceeds from the Father and from the Holy Spirit and receives his birthright from both; Christ has not been the maker of this world and did not create all things; Christ was not conceived by the Holy Spirit nor born from the Virgin Mary; the soul of Christ either was one of the angels made at the beginning of the world or was made anew by the Holy Spirit from the elements; Christ either was the son of Joseph or was born of adultery; Christ was not sinless by nature and possessed two spirits in his heart, one good and the other evil and he was tempted internally by the evil; if Christ had been omnipotent he would have been a fool letting himself be killed; Christ was not crucified, but Simon the Cyrenian in his place; Christ allowed himself to be hung like a brute animal; when Christ died his intellect, memory and will also died; at Christ's death his soul also died; Christ did not die for the sins of all people but only to serve as an example of patience; Christ did not descend into Hell nor did he rise up again; you doubted that the body of Christ was in heaven and that it appeared to the apostles for forty days after his death until the Ascension; Christ is not the object of our beatitude;

you said that God does not exist and that if he did, he would not be in the heavens to be seen; God is air and the other things that we see; God does not look after these things below;

the Holy Spirit is one of the more noble of the angelic spirits created at the beginning of the world; the Holy Spirit is made from the substance of the chaos and created by the Father and not by the Son; the Holy Spirit is given to all men, Turks, heretics, Jews and Christians;

the chaos, from which all things were created, has been from all time; God made nothing by himself or directly, but everything by means of the angels;

the most Blessed Virgin is inferior to the empress Mary of Austria; the most Blessed Virgin was a sinner and adulteress; she was not always virgin and conceived Christ in sin;

all men will be saved, even infidels; it is impossible that all people should rise up again at the Universal Judgment in soul and body; at the Last Judgment Christ will make suggestions to the memory of the Father and God will judge; there are two principles, as the Manichees assert, one for good, the other for evil; angels originated from a putrefied corporal substance; the angels are of the same nature as God, but not made by God, but by nature; Lucifer never sought equality with God; at the beginning of the world a multitude of men was created, not Adam alone, and these men were made not by God but by the angels; men are not made in the image and likeness of God, but of the angels; man's soul is not infused into him while the body is in the mother's womb, but only when the infant leaves it; at the death of their bodies, even the souls of men disappear and nothing remains, except for ashes; the soul and the spirit of man is an angel; souls are not created anew and are made from the four elements; men begin to sin the moment they leave their mother's womb; to blaspheme against God and the saints is not a sin, in fact it should be considered among the callings;

nobody is predestined by God to eternal bliss and those whom God foresees will be blessed, he foresees universally, not particularly; the blessed do not attain their beatitude through the grace of God, but through their own works and merits, actually through the influence of the planets and of fortune; no one is justified through the passion and death of Christ;

the sacred law of God, contained in the New and Old Testaments, is, to put it in the vernacular, human business; in Holy Scripture some things are true, other things that contradict each other have been added by the evangelists; Holy Scripture consists only of a few words and only these come from God, the rest have been added by men and are like the tales of battle; Holy Scripture deceives us and was concocted to deceive men, especially when it affirms that there is a God; among the various precepts, the precept to love one's neighbor is superior to the one to love God;

the supreme pontiff of the Church and the other prelates of the Holy Roman Church are not guided by the Holy Spirit, are lacking in authority, and are preoccupied solely with deceiving the souls of the faithful; the supreme pontiff is not more important than he in dignity and power, but equal; his [the pope's] authority absolutely does not come from Christ, nor are we to understand the words "Whatever you bind on earth"[100] as pertaining to the authority of the popes; the statutes, orders and laws of the Church are not true in any way, nor are men obliged to observe them, since they are, as is vulgarly said, a mere business; ecclesiastics are like the Devil, and you would have traded them all for a coin or two; and if you had not been held back by love for your children, you would have barged into the churches to burn them and kill their priests;

saints are not to be adored in any way, nor their relics venerated, since there is no difference between them and the remains of other men; images are not to be venerated; indulgences do not depend upon the merits of Christ and the saints; we must not pray for the dead or give alms; masses and pious works for the dead are of no value; you disdained fasting and its institution and for your entire life never

---

[100] Mt 16: 19.

observed Lent; the words of the saints and of the apostles should never be cited in sermons, because they are, as it is said, a mere business;

the sacrament of baptism is not necessary, nor instituted by God; every man as soon as he is born, is baptized by God and baptism is a human invention to devour the souls of men;

the sacrament of confirmation is not a sacrament, it is not necessary, nor was it established by Christ; it is a human convention, and, as vulgarly said, a business of the religious;

marriage is not a sacrament, nor instituted by God, nor ordered by God, but a pure invention of men;

confession made to a priest is of as much value as if it had been made to a tree or to a plant; it suffices to confess one's sins to God, and if someone also wants to confess them to priests, this confession works only to establish the penances for the sins; any layman, if he knows how to assign the penances, can properly hear confession, in fact can remit the sinner's sins;

while you were observing an unconsecrated wafer and you saw in it the image of our Lord Christ crucified, you uttered terrible and unheard of words: "That is a great beast"; of the most holy Eucharist you said "It's a piece of dough," and that the true body of Christ does not remain in these elements, and, in addition, totally novel and incredible, that into the consecrated host it is the Holy Spirit that descends and not the Son; you believed that the holy Eucharist was not instituted by Christ, but is a pure human invention;

all men can be priests, without being initiated in sacred things; the sacrament of Orders was not instituted by God, but, as vulgarly said, is a new business for the religious;

extreme unction is not necessary, nor is it of any value nor established by Christ;

you possessed and read books prohibited by the Holy Apostolic See.

Coming, however, to a more salutary decision, as it seemed, you abjured, rejecting and revoking these heresies publicly in this same church of S. Andrea in the city of Portogruaro, in accordance with the prescribed usage of the Church. Therefore, our predecessors, believing you to be truly converted, granted you the grace of being absolved from the sentence of excommunication by which you were bound, readmitting you to the bosom of the Holy Church of God if you would return to the unity of the Holy Church with a true heart and unfeigned faith, out of mercy granting you your life and condemning you, after imposing certain salutary penances, to weep over your sins in perpetuity and placate the ire of God with fasting and prayer, immured between four walls for the rest of your days, clothed in the garment of penance.

But, even before two years had transpired from your condemnation, that is on 19 January 1586, we Matteo Sanudo, bishop, and the very reverend father of pious memory Evangelista Pelleo, doctor in theology and at the time apostolic inquisitor for the entire patriarchate and diocese of Concordia, moved by your and your children's humble supplications, believing you to be truly converted and restored to the faith, mitigated and commuted your sentence, granting to you Montereale as your prison, and even relaxing some of the salutary penances that had been imposed, treating your wounds with oil and wine as our Savior taught us,[101] because we believed that you had truly recanted.

On the contrary, after all that transpired, and after the passing of many years, you were accused to us anew of having relapsed into many of the heresies that you had abjured, and into new ones. After we, with heavy heart, heard such things about you, compelled by the demands of justice, we decided to begin an inquiry, examine witnesses and question you under oath, and to do all the things, as a whole and individually, which we were obliged to do according to the canonical norms. Therefore, wishing to bring the present case to a suitable conclusion, we summoned a full assembly of doctors in sacred theology and experts in canon and civil law, with the presence and participation of the most worthy Pietro Zane, distinguished *podestà* of Portogruaro, invited and requested by us. And after obtaining their counsel, mature and fully pondered, regarding each and every item, and after discussing the merits of the trial and weighing on the scales of justice every individual item, as we were obliged to do, we discovered both by means of witnesses and by your own confession obtained judicially that you have relapsed into the heresies you had abjured and into new ones.

We discovered, in fact, that not only were you negligent about fulfilling the penances imposed on you and commuted by this Holy Office—not wearing the penitential garment, called in the vernacular the *abitello;* not consigning the testimonial letters, which you were obliged to bring each year according to your sentence, attesting that you had been to confession six times and had received Holy Commun-

---

[101] A reference to the parable of the good Samaritan (Lk 11: 34).

ion; transgressing the [geographical] boundaries that had been imposed on you; discussing the faith on many occasions despite the prohibition in the sentence. But even you admitted that you had spoken jestingly often about the things of the faith, and told lies about it.

You confessed that you believed and taught that to enter into the approved monastic orders "is a thing for beggars," and for this reason you urged others not to enter;

you confessed believing only part of the Gospel message, or, as you yourself said, "that which is the truth," because you stated that the Gospels were written by priests and monks who have studied;

you have believed and affirmed that God is air, water and all the other things;

you have believed and said that we do not know which is the true faith; that the will to remain in the sect of the Turks, in the perfidy of the Jews and in the other condemned sects is good and comes from God; that Turks, Jews and other infidels sin when they embrace the law of Christ and become Christians.

You stated that you want to be a Christian because your father, grandfather and other relatives were Christians, but if you had been born a Turk, you would want to die in their impiety; you asserted that you believed you were a prophet and that even prophets have erred in their prophecies.

You denied the existence of Paradise; you went to pains to persuade others that we do not know if saints, especially the hermits and others who met death for God's sake, ascended to Paradise.

Openly denying the divinity of Christ, our Lord, you dared to affirm that if Christ had truly been God, he would have been very foolish allowing himself to be hung on a cross; you also stated that Christ had the humanity but not the power of the Father.

You were not ashamed to say, when we were talking about the articles of the faith, that you only believed what you could see; and that Christ could not descend from the cross.

You are held to be vehemently suspected [of heresy] concerning the virginity of the immaculate and most blessed ever Virgin Mary.

For these reasons and in accordance with the opinion of the above mentioned [experts] we have considered you and consider you now relapsed in light of the canonical law, which we communicate to you with sorrow. But since for our edification and that of upright Catholics, thanks to the inspiration of divine grace, you have returned anew into the bosom of the Church and of its unity, detesting the aforesaid errors and heresies and believing in a Catholic manner, as you have asserted, and affirming the Catholic faith, we have admitted you to receive the ecclesiastical sacraments of penance and of the Eucharist, which you have humbly requested, as the canonical statutes permit to the relapsed who repent and humbly request them.

However, since the Church of God has nothing more to do with you, having comported itself with such mercy with you, as we said above, and you abused her, relapsing into the heresies that you had abjured and into others, therefore we, bishop and inquisitor, seated as a tribunal in judgment, with the sacred Gospels before us so that our judgment may emanate from the countenance of God and our eyes may behold what is just, and having before our eyes only God and the unshakable truth of the holy faith and the necessary extirpation of heretical pravity, in this place, on the day and hour previously established for the definitive sentencing, we determine that you Domenico Scandella have truly relapsed into heretical pravity, even if you are now penitent, and as a true recidivist we expel you from our ecclesiastical forum and consign you to the secular arm. We beseech the aforesaid secular arm, however, that it carry out its sentence upon you avoiding the spilling of blood and the danger of death. Thus we state, pronounce, declare, sentence, expel, consign and pray.

So be it, Matteo Sanudo, bishop of Concordia.

So be it, Fra Girolamo Asteo, apostolic inquisitor General.

The above sentence was issued, read and promulgated by the aforesaid most illustrious and most reverend bishop and most reverend father inquisitor, and it was read out by me, Orazio Crasso, notary, in the Church of S. Andrea in the city of Portogruaro, Sunday morning, the eighth day of August 1599, in the presence of many in attendance, and especially of the worthy gentlemen Pasquale de Federicis, Pietro da Mestre, Ortensio Claudio, residents of Portogruaro, as witnesses.

The same day

It was reported by the emissary Annibale, that by order of the most illustrious and most reverend bishop and the most reverend father inquisitor, he had that morning consigned to the secular court of the *podestà* of the city of Portogruaro the forenamed Domenico Scandella.

Appendix

Letters from the Supreme Congregation of the Inquisition in Rome to the Inquisitor for the Friuli, Girolamo Asteo.[*]

Cardinal Giulio Antonio Santoro to Fra Girolamo Asteo
Rome, 5 June 1599

Reverend Father. The letter from your reverence of the 7th, received on 27 May, was read to His Holiness in congregation and he has ordered that you should not fail to use every diligence to apprehend that person of the diocese of Concordia, who has denied the divinity of Christ, our lord, as was attested by two witnesses, although individually. And proceed in such a manner that his incarceration take place safely without possibility of flight since his case is extremely grave, especially since he has been condemned as a heretic on other occasions. At the moment of capture, conduct a perquisition of his books and writings and proceed with that diligence called for by the gravity of the case and inform us of everything.[1] As for the information you seek, whether one should proceed against denounced persons when there is danger to the life of witnesses who have testified or denounced them, His Holiness orders your reverence to send a copy of the charges so that they can be carefully pondered here.

About the concern raised in your letter, whether you should proceed to an arrest when you have one witness against the defendant, let me say that in this matter you should let yourself be governed by the dictates of justice. You should know that when there is one witness who testifies about a crime and he suffers from no exceptions (legal

---

[*] AAUd, *S. Officio*, b. 59, under their respective dates.

[1] The letter was received in Gorizia on 14 June and the inquisitor noted on it: "Concerning the apprehension of Menocchio." The arrest, decided on 12 May, was executed the 21st of June.

disabilities) of any kind, one can proceed even to torture, as well as capture and prosecution, especially since the holy faith works in favor of the Holy Office in its cases. Since I have nothing more to add, stay well and may the Lord preserve you in his blessed grace.

the same
Rome, 17 July 1599
Reverend Father. In reply to your letter of the 2nd of this month, I inform you that by order of His Holiness I am writing to monsignor the nuncio in Venice to perform every office necessary to obtain custody for the Holy Office over that peasant who uttered those horrible and heretical blasphemies against the most Blessed Virgin while the litany was being sung on her feast day. If you have additional information, you may advise monsignor the nuncio.[2]

We have been pleased to learn that your reverence has arranged for the incarceration of that heretic, nay heresiarch, of the diocese of Concordia and that it all took place without fuss of any kind. Therefore, you should now proceed, gathering the necessary information and arraigning the defendant using every diligence required by the gravity of the case, keeping us informed of everything.[3] Meanwhile, I bid you farewell and commend myself to your prayers.

the same
Rome, 14 August 1599
Reverend Father. Your letter of the 14th of the past month containing the three denunciations that you sent was read in the congregation before His Holiness last Thursday. As for Signor Savorgniano Savorgniani, residing in the village at Martignacco, it was resolved that your reverence should have him observed to see if he keeps Lent and how he behaves in matters of the holy Catholic faith. The other two denunciations do not appear to be of great moment and, thus, call for no action at this time.[4]

As for those who have brought cases of prohibited books from Germany, your reverence should use all possible diligence to gather

---

[2] The person being discussed was Lorenzo Furia of Palazzolo, as the inquisitor noted on the paper. His trial is preserved in AAUd, *S. Officio*, b. 16, fasc. 335.

[3] The letter was received at Portogruaro on 28 July, and the inquisitor noted on it: "About Domenico Scandella called Menocchio."

[4] See AAUd, *S. Officio*, b. 17, fasc. 335.

more information and communicate everything that you know to monsignor the patriarch so that no stone can be left unturned to discover the truth.

In the case of that relapsed person, who reveals himself to be an atheist in his interrogations, proceed to the full extent of the law, also for the purpose of uncovering his accomplices. And since his case is of extreme gravity, your reverence should send a copy of his trial, or at least a summary of it.[5] With which I commend myself to your prayers.

the same
Rome, 16 October 1599

Reverend father. Your letter of the 5th was received on the 23rd of last month, from which we learned about the conclusion of the case of Domenico Scandella of the diocese of Concordia, relapsed heretic, and thus consigned to the secular authorities.

As for the other prisoner of the same diocese, accused of formal heresy and of heretical blasphemy, we shall give an accounting to His Holiness so as to provide for the difficulties that you mention. . . .[6]

---

[5] The letter was received on 15 September, by which date the sentence against Menocchio had been carried out. The inquisitor scribbled on the sheet: "About Domenico Scandella."

[6] The reference is to the case of Antonio Scodellaro: see cxii. The letter continues on other matters.

Index of Names

The trials in *Domenico Scandella Known as Menocchio: His Trials Before the Inquisition (1583–1599)* were the sources of the well-known study by Carlo Ginzburg, *The Cheese and the Worms,* translated by John and Anne C. Tedeschi, in which the relations between popular and learned cultures were analyzed through the ideas of the Friulan miller. In this volume, Andrea Del Col makes use of new documents and offers a fresh interpretation of the inquisitorial trials. He explains how the Holy Office in Friuli functioned, the different ways in which the judges operated and conducted inquiries, and the manner in which the notaries laid down the records, all crucial elements for a correct understanding of the sources. Some of Menocchio's ideas do not, as previously thought, arise from popular culture, but can instead be interpreted as a continuation of certain Cathar concepts from the late Middle Ages. This view varies from Ginzburg's, setting forth differently the fundamental issues of the transmission of ideas and the relations between cultures in European history.

◆

Andrea Del Col, on the faculty at the University of Trieste, is a member of the advisory committee of the Istituto di Studi Rinascimentali of Ferrara and of the editorial board of *Metodi e Ricerche.* He has published widely in the field of the inquisition. John Tedeschi and Anne C. Tedeschi have translated three books by Carlo Ginzburg: *The Cheese and the Worms* (1980), *The Night Battles* (1983), and *Clues, Myths and the Historical Method* (1989). John Tedeschi's *The Prosecution of Heresy: Collected Studies on the Inquisition in Early Modern Italy* was published by MRTS in 1991.